MARVEL

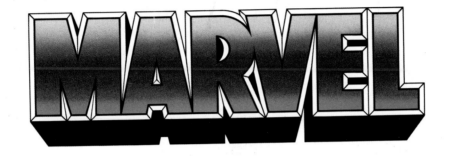

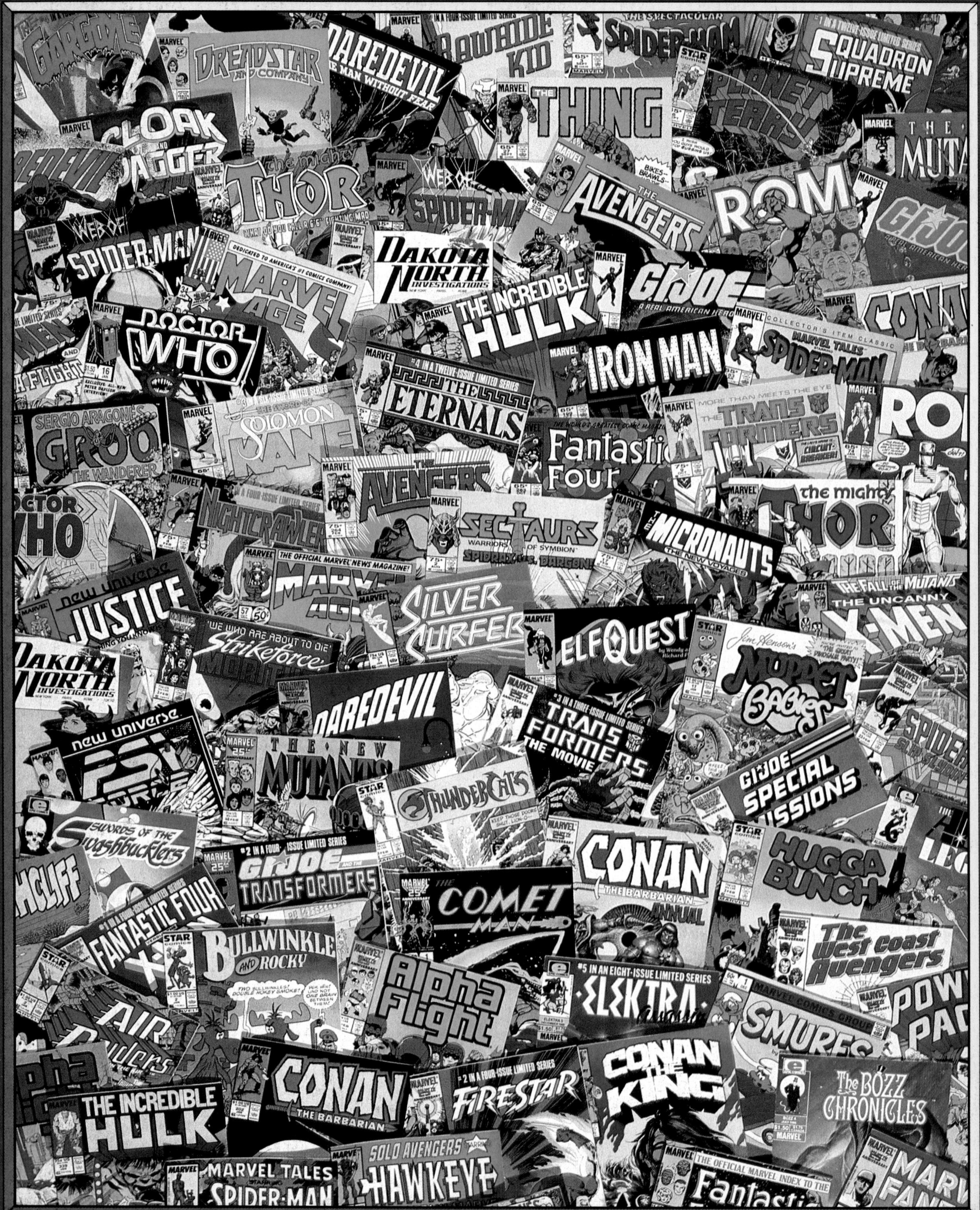

DREADSTAR AND COMPANY
DAREDEVIL THE MAN WITHOUT FEAR
RAWHIDE KID
THE SPECTACULAR SPIDER-HAM
SQUADRON SUPREME
THE THING
CLOAK AND DAGGER
THE MIGHTY THOR
WEB OF SPIDER-MAN
THE AVENGERS
ROM
G.I. JOE
DAKOTA NORTH INVESTIGATIONS
MARVEL AGE
THE INCREDIBLE HULK
IRON MAN
DOCTOR WHO
MARVEL TALES SPIDER-MAN
THE ETERNALS
SERGIO ARAGONÉS GROO THE WANDERER
SOLOMON KANE
FANTASTIC FOUR
THE TRANSFORMERS
NIGHTCRAWLER
SECTAURS
MICRONAUTS THE NEW VOYAGES
THE FALL OF THE MUTANTS
THE UNCANNY X-MEN
JUSTICE
SILVER SURFER
ELFQUEST
STRIKEFORCE
MUPPET BABIES
DAREDEVIL
TRANS FORMERS THE MOVIE
THE NEW MUTANTS
THUNDERCATS
G.I. JOE SPECIAL MISSIONS
SWORDS OF THE SWASHBUCKLERS
G.I. JOE AND THE TRANSFORMERS
CONAN THE BARBARIAN ANNUAL
HUGGA BUNCH
THE COMET MAN
FANTASTIC FOUR
BULLWINKLE AND ROCKY
ALPHA FLIGHT
ELEKTRA
THE WEST COAST AVENGERS
SMURFS
AIR RAIDERS
CONAN THE BARBARIAN
FIRESTAR
CONAN THE KING
THE BOZZ CHRONICLES
THE INCREDIBLE HULK
MARVEL TALES SPIDER-MAN
SOLO AVENGERS HAWKEYE
THE OFFICIAL MARVEL INDEX TO THE FANTASTIC

MARVEL

Five Fabulous Decades of the World's Greatest Comics

by
Les Daniels

Introduction by
Stan Lee

Harry N. Abrams, Inc., Publishers

Art Direction: **David Kaestle, Inc.**

Designer: **David Vogler**

Assistant designer/Production artist: **David Wilson**

Editor: **Judy Fireman**

Cover art and chapter dividers: **John Romita**

Title lettering: **Alex Jay**

Comic lettering: **Ken Lopez**

Super hero profile coloring: **Gregory Wright**

Endpapers: **Tom Morehouse**

Archival photography: **Eliot R. Brown**

Location photography: **Michael Melford and Jim McCrary**

Merchandise photography: **David Arky**

Library of Congress Cataloging-in-Publication Data

Daniels, Les. 1943-
    Marvel: Five fabulous decades of the world's greatest comics
    Les Daniels: introduction by Stan Lee.
        288 p.   cm
        ISBN 0-8109-3821-9 (cloth)
        1. Marvel comics group. 2. Comic books, strips, etc.—United
    States—History and criticism. 1. Title.
    PN6725.D195   1991
    741. 5' 0973—dc20   91-8783
    ISBN 0–8109–2566–4 (pbk.)

Acknowledgments

It may be a cliché to say that a book would have been impossible to produce without help, but in this case it's true. I owe a debt to everyone who has ever worked at Marvel; without their work I would have had no subject. Beyond that, special thanks are due to the many individuals listed below who generously agreed to grant me interviews. Not only did they offer valuable insights and information, but they proved to be a wonderfully intelligent and entertaining crew.

While everyone's cheerful cooperation went well beyond the call of duty, additional acknowledgment is gratefully offered to publisher Stan Lee, who not only contributed a lively introduction, but has been actively involved in all aspects of this project from its inception; to executive art director John Romita, who drew the book's jacket and the spectacular super hero portraits that introduce each chapter; and to executive editor Mark Gruenwald, Marvel's resident historian, who cast his keen eye over the book at several crucial stages. While acknowledging his inestimable efforts, I hereby absolve him of any responsibility for my theories and for any errors that may have inadvertently crept into the text.

Quotations from the late Bill Everett are from an interview conducted by Roy Thomas, and are reprinted with his permission.

Paul Levitz of DC Comics kindly consented to illuminate the relationship between the two giants of the comic book business.

Judy Fireman, my editor, provided the energy, enthusiasm and expertise to keep the book on track over a long, hard course. Holly Reandeau, publishing coordinator at Marvel, cheerfully solved countless problems and made it seem easy. Pam Rutt of Marvel publicity and Michelle Gagnon, Marvel's vice president of international licensing, helpfully provided much-needed illustrations. And editor Sid Jacobson got things off to a good start.

David Kaestle, David Vogler and David Wilson of David Kaestle, Inc. are responsible for the book's handsome design and layout. Working together, Vogler and I managed to keep both Federal Express and AT&T solvent until the end of the century. Danny O'Brien offered a helping hand at every turn. Eliot R. Brown produced the meticulous and painstaking archival photography, and Tom Morehouse created the amazing collage that embellishes the endpapers.

Thanks also to Paul Gottlieb at Harry N. Abrams for his strong and continuous commitment to this book, and to Eric Himmel for his cheerful and efficient guidance throughout the publication process.

Thanks to my agent, Merrilee Heifetz, for so capably taking care of business; to my sister, Diane Manning, for helping to transcribe the interviews; to my old friend Donna Rose for keyboarding the entire manuscript; and to John and David Buskin for the job recommendation.

My gratitude goes as well to the collectors who made material available for research and reproduction: John Andreozzi, Steve Bissette, Mike Chandley, Paul Dobish, Ed Fuqua, Fred Ganczar, David Anthony Kraft, Arthur E. Moore, Will Murray, Warren Reece, Rick Roe and Larry Stone. And a special tip of the hat to the inexhaustible Mad Peck Studios Archives.

And thanks to my mom, who bought me my first comic books.

SPECIAL THANKS TO...

John Buscema
John Byrne
Chris Claremont
Gene Colan
Gerry Conway
Tom DeFalco
Vince Fago
James Galton
Steve Gerber
Chip Goodman
Archie Goodwin
Mark Gruenwald
Don Heck
Michael Z. Hobson
Carol Kalish
Jack Kirby
Stan Lee
Todd McFarlane
Frank Miller
Jerry Perles
John Romita
Jim Salicrup
Jim Shooter
Ed Shukin
Joe Simon
Louise Simonson
Walter Simonson
Flo Steinberg
Terry Stewart
Roy Thomas
Len Wein
Marv Wolfman

Contents

SUPER HERO PROFILES

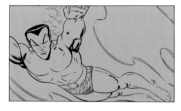

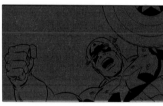

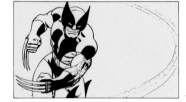

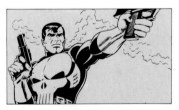

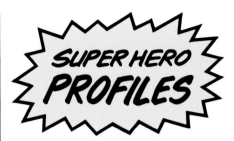

Introduction
by Stan Lee

Welcome to the wonderful, way-out world of Marvel! After more than half a century of creating comics, we decided to settle back, catch our collective breath and take stock of where we are and how we got here. And what better way to do it than by creating a book such as this?

Author Les Daniels meticulously researched our history, leaving no stone unturned and interviewing anyone and everyone he could find who had a part in the evolution of the Marvel mythos. Not only will new readers find a treasure trove of comicbook lore, but even those of us who were there will be amazed by all the colorful events and illustrations we had long since forgotten.

As for me, I love writing introductions. Guys like Les do the hard part, but the one who writes the intro gets to meet the reader first, while the reader is still in a good mood. As a matter of fact, I've probably done more introductions than anybody except the manager of a lonely hearts club. But never have I approached the task with more unbridled enthusiasm. To me, this is more than a book; it's a chance to visit again with old friends, with some of the most wonderfully talented artists and storytellers of our time. The mind boggles.

But what about you? As with everything we publish, the reader is always our first consideration. We want you to share every bit of the fun and excitement that we ourselves experience with every comicbook we create. We want you to savor again the thrill of discovery that you enjoyed when you were younger, when comics were your magical introduction to worlds of indescribable wonder and thrilling fantasy. We want to show you how we did it, why we did it, when we did it and, perhaps most important of all, we want to show you *who* did it, to have you meet the brilliant creators behind the names in the credits.

That's not all. Marvel's fame lies mostly in its characters. As you know, we've never been shy about talking about our heroes and heroines, and this is our greatest opportunity to go at it with both barrels. You're about to discover a cornucopia of facts and fables about our rollicking roster of super heroes and villains. In fact, if you pay strict attention, you might

Publisher Stan Lee, disguised as almost every Marvel hero, on a 1990 trading card. The original 1977 painting is by Arnold Sawyer.

Stan Lee in the 1950s with Joe Maneely, one of the finest — and fastest — Marvel artists.

even qualify for a rare, prestigious No-prize for being an M.M.M. (Mighty Marvel Maven), a highly-coveted bullpen award, somewhat on a par with a Pulitzer nomination.

Hard though it may be to believe, there's even more in store for you. You'll go behind the scenes to learn how comics are actually created and produced. You'll see for yourself how the magic happens, how we progress from the birth of an idea to its ultimate metamorphosis into a stellar feature between the covers of a Marvel comicbook. But let me digress for a moment to explore a subject dear to my heart, the oft-discussed, though highly elusive "Marvel style."

Ask any dedicated Marvel fan why he favors our line of comics and he'll probably say something to this effect: "They have a certain style that I like." Press him to define that style and he may become a bit vague; certain things are difficult to put into words. But allow me to try.

Perhaps the most important element in the so-called Marvel style is the fact that we strive to stress realism in every panel. I can imagine the scoffers among you leaping to their feet and exclaiming, "How can he speak of realism when Marvel specializes in fantasy?" Glad you asked.

The trick, as we see it, is to create a fantastic premise and then envelope it with as much credibility as possible. Case in point: Spider-Man. Here's a character who can walk on walls like an insect and shoot webs that enable him to swing from building to building. Hardly an overdose of total reality, I grant you. Well, having established the parameters of the unreal, we then do our best to treat ol' Spidey as if he could be your next door neighbor. Despite his super powers, he still has money troubles, dandruff, domestic problems, allergy attacks, self-doubts and unexpected defeats. In other words, we think of him as real and try to depict him accordingly.

The same applies to our other dazzling derring-doers. Despite their fantastic super powers, they still have woes, worries and weaknesses, and each has his or her Achilles heel.

Another way we strive for realism is through dialogue. We try to ensure that you'll never hear Wolverine speaking in the same manner as Reed Richards; the Silver Surfer will most definitely not sound like Nick Fury; Dr. Doom and Thanos will be miles apart linguistically; and Thor isn't likely to be mistaken for The Punisher if you happen to overhear him on the phone.

I'd be shamefully remiss if I neglected to mention another important element in the making of our mighty mythos. No matter how somber a story might be, you'll usually find an element of humor lurking in the background. For, above all else, our overriding credo emphasizes the fact that Marvel stands for fun, for slyly savoring the madness

Stan Lee in uniform during World War II. He never smoked cigarettes, but used one in this photo as a prop.

and mirth in the wacky world around us.

There's one other paramount rule drummed into every Marvel staffer and free lancer alike. We must never ever talk down to our readers. We've always been proud of the fact that we create stories for younger people which respect the intelligence of our older readers. Or, we could just as easily state the converse; we fashion stories for adults which can be read and enjoyed by younger readers. As a matter of fact, we're proud that Marvel was largely responsible for transforming comicbooks from a children's medium into a form of entertainment which today appeals to readers of all ages.

Next, onto a most urgent philosophical matter. Consider the word "comicbook." I've been fighting a losing battle with the rest of the world over that word for years. Most everybody spells it "comic book," as if it's two separate words. You'll even see it spelled that way throughout this very book, except in my introduction, of course! Now here's the crucial point, and you may take

notes if you wish. Any school kid can tell you that "comic" is an adjective which, in this case, modifies the noun "book." Thus the two words can only mean a comical book. Such an interpretation would certainly give a casual reader the wrong impression about our mighty Marvel masterworks.

Stan Lee as Uncle Stan, dressed up for a zany promotional stunt to encourage sales in 1975.

Behind the mask of Spider-Man is Stan Lee, whose writing and editing talents helped make Spidey the most famous and beloved of Marvel's super heroes. The drawing is by Lee's longtime collaborator John Romita.

Now, let's consider the single word "comicbook." Ah, what a world of difference doth lie herein! Suddenly, it is no longer an appellation indicative of humorous reading matter, but rather a generic term denoting a specific type of publication. That is why, to me, this tome is all about comicbooks rather than comic books. The defense rests.

But no matter how you spell it, our artists, writers and editors are among the most talented, dedicated and creative people you'll find on this planet. (We tend to think in planetary, cosmic terms). Each Marvel comicbook is like a mini-motion picture, with a bigger-than-life story that has to hold your interest from the first page to the last. Since most of our titles are published monthly, the writer's task is the equivalent of dreaming up plots for twelve movies a year. But that's just the beginning. Bear in mind that we publish close to a hundred different titles a month which, multiplied by twelve, creates an annual output of over a thousand issues, all compelling enough to make eleven million readers return month after month to peruse eagerly each action-packed tale.

How many writers and editors does it take to produce such a monumental quantity of work? A comparative handful! A few staff editors and a couple of dozen script writers. That's all! Finito! They're geniuses, each and every one!

But the scripts are only part of the process. Our artists, who are among the world's most famous illustrators, must not only draw the stories but must draw them quickly because of their never-ending deadlines. What's more, they must draw them dramatically, clearly and excitingly. Though they create more than a hundred panels for each typical comicbook, no two drawings can be alike. Each must be a different pose, a different angle, a different perspective, with different facial expressions and an endless variety of layouts, as well as all the subtle permutations of light and shading.

Perhaps that's why thousands of people all over the world inundate us with mail, enthusiastically commenting about our artwork and stories, offering a plethora of suggestions and critiques. It gives us the wonderful feeling that our readers are more than just fans, they're something far more valuable — they're our friends. They really care — and the feeling is quite mutual.

Since you too are a friend, it's time for me to end this rambling dissertation and let you get to the heavy stuff. But I'd like to close by reprinting a couple of paragraphs I wrote for my Soapbox column some time ago. They sum up the way I feel about Marvel Comics, and I'd like to share that feeling with you:

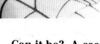

Can it be? A case of sibling rivalry!

To me, Marvel is more than a group of magazines. It's a cornucopia of fantasy, a wild idea, a swashbuckling attitude, an escape from the humdrum and the prosaic. It's a serendipitous feast for the mind, the eye and the imagination. It has a spirit you can almost feel, a sense that every Marvelite is an equal among equals as we share the fun and the foibles together. Finally, it's a gleaming tribute to our love of satire and excitement, a literate celebration of unbridled creativity coupled with a touch of rebellion and an insolent desire to spit in the eye of the dragon.

Or, to put it another way, if there were no Marvel, we'd have to invent it! Hey, come to think of it — we did!

Excelsior!

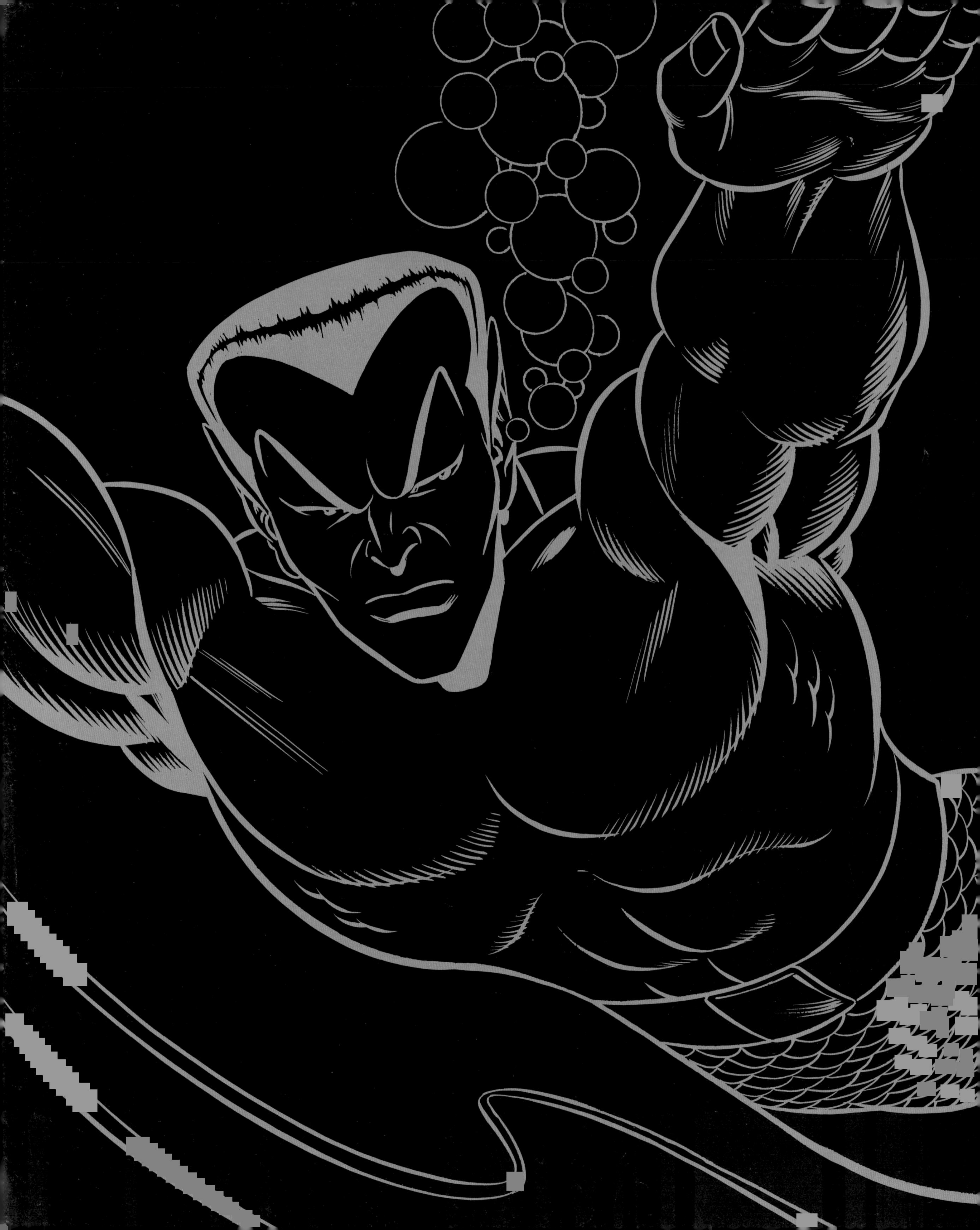

CHAPTER ONE

At the Corner Newsstand (1896–1939)

Comic books are born out of the marriage of newspaper comic strips and pulp fiction magazines. Fantastic heroes like Superman and Batman help define the new art form, and a young publisher named Martin Goodman decides to take a chance with *Marvel Comics* #1.

Marvel got its start in the 1930s by publishing imaginative fiction in pulp magazines. The covers already looked like comic books.

By the 1940s super heroes had turned comic books into a big business, and Marvel's top characters were fighting World War II.

In the 1950s comic books diversified, and unorthodox genres like horror created new audiences and then a public outcry.

A dazzling figure of living flame streaks dramatically across the night sky. Beneath him, an uncannily agile young man swings from a dark rooftop on threads of gossamer webbing. And in the shadowy street below, a lonely stranger is suddenly transformed into a rampaging beast.

This is the world of Marvel Comics, home to fabulous characters like The Human Torch, Spider-Man and The Hulk. Here an endless array of heroes and monsters sometimes pass each other in the night, but they are more likely to turn and erupt into exuberant conflict, creating pyrotechnical displays of thundering action. Marvel's tales of fantastic adventure, which entice and reverberate like the myths of ancient days, have entertained readers in America and around the world for more than half a century.

As the wellspring of vivid, archetypal heroes and the lasting memories they have brought to so many generations, Marvel is an enterprise of continuing commercial success and cultural resonance, one that maintains its power through the seamless integration of the creators' imaginings and the readers' fantasies.

The writers and artists who create the comics have always endowed their characters with such dynamic life that they have become, in Shakespeare's words, "such stuff as dreams are made on." Popular heroes like Captain America, The Sub-Mariner, The Fantastic Four, Iron Man, Thor, The Avengers, Daredevil, X-Men, The Silver Surfer, Conan the Barbarian, Wolverine and The Punisher, flamboyant figures with touchingly human flaws, are only a handful of the stars in a colorful cast of characters that numbers in the thousands and sells millions of comic books every year.

Through vigorous drawing, enthusiastic writing and energetic marketing, Marvel has succeeded in producing the most popular line of comic books in the United States today, one that commands tremendous loyalty in its readers.

And today's typical readers are not necessarily kids. While comics are sometimes dismissed as childish, they are—paradoxically—childlike in the best sense: they display uninhibited inventiveness and a sometimes startling capacity for candor. Comics are about what we are thinking, whether as children or adults. The comic book medium

has great potential to entertain and communicate, a fact that has been recognized more enthusiastically in Europe and Japan, where comics are much more popular than they are in America and where they have a predominantly adult audience. Yet the respect accorded comics internationally has begun to grow in the land of their birth, as more people come to realize that the escapism comics provide can be psychologically valuable, and that the direction in which we choose to escape can give us a new perspective on where we are and where we have been. In this freewheeling kingdom of popular culture, Marvel has created a symbolic history of America's psychological and social history over the past fifty years.

Comics as Culture

The comics show us ourselves and our attitudes in a funhouse mirror, the images exaggerated but still recognizable. The books record angry rebellion at the end of the Great Depression, a surge of self-confident patriotism and purpose in World War II, and then the confusion, disillusionment and search for suitable enemies that characterized the postwar era. The 1960s brought introspection and a quest for identity and meaning, while the 1970s felt nostalgia for the popular culture of the past, undercut by modern skepticism. The 1980s pushed boundaries with wild self-parody and a frank acknowledgment of the human capacity for cruelty, yet these have been tempered by the idealism inherent in the comic book heroes themselves. By their very existence, these characters affirm the hope that we may someday transcend our mortal failings and transform ourselves into something truly marvelous.

The story of Marvel Comics is also the story of an art form, one as uniquely American as jazz or rock and roll, and one that has also proven to be a universal language. The techniques of drawing, design and narrative are fascinating in themselves, and the creators are often as interesting as their creations.

These fantasies in words and pictures have captivated and delighted millions over the years; hardly a kid in America has grown up without them. They have become part of the modern consciousness, and their influence has spread into

A 1940s New York newsstand specializing in foreign periodicals had space for American comics.

other arts from painting to literature to cinema.

Most of all, however, comic books are fun. They present visions of speed, strength, heroism and secret powers. They offer excitement, adventure and spectacle. They appeal to the dreamer in all of us.

Ancestors of the Comic Book

The idea of creating a narrative through a series of pictures is as old as art itself, but the comic book as we know it today is a hybrid mating of two late-nineteenth-century forms, the newspaper comic strip and the pulp magazine. In the late 1930s the comic book became the reflection of a generally unacknowledged side of the American character: a new nation built on puritanism, rationalism and the work ethic nonetheless had a longing for the grotesque, the absurd and the fantastic. Other, older cultures treasured legends of heroes and clowns and monsters that dated back to antiquity, but this new land, a civilization without a history, had to invent its own myths.

Comic book artists looked to the past for inspiration, but ultimately the best ideas were new. Science and progress became dominant values in the new country, and fictional characters with astonishing powers were the result of humanity's experiments rather than divinity's whims. The new science fiction genre, which developed in the late nineteenth century, promoted serious artistic speculation and also allowed mythology to emerge in modern form. The "science" in many stories may have been nonsense, but the visions of fabulous transformations were powerful indeed. And when they were discovered by the pulp publishers, America's wildest dreams and nightmares began to be peddled for pennies at every corner newsstand.

Pulp magazines, with their lurid tales of brave men battling exotic menaces, provided the editorial content for comic books, as well as the all-important network for publication and distribu-

tion. Newspaper comic strips, with their rows of colored pictures and their dialogue in speech balloons, provided the comic book with its form. Coincidentally, both antecedent forms, the pulps and the strips, got their start in 1896.

Richard F. Outcault's "The Yellow Kid," generally regarded as the first modern newspaper comic strip, made its debut in 1896 in William Randolph Hearst's *New York Journal*. Use of the color yellow represented a breakthrough in printing techniques that, added to red and blue, made full color in newspapers possible for the first time, and it was this innovation that made Outcault's one-panel feature a landmark. The term "yellow press" came to be applied to papers that featured appeals to popular taste like reportage of political scandals, muckraking, descriptions of lurid crimes—and single panel or strip cartoons. Strips that followed the Kid continued to emphasize humor, hence the term "comics."

In the same year, publisher Frank Munsey "invented" the pulp magazine by printing his magazine *The Argosy* on the cheapest possible paper, known as wood pulp or pulp. Simultaneously, he switched from children's stories to tales of action and adventure, emphasizing a type of fast-moving fiction that is still called "pulp" today, more than three decades after the last magazine of that type gave up the ghost.

The standards for the pulp industry were set by Munsey's top writer, Edgar Rice Burroughs, who depicted an earth man conquering the planets and a white man dominating the "dark continent" of Africa. Burroughs' science fiction story "Under the Moons of Mars" appeared in 1912 in Munsey's pulp *The All-Story*, and was followed the same year by an even bigger sensation, "Tarzan of the Apes." The nearly-naked jungle man who battled against overwhelming odds became the prototype of the pulp hero, and his first adventure gave birth to countless sequels and imitations. The pulps proliferated, filling the nation's newsstands with hundreds of titles during the years following World War I.

Richard F. Outcault's "The Yellow Kid," the forerunner of American comic strips. Here, The Kid's debut on February 16, 1896, without his yellow nightshirt.

A new wave of super heroes, whose personal problems were as interesting as their powers, heralded the renaissance of the 1960s.

Experimentation and innovation in the 1970s brought about new interest in Marvel's mutants— misunderstood heroes who banded together to protect mankind.

Long established as the leading comic book publisher, Marvel in the 1980s reflected the new public interest in tough, streetwise characters.

► The most popular pulps were devoted to the exploits of a recurring character, often a vigilante like The Spider. This hero got his start in 1933, usually written by Norvell Page under the name "Grant Stockbridge." Marvel's Stan Lee remembered The Spider when he introduced Spider-Man in 1962.
Cover: John Newton Howitt.

◄ *Weird Tales* gained a reputation as one of the most literate pulp magazines. It introduced many important writers during its run from 1923 to 1954.
Cover: Virgil Finlay.

THE PULP WAVE

Pulp magazines bloomed and boomed during the era between the two world wars. Titles featured fiction on every subject from baseball to romance. But the pulps best remembered today are those that featured the outlandish, fantastic, aggressive heroes that helped inspire comic books.

The most important detective story pulp, *Black Mask*, made its debut in 1920 and showcased the tough private investigator heroes of writers Dashiell Hammett and Raymond Chandler. The first science fiction pulp, *Amazing Stories*, got off the ground in 1926, and two years later published a story by Philip Nowlan about interplanetary adventurer Buck Rogers. *Weird Tales*, a horror pulp that first appeared in 1923, featured tales by H. P. Lovecraft, Ray Bradbury and a young Texan named Robert E. Howard, whose stories about a bloodthirsty bar-

barian called Conan would eventually inspire a successful Marvel comic book series, as well as two feature films.

The popularity of certain pulp heroes led to magazines featuring them individually. Perhaps the best known was *The Shadow*, starring a hero who also had his own radio program. In print, The Shadow was a black-clad, gun-toting crime-fighter, but over the airwaves The Shadow had the added hypnotic power of being able to make himself invisible. In 1933, using the name "Kenneth Robeson," Lester·Dent created superscientist *Doc Savage* and a team of five colorful helpers. That same year, Robert Jasper Hogan recounted the daring aerial exploits of *G-8 and His Battle Aces*. From such stories, and the lurid illustrations on their covers, came influences that would shape the world of comic books for years to come.

The Pulps Go Daily

The marriage of the pulps and the comic strips took place on January 7, 1929, when two protagonists who had previously been confined to purple prose appeared at last in full color in newspapers across the country. "Tarzan" was transformed into strip form by artist Hal Foster, while Dick Calkins did the same for Philip Nowlan's futuristic "Buck Rogers," from the pulp *Amazing Stories*. Before this the strips had been truly comic, but now the influence of the pulps opened the way for more melodramatic fare.

The stock market crash of October 1929, and the long depression that followed, helped guarantee that the new serious note of the comics would not be just a passing fad. Readers wanted more than laughs; they also wanted images of strong men taking control of their world.

Crime fighting moved into the funny papers with Chester Gould's grim detective "Dick Tracy" in 1931, and pulp writer Dashiell Hammett got into the act in 1934 with "Secret Agent X-9," illustrated by Alex Raymond. In the same year, Raymond introduced his spectacular science fiction strip "Flash Gordon." Lee Falk and Ray Moore's "The Phantom" had a mask and a secret identity, and was the first comics character to dress in tights from head to toe.

The Birth of the Comic Book

The comic books that were about to burst into the country's consciousness in the early 1930s had actually been around in another form for decades. A book featuring The Yellow Kid had been published as early as 1897, but, like many subsequent efforts, it was a collection of comic strips rather than a comic book. Surveys showed that comics were the most popular feature in newspapers, but the ideal way to package the product remained undiscovered.

Two salesmen finally found the answer in 1933. Harry Wildenberg and M. C. Gaines worked for Eastern Color Printing, a concern whose giant color presses produced Sunday funnies for many newspapers. Casting about for something new to sell, one day Wildenberg folded up a newspaper page and saw that he had created a booklet measuring roughly seven inches by ten inches. He

Early newspaper strip heroes Tarzan by Burne Hogarth, Buck Rogers by Dick Calkins and Dick Tracy by Chester Gould.

acquired reprint rights to some comic strips, put together *Funnies on Parade,* and sold the book to Procter & Gamble to use as a promotional giveaway. The comic book was born. *Famous Funnies,* another giveaway, appeared later that year. Gaines thought up the next step: he affixed a ten-cent price sticker to some copies and tested them on a few newsstands. The copies sold, and *Famous Funnies* thus became the first recognizable comic book to enjoy retail sales.

Comic books reprinting old strips began to sprout like mushrooms, but the real breakthrough was to come with original material created specifically for the new format. The principal pioneer of this new idea was a retired army officer and former pulpwriter named Major Malcolm Wheeler-Nicholson. More of an editorial visionary than a businessman, Wheeler-Nicholson published *New Fun Comics* in 1935, followed it with a few more innovative titles, and was eventually absorbed by an entrepreneur more experienced in the battle for newsstand space, pulp publisher Harry Donenfeld. The company that evolved would eventually be known as DC, after its publication *Detective Comics.* One of DC's early experiments unleashed the character who was to define the comic book for the future: Superman. A runaway success, the Man from Krypton appeared in the first issue of *Action Comics,* dated June 1938.

Enter Mr. Marvel

By this time the enterprise that would become Marvel Comics was already in operation, headed by a young publisher named Martin Goodman. In fact, Goodman began publishing before DC, but initially his field was the pulps.

Born in Brooklyn in 1910, Martin Goodman was fascinated by periodicals throughout his childhood; as a child he cut and pasted stories together in an attempt to create magazines. As a young man, just prior to his involvement in the business that would become his life, Goodman set out from his modest beginnings in Brooklyn to explore America. According to Jerry Perles, Goodman's lifelong friend and legal counsel, "Martin's strength was in circulation and distribution. When he was young he traveled around the country, bumming in hobo camps, cooking over campfires. He knew every town and it helped him to know markets."

His explorations over, Goodman took a job as a

MEET MARTIN GOODMAN, PUBLISHER

THE SUPER HERO COSTUME

The standard super hero costume, which might seem more appropriate for gymnastics than hand-to-hand combat, immediately became all but obligatory for the first comic book heroes in the late 1930s; in the present the costume is a comic book convention. Artists laughingly refer to such outfits as "long underwear."

In truth, comic book artists, many of whom have at least some classical art training, and all of whom are pressured by deadlines to draw quickly, enjoy rendering what is in effect the nude figure in action. The reader responds with the unconscious understanding that gaudily colored near-nakedness is the proper attire for fictional characters enacting dreams and fantasies, as did the ancient gods. For generations of comic book readers, the skintight costume has seemed the appropriate garb for heroes who embody their deepest dreams of freedom and power.

▶ **Martin Goodman's first magazine was** *Complete Western Book.* **This issue, from February 1938, has a cover by J. W. Scott.**

salesman for a publisher in New York, and shortly thereafter set out to conquer the newsstands for himself. He was twenty-two years old.

In 1932, with the economy in disarray, Martin Goodman and Louis Silberkleit formed Western Fiction Publishing with borrowed capital, and produced their first pulp, *Complete Western Book.* Nostalgic stories about cowboys were in great demand as Americans attempted to create an epic of self-sufficiency and progress out of the conquest of the frontier, and the firm continued to produce similar pulps, like *Best Western* and *Quick Trigger Western Novel.*

Goodman quickly developed a philosophy of publishing that involved seizing on an appealing idea, whether it was his or another company's, and flooding the market with similar products for as long as public interest continued. He summed up his approach in a remark that has been often quoted in the industry: "If you get a title that catches on, then add a few more, you're in for a nice profit." On the face of it, this idea is simply common sense, and in fact it did enable Goodman to survive in the cutthroat world of magazine distribution while competitors fell by the wayside. Yet the idea was also a two-edged sword. By jumping from one hot concept to another, and exploiting each until it was exhausted, Goodman ran the risk of losing a distinct identity and the loyal following it could bring.

If he sometimes appeared to be a trend follower, in other ways Goodman was very much his own

man. He and Louis Silberkleit agreed to disagree in 1934, and Goodman became sole proprietor of his small empire. Silberkleit hardly disappeared into the void, however, since he soon became a partner in MLJ, publisher of the popular adventures of the orange-haired adolescent known as Archie.

Goodman exhibited shrewdness in the way he structured his business. Western Fiction was only the first of his many companies, which would eventually number—on paper anyway—more than fifty. There were two reasons for this diversification: a small, individual company in trouble could fail without affecting the others, and maintaining a number of small companies meant that each was taxed in a low bracket. Western Fiction was soon joined by Manvis Publications, Postal Publications, Emgee Publications and dozens more. The name of one, Newsstand Publications, exemplified Goodman's concern with distribution; the name represented a tribute to the ubiquitous vendors who provided the public with newspapers, pulp magazines and comic books. And for publishers, what happened at the newsstand was the bottom line.

Predictably, Goodman's employees had diverse opinions of him. In interviews years later, several referred to him as "a nice guy"; another attempted to be complimentary but ended up lapsing into obscenity; and one refused to comment. What they all seem to remember with amusement was

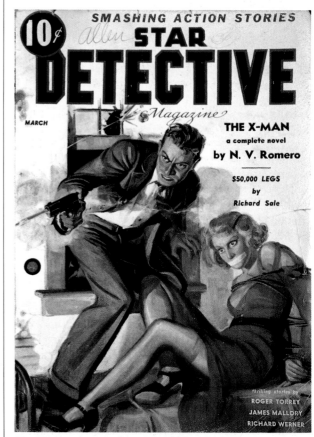

The X-Man, featured in this 1937 pulp, had no connection to Marvel's X-Men who, fifty years later, were wildly popular. Cover: J. W. Scott.

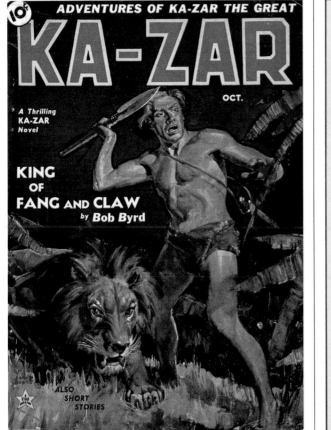

Ka-Zar had only a short pulp career, but he appears intermittently in comics. Cover: J. W. Scott.

his habit of stretching out on the office couch after lunch to take a nap. Despite such snoozes, or perhaps because of them, the Goodman empire continued to grow. He added pulps featuring sports, detective and adventure stories.

In 1936 came the debut of *Ka-Zar,* the first Goodman pulp based on a continuing character. In an ad prepared for retailers, the new hero is described in these glowing terms: "*Ka-Zar* is more than a fiction magazine. It is the old, never-ending, yet most thrilling of all stories, the fight of man against wild nature." In short, Ka-Zar was a fairly transparent imitation of Tarzan, one of the great pulp successes; even the names were similar. And yet the magazine folded after three issues.

Marvel Looks to the Future

Goodman got at least the title right when he began *Marvel Science Stories* in August 1938. This entry in the comparatively uncrowded science fiction field was not a notable success, but Goodman realized there was something about the ring of that first word, and he stuck with it as the title changed to *Marvel Tales* and then *Marvel Stories* before the magazine gave up the ghost in 1941.

But *Marvel Science Stories* did have its moments. It included work by recognized science fiction writers, even if the offerings were rarely their best. The lead story in the first issue was "Survival," by the

MARVEL'S ZANIEST PULP STORY

Uncanny Stories, a mixture of science fiction and fantasy that lasted only one issue, produced the most enjoyably zany story in any of Martin Goodman's Red Circle pulps: "Coming of the Giant Germs" by Ray Cummings. The title is a gem, and the plot delivers: some criminals steal a spaceship and escape to a planetoid, then grow lonely, return to earth and kidnap all the contestants in the Miss Earth beauty pageant.

The hero is the pageant winner's indignant boyfriend, who sets out to rescue her and the rest of the world's prize pulchritude. He soon encounters the colonized planetoid's original occupiers, the eponymous giant germs: "Little green slimy things like footballs with waving feelers on them. Bouncing footballs the size of a man's head. A million of them, crowded in there, leaping one upon the other in a pulsating mass." These turn out to be only the smaller giant germs; their big brothers soon emerge to reclaim their home, routing the bad guys and allowing Miss Earth and her friends to escape.

Ray Cummings was a recognized name in science fiction, but clearly this was not his finest hour. After this issue, dated April 1941, Martin Goodman abandoned science fiction and fantasy pulps. The Giant Germs proved deadlier than anyone had feared.

Martin Goodman's first science fiction pulp. Cover: Norman Saunders.

This title eventually gave the company a name. Cover: Frank R. Paul.

▶ **Depression audiences took a certain satisfaction in seeing New York, the country's financial center, wiped off the map. Cover: H. W. Wesso.**

prolific pulpster Arthur J. Burks. An editorial blurb describes it in typically breathless fashion: "What will the rebirth of America be, when one day the military forces of the world combine to devastate the greatest nation the world has ever known?" Marvel looked to the future and saw world war, but not every story was this serious. A

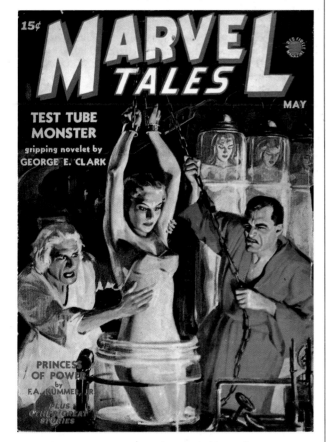

less politically concerned companion piece was Leon Byrne's "Monsters of the Mountain," about a plague of giant squirrels and bunnies.

The Red Circle

A halfhearted attempt to establish an identity for what was usually described loosely as "the Goodman group" was made when a new logo was adopted: a red disk surrounded by a black ring that bore the phrase "A Red Circle Magazine." But it appeared only intermittently, when someone remembered to put it on the cover.

Apparently for legal or financial reasons, different issues of the same title were published by different Goodman companies, and sometimes Goodman was listed as editor and managing editor as well as publisher. Nonetheless, the man who actually edited most of Goodman's pulp magazines was a former advertising copywriter named Robert O. Erisman. An unsung hero of Marvel's formative years, the energetic Erisman was evidently too busy to socialize, and did not leave a very strong impression on his colleagues, but Goodman appreciated all his hard work.

A Pinch of Spice

Several writers recall that Robert Erisman encouraged them to put some sex into their stories, but this was only in the brief period toward the end of the decade when such material was temporarily in vogue. A few publishers had been able to boost sales by upping the erotic octane of their

offerings, notably *Spicy Mystery* and its other *Spicy* sisters. These were produced by an outfit called Culture Publications; its backers included DC's Harry Donenfeld. By today's standards the sex was tame indeed: euphemistic descriptions of partial nudity—no body contact allowed. Perhaps to compensate, exotic forms of depravity flourished, the emphasis on whips and chains.

Goodman got in on this act in 1938 with *Mystery Tales* and *Uncanny Tales,* two "horror" pulps that seem so eager to titillate that modern readers find them merely humorous. Could there be any other response to stories with titles like "Pawn of Hideous Desire," "Cult of the Lusting Carcass" or "New Girls for Satan's Blood Ballet"? Perhaps the most lurid story of the era, "Fresh Fiancés for the Devil's Daughter," by Russell Gray, is hidden away in the back of the May 1940 issue of *Marvel Tales.* The plot has something to do with a crazed nymphomaniac who, to get revenge, forces men who have spurned her to torture each other's wives.

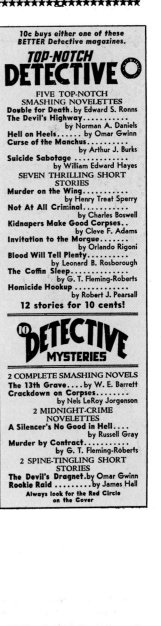

◄This ad, which appeared shortly before the first Marvel comic book, lists every magazine Martin Goodman was publishing in 1938.

▶ **Comic book artists Joe Simon and Jack Kirby provided this illustration for the interior of** *Marvel Tales* **(November 1940).**

Time for a Change

In his efforts to try new kinds of pulp fiction, Goodman produced a string of flops. *Ka-Zar* lasted three issues. *Marvel Science Stories* staggered along for three years while undergoing three title changes. The two horror pulps, *Mystery Tales* and *Uncanny Tales,* averaged a dozen issues apiece, and a follow-up, *Real Mystery,* survived for just two issues. Its stories were mostly retitled reprints from the two earlier sex-and-violence magazines. Someone in the torture-happy Federal Trade Commission must have felt he wasn't getting his money's worth, for Goodman was requested to cease and desist from the practice of recycling old material without designating it as such.

MIND-JOLTING NOVELETTE OF A ROBOT TO END ALL ROBOTS!

A DICTATOR FOR ALL TIME

by RAYMOND Z. GALLUN
Author of "The Time Retarder," etc.

The culmination of all scientific progress, was The Entity, with an inconceivably vast and complicated body comprising every element and compound that could exist, with a brain weighing well over a thousand tons!

What mindless plan would next occupy his colossal intellect?

NOT so long ago, birth had occurred. Maybe a half-billion years. Two stars had swept close; matter was torn from their masses in a brief interlude of unimaginable glory. Then those stars had gone on, like dogs retreating from a fight, to dwindle to pinpoints in opposite distances of space.

But around both, where there had been only emptiness before, tattered streamers had swung, coalescing gradually to form the crude, fiery shapes of primitive worlds.

56

THE BIRTH OF THE SUPER HERO

Jerry Siegel and Joe Shuster's Superman combined all the most intriguing elements of pulp and comic strip characters. Superman fought crime, came from another planet, had a secret identity—and he wore tights. He was also invulnerable and nearly omnipotent. Upon his debut in 1938, Superman immediately became the standard by which all comic book heroes were judged, and most of his successors offered no more than variations on the powers he possessed. Even the term "super hero" is a tribute to his impact and influence: his name became the job description.

The fantastic popularity of this one character guaranteed, and to a large extent defined, the future of comic books. Variations have come and gone, but the typical plot still involves an individual with incredible powers who is devoted to defeating evil wherever it appears. If there was a weakness in Superman, it lay in his very perfection, which made plotting difficult once the novelty wore off. He was also so earnest and upright—perhaps too virtuous.

In contrast to Superman, DC's second major hero was a mortal, obsessed with the idea of revenge. Batman, created by Bob Kane in 1939, was similar to a traditional pulp hero, a dark figure in constant danger who relied on his own brains and brawn. A product of dedication and training, Batman was comparatively believable, but whether that made him more appealing was a matter of individual taste. Humanized by the addition of a kid sidekick named Robin, Batman

further solidified DC's position as leader of the comic book industry during its formative years. In a crowded field, DC was the one company that Marvel would measure itself against for decades. Ultimately they both outlasted all competition, and became the two dominant forces in the industry today.

▲ **The Sub-Mariner was created for this comic book.**

Bill Everett shortly before he introduced Marvel's first super hero, The Sub-Mariner.

Yet all this time Goodman had been moving steadily toward the three elements that were essential to comic books: horror (without sex), science fiction and a hero who appeared in every issue. It was time to change to the new medium.

Some historians of popular culture have suggested that comic books replaced the pulps. This is not strictly true, since pulps continued to be published until 1955. And pulps appealed to an older audience. Yet comic books began to outsell the pulps almost at once. They were new; they were gaudy; they siphoned off many of the most exciting ingredients of the pulps, and simultaneously repackaged the most popular feature of newspapers. They began immediately to rake in a healthy portion of the dimes and quarters spent at the newsstand. Publishers like Goodman, who were successful with the new form because of their background in distribution, tended to lose interest in the pulps, especially when wartime paper rationing forced them to make a choice. In 1938 Goodman had twenty-seven different pulp titles on the stands; by 1944 only five diehard western titles remained. Yet his experience putting pulps into retail outlets gave him distribution expertise that many comics publishers lacked.

A salesman named Frank Torpey is credited with convincing Goodman that comic books were the coming thing. In 1939, Torpey was sales manager for an outfit called Funnies, Inc., a collection of artists and writers who had talent and ideas, but lacked the wherewithal for printing and distribution. Consequently, Funnies, Inc. was creating complete comic book packages to be sold to established publishers. With these packages Torpey enabled Goodman to venture into comics without having to hire a single person at the start. The arrangement worked so well that Torpey was soon hired as a salesman by Goodman, who always referred to him as "my lucky charm."

Marvel Comics Finds a Hero

Early in 1939 a bizarre character called The Sub-Mariner, part man and part fish, had been fea-

tured in the black-and-white *Motion Picture Funnies Weekly,* a failed promotional theater giveaway that Funnies, Inc. had produced. The creator of the story was a struggling young artist from Massachusetts named Bill Everett. "I wanted it to be different, totally different, from anything else," Everett said. "It was pretty darn hard to do, because almost everything was being done at the time. The Sub-Mariner happened to be a lucky guess." He was also one of the first great characters to emerge from the early days of the comic book.

The Sub-Mariner, furthermore, became the first Marvel hero: he was created by Everett before any other comic book character published by the Goodman group. Everett and his fish-man might have been dead in the water, but happily for all concerned, the story from the theater giveaway was repackaged for the first issue of Goodman's first comic book. Thus the big one that almost got away became part of an ongoing series with a title that would eventually give its name to a comic book empire.

The title, of course, was *Marvel Comics.*

Rough cover design by Bill Everett for an early issue of *Marvel Comics,* drawn in 1939 but never published.

CHAPTER TWO

The Golden Age (1939–1950)

Marvel introduces classic super heroes like Captain America,
The Human Torch and The Sub-Mariner, who thrive during
World War II but fade as the decade ends.
A creative scramble is on as Marvel experiments
with westerns, romances and crime comics.

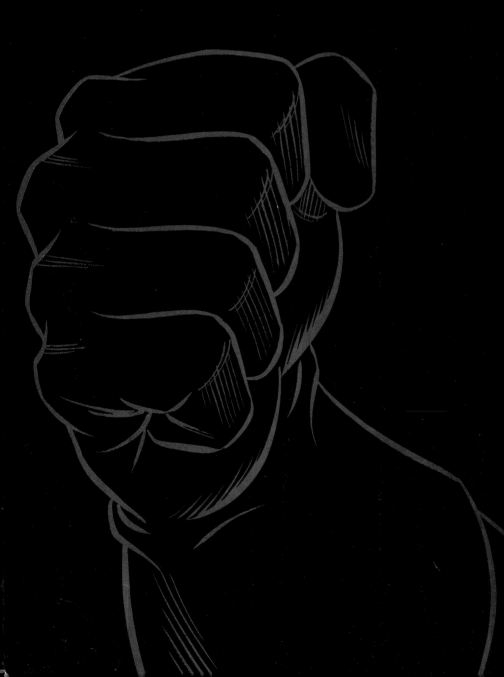

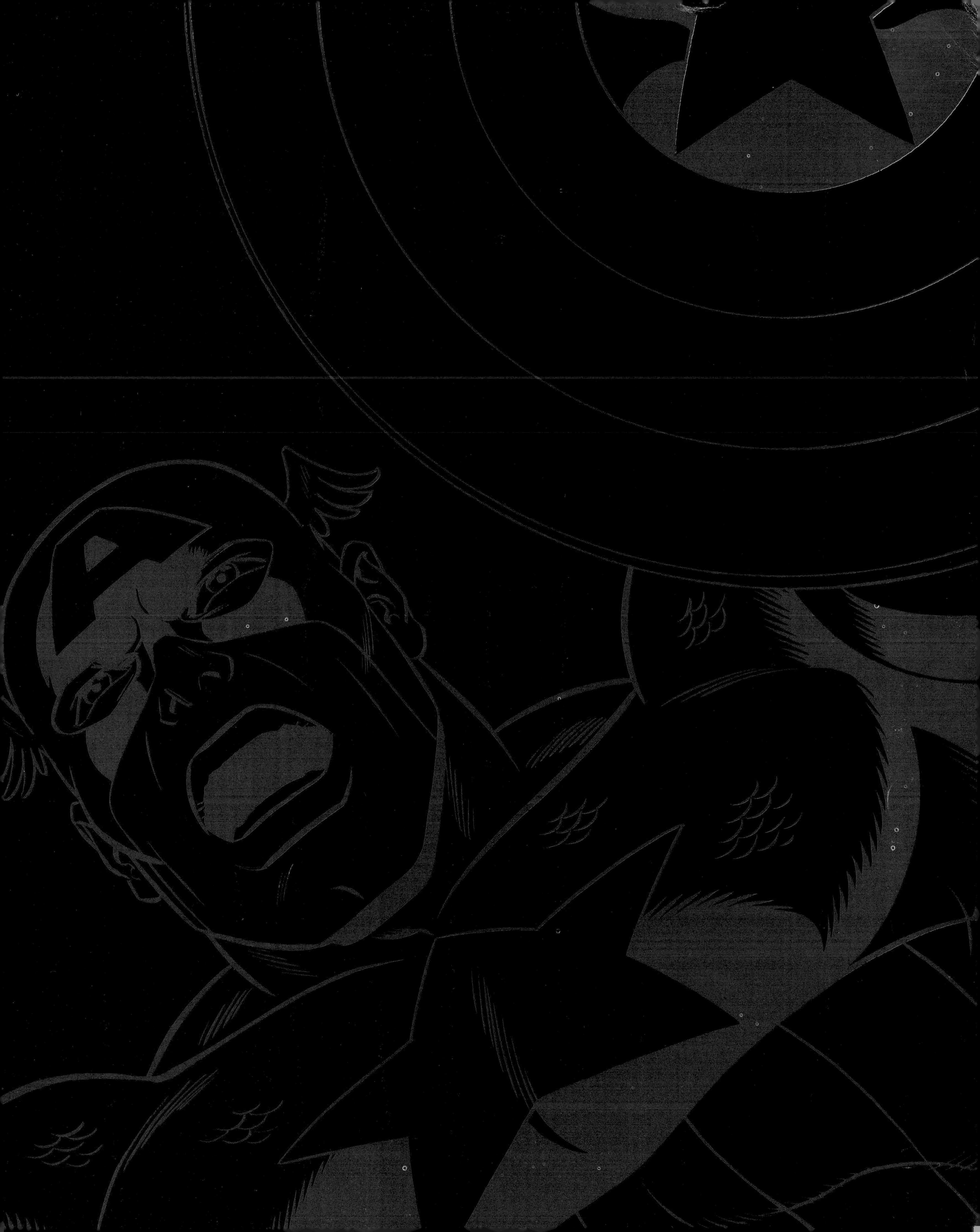

In 1990, Marvel reprinted the first issue of *Marvel Comics* #1 as a hardcover book priced at $17.95.

Marvel Comics was hot: the cover of the first issue depicted The Human Torch melting his way through a circular steel door to confront a crook armed with a pistol and a hand grenade. This fiery super hero, created by Carl Burgos, joined Bill Everett's aquatic avenger The Sub-Mariner to become one of the twin stars of the immediately successful *Marvel Comics*. The debut of two major heroes in one comic book was especially appreciated by Depression-era kids looking for thrills and adventure at bargain prices.

This first issue of *Marvel Comics,* originally priced at ten cents, has become perhaps the most valuable comic book ever published. In 1987 a rare copy in mint condition changed hands for $82,000. Its status as the maiden effort of the Marvel line, coupled with its atypical introduction of two classic characters, has made it a cherished milestone of popular culture.

Published in October 1939 and reprinted the following month, this comic book is the embodiment of what fans call The Golden Age, that period of happiness and innocence when both the fans and the comics themselves were young. It was a time of tremendous excitement and enthusiasm; because comic books were new, every page promised something fresh and interesting. Although the writing and drawing are unsophisticated by today's standards, the exhilaration of a new medium shines through, for this was a golden age for the comic book creators as well. These young men had grown up in hard times. The chance to earn a living writing and drawing wild fantasies was itself a fantasy come true.

A Bright New Flame

Carl Burgos was typical of the early comic book creators. He was young and full of fire. Like most of his colleagues, he was a gifted amateur—at this time there was no such thing as a comic book professional. Seasoned artists worked on newspaper strips; the young comic book artists were inventing a new form and they relied on energy rather than experience. The infant medium was a private playground, free of any demands of tradition or technique.

Burgos did it all: he invented the Torch character, wrote the story, did all the artwork and the lettering too. This one-man-band approach to the creation of comic books eventually gave way to something more like an assembly line, but at this point, as Burgos later recalled, "The miserable drawing was all mine."

The Human Torch, purists inevitably point out, was not really human at all. More accurately, he was an android, an artificial being created in a gigantic test tube by one Professor Horton, whose sloppy science caused his new creature to burst into flame upon exposure to oxygen. For safety's sake, the android was sealed in concrete, which could have ended the story right there, had it not been for a convenient leak. The Torch escaped and burst forth on an incendiary rampage, setting the city on fire while he screamed, "I'm burning alive! Why must everything I touch turn to flame?" By the end of the first episode, he had become involved with gangsters and had caused a death.

This was almost a horror story, with strong overtones of the Frankenstein theme. Confused, combustible and unstable, The Human Torch was hardly the ideal hero, especially when compared to the dignified and altruistic Superman. Gradually The Torch acquired some self-control, but his tortured beginnings helped establish a precedent for the flawed protagonists that would eventually become the Marvel specialty.

► The comic book that launched a company. It was published in 1939 and is valued today at up to $82,000. Cover: Frank R. Paul.

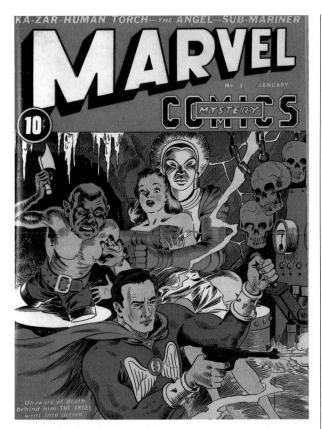

Dangerous When Wet

If The Torch had a wild streak, The Sub-Mariner was completely out of control. Bill Everett's work had the look and feel of a pulp terror tale, and in fact Namor The Sub-Mariner was actually a monster. His father was an American naval officer and his mother the princess of an undersea realm; their son grew up swearing vengeance on the surface people who had destroyed his idyllic undersea Antarctic kingdom.

With pointed ears and a wedge-shaped head, Namor was a freak in the service of chaos. Although The Sub-Mariner acted like a villain, his cause had some justice, and readers reveled in his assaults on civilization. His enthusiastic fans weren't offended by the carnage he created as he wrecked everything from ships to skyscrapers.

Undirected anger was one of the chief products of the Depression, and innocent characters driven to destructive behavior are among the icons of the age, notably in popular films like *King Kong* and *Frankenstein*. There was a widespread if not necessarily acknowledged feeling that civilization had failed and might as well be swept away; in some parts of the world this frustration led to Fascism instead of fantasy. But Namor embodied discontent more or less harmlessly; he also embodied the natural rebelliousness of youth. If Superman was America's superego, then The Sub-Mariner was its id. Bill Everett referred to both himself and his creation Namor as angry young men, and in 1939 his moody introduction of The Sub-Mariner was the best-looking and most interesting thing in *Marvel Comics.*

New Kids on the Block

Everett and Burgos began at once to alter the upright paradigm of the super hero as it was developing throughout the industry. *Marvel Comics* was something new, offering troubled characters who were rebels rather than role models for the youth of America. While The Human Torch and The Sub-Mariner were grandiose figures, both spoke in slang and exhibited adolescent attitudes; often they accompanied their violence with corny wisecracks. The danger of The Torch's flame and Namor's madness gave them an extra edge. They stood out at once from their rival heroes, who really didn't understand the glorious fun of making a terrible mess.

Publisher Martin Goodman didn't immediately realize just what he had: a great title and two dynamic heroes. He insisted that *Marvel Comics* also include his failed pulp hero Ka-Zar, whose jungle antics were dutifully revived by Ben Thompson. Goodman's eclectic taste was further reflected by the appearance in the comic of Al Anders' western character, The Masked Raider. Closer to current popular trends in the field was a costumed crime fighter, Paul Gustavson's The Angel, who had no uncanny powers but did sport a trim mustache. Goodman had hopes for this blue-clad adventurer and put him on the cover of the comic book's next two issues. He also inexplicably changed the title to *Marvel Mystery Comics.*

The changes didn't matter. Goodman had beginner's luck, and *Marvel Mystery* was a solid hit. Timely Publications became the name under

◄The Angel, temporarily missing his mustache, was cover boy for *Marvel Mystery Comics* in January 1940. Cover: Alex Schomburg.

Sub-Mariner v. Nazis in his first issue (Spring 1941).

Sub-Mariner v. Japanese at the Panama Canal (Summer 1942).

◄ Marvel remembers its early days in a page from a 1947 pamphlet called *Secrets Behind the Comics.* Script: Stan Lee.

► **The first page of the first story featuring the first Marvel super hero: Bill Everett's Sub-Mariner. From the first Marvel comic book:** *Marvel Comics #1.*

SUB-MARINER

The Sub-Mariner, Marvel's first super hero, remains one of the most remarkable. Created by Bill Everett more than fifty years ago, at a time when most comic book heroes were noble benefactors with no real personalities, Prince Namor was a troubled rebel with a short temper and a bad attitude. He was almost a villain, but fought to protect his people and his home from an aggressive civilization that respected neither other cultures nor the balance of nature. This monster from the ocean floor symbolized the battle against racism, exploitation and pollution; as a result, he was a particularly modern sort of antihero.

While many super heroes spring from scientific experiments, The Sub-Mariner is a throwback to ancient myths about mysterious species who share the earth with human interlopers. The Sub-Mariner's elfin appearance suggests that he is an elemental spirit who possesses magical talents for bedeviling mere mortals; in fact he is half human, and thus no closer kin to his undersea subjects than to the surface dwellers he professes to despise. Underneath it all, Namor is always at war with himself; his fierce desire to be a leader may mask a fear that he doesn't really belong anywhere.

The mellowed, almost middle-aged Sub-Mariner of today is a less startling figure than the half-crazed kid who rose out of the sea in 1939 to take on the entire world. Namor has even become comparatively resigned to the presence of the human race. Although The Sub-Mariner has grown up, his original incarnation of half a century ago established a landmark in Marvel's development. Here, for the first time, was a hero who exhibited convincing weaknesses; he might be brave, loyal and righteous, but he was also arrogant, obtuse and antisocial.

Protagonists with flaws in their makeup didn't really become common until the 1960s, but the unpredictable Sub-Mariner was a significant precursor. His status as Marvel's first great character is more than a matter of mere chronology.

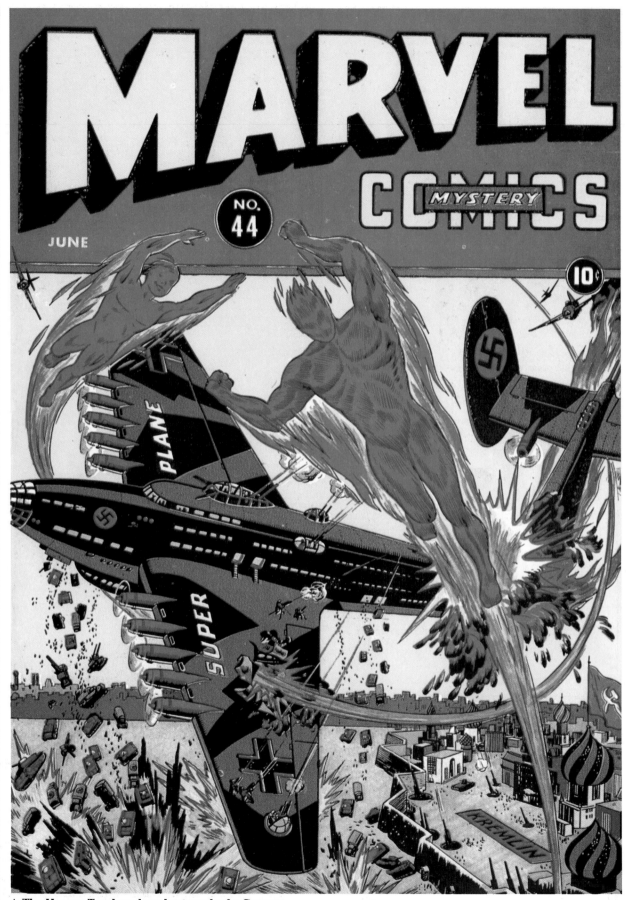

▲ The Human Torch makes short work of a German
"super plane" with help from Toro. This June 1943
spectacle is the work of Alex Schomburg.

PROFILE

I t was no accident that The Human Torch was emblazoned on the cover of Marvel's first comic book; he was, and still is, one of the most visually impressive super heroes ever invented. Part of his appeal may simply be due to the splashy use of the vibrant primary colors red and yellow. The blazing figure of The Torch embodies the very essence of the super hero: a pure distillation of energy and power.

If the simple sight of The Human Torch burning his way across a cover was good for extra sales in 1939, his personality was more problematical. He ignited in a burst of inspiration and then gradually dwindled to a mundane character with little to offer but candlepower. Carl Burgos conceived of The Torch as an android, a synthetic creation who sprang to life full grown, his powers honed to a dangerous edge, his mind a mere blank slate. The combination shot off sparks at once, but naiveté is a difficult quality to maintain. Each successive story made him wiser in the ways of the world, and thus made him less unusual. It was perhaps inevitable that he would turn to fighting crime, but the formerly alienated Torch strained credibility when he joined the police force. Before long, both the character and his writers seemed to have forgotten his artificial origin, his personality and his unique outlook.

The Human Torch was so thoroughly transformed, from a baffled innocent to a responsible adult, that he was ready within a year of his debut to take on an avuncular role as the guardian and instructor of a kid named Toro. A junior version of The Torch,

with similar but less spectacularly developed powers, Toro was an early example of the young companions who were grafted onto many super heroes during The Golden Age. And since he possessed no special attributes, Toro's addition merely provided readers with one and a half Human Torches.

Unlike his contemporaries The Sub-Mariner and Captain America, the original Human Torch was not revived during Marvel's spectacular renaissance of the 1960s. Instead, editor Stan Lee created a new Torch by transferring the striking appearance of the old Torch onto a new character: Johnny Storm, the hothead adolescent member of The Fantastic Four. This new Human Torch, who has now endured for far longer than his predecessor, possessed the lively personality to survive.

Whoever inhabits his form, the blazing image of The Human Torch remains. The power of fire continues to elicit an instinctive response, and The Human Torch is one of the great icons in the history of comic books.

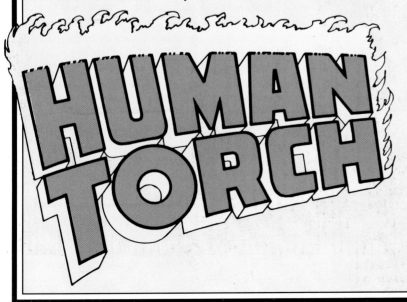

HUMAN TORCH

Young Joe Simon, Marvel's first editor.

Jack Kirby, Simon's long-time artistic collaborator.

▼ This handsome panel was the first Marvel work by writer, artist and editor Joe Simon. From *Daring Mystery* #1 (January 1940).

which Goodman first published a comic book line. He eventually created a number of companies to publish comics (as well as his other magazines), but Timely was the name by which Goodman's Golden Age comics were known.

A Triple-Threat Talent

Emboldened by his success, Goodman hired an in-house staff of his own. The new "staff" consisted of an artist, a writer and an editor—all embodied in one talented twenty-four-year-old named Joe Simon. A native of Rochester, New York, Simon had been supporting his family since he was eighteen, first as a newspaperman and later through work in comic books. In fact, he was working at Funnies, Inc., the company that supplied the stories for *Marvel Mystery Comics.* Goodman's pulp rates were lower than most, but Simon recalls that what Goodman paid for comic book work was "probably better than average. Only thing, by the time Funnies, Inc., got their cut, it was a lower rate." It was advantageous to both artist and publisher to eliminate the middleman. Simon says, "Eventually Goodman phased out Funnies, Inc., because he had me as editor. He didn't need them anymore." For the time being, however, Everett and Burgos and others stayed with Funnies. "They continued to work there and we edited them," Simon says.

Joe Simon's principal task when he arrived at Timely in the fall of 1939 was to develop new comic books. This meant experimenting with new characters, at least some of whom would be successful enough to grab readers by the throat and shake dimes out of their pockets. During the Golden Age, Timely created more original heroes than any other company. Inevitably, a lot of them were duds, but Martin Goodman realized that a winning combo like The Sub-Mariner and The Human Torch didn't happen every day.

Mystic Comics started in March 1940 and ran for only ten issues. It returned with this "first" issue in October 1944.

Daring and Mystic Experiments

Daring Mystery Comics and *Mystic Comics*, Timely's second and third titles, show just how tough the business could be. The characters in these comic books shifted crazily as hero after hero was tried and then dropped. Publishing schedules became erratic, and sometimes *Daring Mystery* and *Mystic* would disappear for months at a time before reappearing with a fresh new lineup.

Daring Mystery's constantly changing characters included such forgettable individuals as The Phantom Bullet and The Phantom Reporter, Rudy the Robot and Marvex the Super Robot, Dynaman and even Stuporman. One story featured a character with the interesting name of Marvel Boy, but he didn't make much of an impression, even on Simon, who shared credit for his creation. "I don't recall that one," he says today. "Probably another dog, huh?" The name survived, however, bestowed on a new hero called Marvel Boy who first appeared in 1950.

Perhaps the only character to debut in *Daring Mystery* that created something of an impact was The Fin, another aquatic adventurer from Bill Everett. "He was really just a frogman," said Everett. A fairly foolish-looking one, however, since his costume consisted of a two-foot-high fin strapped to the top of his head, apparently

intended to convince people he was a shark. Hardly anyone was fooled.

Mystic Comics did not fare much better. The cover character, The Blue Blaze, appeared in March 1940 and lasted only four issues. At that he did better than most of his *Mystic* companions, a gang that included Master Mind Excello, Merzak the Mystic and Flexo the Rubber Man. (Just for the official record, *Mystic* did include the company's first hero group, The 3 Xs, and its first female star, The Black Widow.)

Since most of these failed efforts came from studios or freelancers, an increase in the in-house staff seemed to Goodman to be a good idea. Thus in 1940 editor Joe Simon was joined by artist Jack Kirby. He proved to be a valuable addition indeed.

An Animated Artist

Jack Kirby, born Jacob Kurtzberg in New York City in 1917, had worked on newspaper strips and animated cartoons for the Max Fleischer studio before coming to comic books. Along the way he acquired a number of pen names, including Jack Cortez and Jack Curtis. The practice of using multiple pseudonyms was commonplace in the comics business—it was a way of creating the illusion that a small staff was larger. Ultimately Jack Kirby was the name that stuck.

Simon and Kirby were not strangers, having met while employed by another publisher. They soon combined forces to begin one of the great collabo-

When The Human Torch got his own comic book (Fall 1940), he also acquired Toro, who had started out as a circus fire-eater. Story and art: Carl Burgos.

rations of the Golden Age. Not only did they work at Timely, but they had an office together from which they created features for several other comic book publishers.

In their first year together, the team illustrated a number of pulp stories and came up with several characters, none of which really worked. Early on, they were involved in Timely's most devastating flop, *Red Raven Comics,* which never surfaced again after its one appearance in August 1940.

The most interesting hero Simon and Kirby created during their first year was The Vision. An eerie, green-hued being who came forth to battle supernatural evil, The Vision used smoke to travel back and forth between his world and ours. This idea rose from the smoke-filled office occupied by its creators, both inveterate cigar smokers. The Vision began his sinister career in the thirteenth issue of *Marvel Mystery Comics,* still the company's only truly successful title.

When Heroes Meet

Marvel Mystery Comics pioneered one of the most successful devices in comic book history when The Human Torch and The Sub-Mariner got together in the eighth issue (June 1940). This gimmick—known in the trade as a crossover— eventually led to countless multi-hero epics and thus helped establish the idea of "The Marvel Universe," a crowded, complex social structure in which all characters know each other.

Bill Everett and Carl Burgos worked on that first crossover story together, brainstorming to devise a plot which was then handed over to writers John Compton and Hank Chapman. The idea that the characters would be hostile to each other was a natural because, as Everett noted, "The two opposite elements had their own stories. What would happen if we got them together as rivals to fight one another?"

The clash of fire and water ended in a draw, so that nobody's fans would be disappointed. It's also not unlikely that each artist was protective of his own character. In any case, the precedent had been established that the crossover was just a good old American brawl.

Everett and Burgos each drew the hero he knew best, and the Torch versus Sub-Mariner story was extended for three issues, encouraging readers attracted by the stunt to keep coming back. "Everything was done with an eye for sales," recalled Everett. "We had such tremendous competition."

The cliff-hanger, like the crossover, would later spread throughout the Marvel line, but both were temporarily set aside during the war years. The serial story that took months to tell was perhaps too leisurely for the hectic pace of a world at war, and during the emergency there would be less tolerance for the rebel hero or for characters who wasted their energy in private feuds. These

The Angel of the 1940s had no super powers; in the 1960s his name was bestowed on one of The X-Men.

The Vision of the 1940s was an uncanny being from another dimension; the 1960s version was a hero of another color.

Marvel wasn't always Marvel; in the early 1940s the company was known as Timely Comics, and some covers bore this shield.

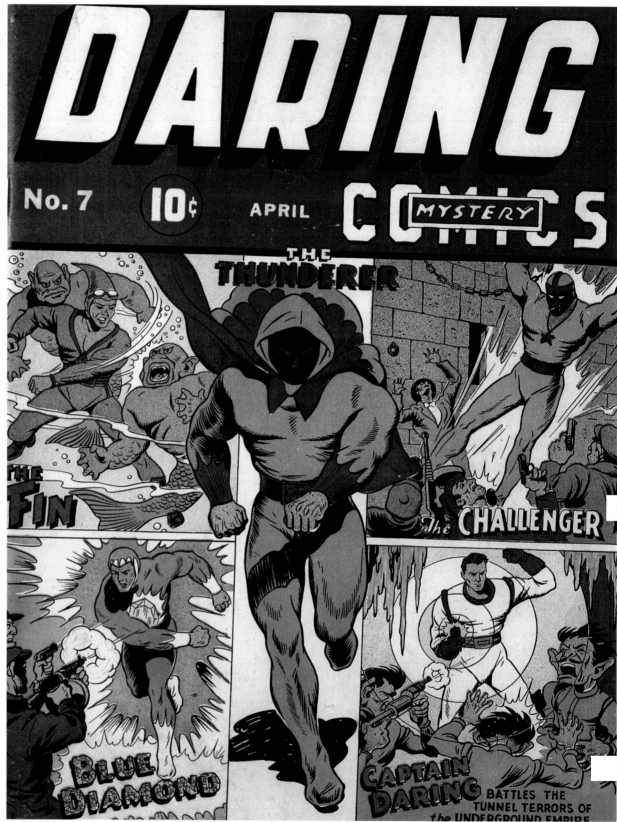

The search was on to find new characters who could achieve the star status of Sub-Mariner and The Human Torch, but it wasn't easy. The cover of *Daring Mystery* #7 (April 1941) introduced five new heroes and not one was a real hit, even though Carl Burgos created The Thunderer, Bill Everett created The Fin, and Joe Simon and Jack Kirby created Blue Diamond. Cover: Alex Schomburg.

▲ Sometimes it looked as if the same unemployed super hero was showing up at the office every month, looking for work, with a new name and his costume dyed a different color. Simon and Kirby drew The Defender for the cover of *U.S.A.* #1 (August 1941), but replaced him in the next issue with Captain Terror.

▲ More look-alike heroes. The Black Marvel showed up in *Mystic* #5 and lasted only three issues; Captain Wonder made only one more appearance after his debut in *Kid Komics* #1 (February 1943). Covers by Alex Schomburg (above) and Syd Shores (below).

MARVEL'S FIRST CROSSOVER

The confrontation between The Human Torch and The Sub-Mariner in the June 1940 issue of *Marvel Mystery Comics* inaugurated a tradition of encounters between super heroes that became one of the company's most popular features. Artists Carl Burgos and Bill Everett are generally credited with creating the concept, although Everett acknowledged that Martin Goodman "had an awful lot to say about the editorial content."

By the time this innovative epic was published, The Torch had learned to control his flame, taken on a human identity and become a New York City cop. Thus it became his duty, not to mention his pleasure, to take action when the antisocial Namor ran amok and wrecked a ferryboat, a train and even the top of the Empire State Building. When he learned that The Torch was on his trail, The Sub-Mariner became really annoyed: "Imbeciles! What shall I do next to impress them?" He flooded a tunnel, then destroyed The Bronx Zoo, but proved he was just a diamond in the rough by saving an infant from the stampeding elephants. Then he ripped up the George Washington Bridge.

Almost anything would have been anticlimactic by the time The Torch showed up, so most of the fight was put

off until the next issue, in which twenty-two pages of furious action ended in an elaborate standoff, followed by the cliff-hanging question, "What's your solution?" Readers had to wait another month for the one-page ending that enabled both heroes to walk away. By then circulation had jumped and hundreds of thousands of kids had gone crazy with excitement. The battle is still recalled as one of the great events of The Golden Age.

Joe Simon's original sketch of Captain America, the company's superstar.

editorial innovations were postponed for the duration, and did not come into their own again for more than twenty years.

Marvel Declares War

Martin Goodman was one of many Americans concerned about Hitler's aggression in Europe, even though isolationism remained widespread in the U.S. until the Japanese attack on Pearl Harbor on December 7, 1941. Goodman's concern was reflected in his comic books, which declared war more than a year before the United States government did. The comic book medium may have been humble, but the message got through to American youth as Timely's violent heroes found a suitable target for their hosility in the menace of Fascism.

The Sub-Mariner took on a Nazi submarine as early as the fourth issue of *Marvel Mystery* (February 1940), and both he and The Torch fought the good fight separately in the premiere issue of *Human Torch Comics* (Fall 1940). The two rivals even buried the hatchet and teamed against the Axis in *Marvel Mystery* #17 (March 1941).

Martin Goodman and many of his employees

were Jewish, and no doubt their anti-Nazi sentiment was partly a reaction to Hitler's insane policies. But there is also the fact that many of the Marvel pioneers were young men who had grown up in tough neighborhoods and knew a bully when they saw one. The same economic conditions that had produced Fascism had produced a generation that was ready and willing to do battle with it.

Goodman's son Chip, today a magazine publisher himself, suggests that his father also possessed the deep patriotism of the self-made man who sees the American ethic embodied in his own success. For all of these reasons—and because conflict sold comics—Marvel was ready to take on the world.

The war, not entirely incidentally, provided the company with a shot in the arm. Except for a new *Human Torch* quarterly, throughout 1940 and most of 1941, Timely was still publishing little more than a monthly issue of *Marvel Mystery*. It was time for Joe Simon and Jack Kirby to come up with a winner. And they did, with bombs bursting and flags waving patriotically.

The sketch Simon sent to Goodman still exists. A note at the bottom reads: "Martin—Here's the character. I think he should have a kid buddy or he'll be talking to himself all the time. I'm working up script—send schedule. Regards, Joe." The "character" was Captain America.

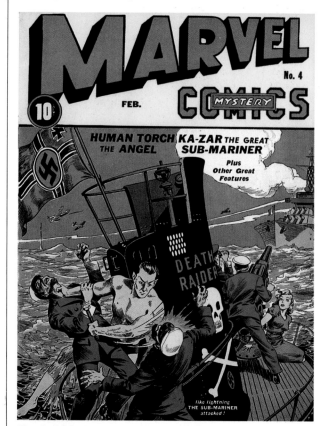

The Sub-Mariner was often grouchy, but when he lashed out at the Nazis, he became a veritable good guy. This first shot in Marvel's war against the Axis powers was fired in February 1940, almost two years before Pearl Harbor. Cover: Alex Schomburg.

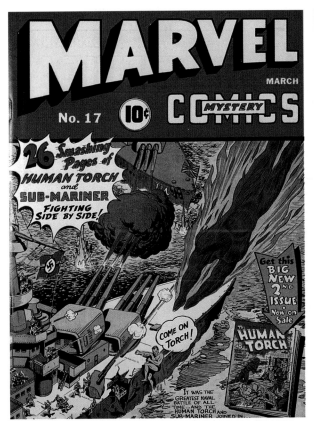

Super heroes were teaming up to fight World War II in this issue dated March 1941, while the United States was still waiting on the sidelines.

The All-American Hero

Captain America was the hero who put Timely into the top rank of comic publishers. The time was ripe for an idealized freedom fighter who possessed, in Jack Kirby's words, "the character to win and to triumph over evil. It is a simple formula, but very effective and powerful."

"Basically," says Joe Simon. "we were looking for a villain first, and Hitler was the villain." This idea was made quite clear by the cover of *Captain America* #1, which showed the new hero, dressed in red, white and blue, punching Adolf Hitler in the face. The date was March 1941, nine months before Pearl Harbor. The timing was perfect, and the unusual move of starting a new character in his own comic book would prove to be very successful.

"*Captain America* was exceptional, a sellout," says Simon. "We were up to, after the first issue, close to the million mark, and that was monthly." A circulation figure like that, far above what most popular comics achieve today, put Captain America in the same league with Superman and Batman as one of the true giants of The Golden Age. As a contrast, consider that the weekly circulation of *Time* magazine during the same period was 700,000 and that there were dozens of comic books on sale for every news magazine. "We were entertaining the world," Simon says.

Captain America's appeal was novel; he was not

born with great power, but rather had it bestowed upon him as a gift. The champion of freedom started out as Steve Rogers, a scrawny 4-F rejected by the army and then redeemed by a dose of a "strange seething liquid" that turned him into a strapping specimen of heroic young manhood. It could happen to anyone, even the ordinary reader. And part of the attraction was that Steve Rogers never became excessively gifted; he wasn't invulnerable—he was just tougher and braver and smarter than anyone else.

The secret formula and its inventor were destroyed by saboteurs, and therefore Captain America was the only one of his kind, assigned by the government to disguise himself as a private in the army. The fact that many readers would soon find themselves in that very same army helped ensure "Cap's" popularity; the new soldiers remained comic book fans, and they, too, hoped to be heroes in disguise. Meanwhile, the "kid buddy" showed up as Bucky Barnes, the teenage "mascot of the regiment" at Camp Leigh. Timely had already established the precedent of a younger, less powerful sidekick with The Human Torch's companion Toro, so readers without quite

THE MAN BEHIND THE COVERS

The chief cover artist for Marvel throughout The Golden Age was Alex Schomburg, a master at depicting scenes of mass confusion. His work, at once spectacular and meticulous, was often the best part of the books it graced. Publisher Goodman, who appreciated getting his money's worth, said that when Schomburg drew a bridge, you could see every rivet.

Schomburg worked in his own studio without direct supervision, although some of his covers were reportedly

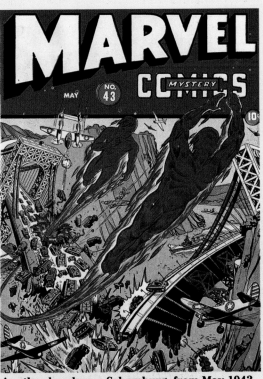

Another handsome Schomburg, from May 1943.

elaborations of roughs prepared by staff artists. His first Timely work appeared on the first issue of *Daring Mystery* in 1940, but he really came into his own during the war, when he began to produce phantasmagoric riots of men, machinery and monsters, plus as many super heroes as he possibly could squeeze onto the page. Schomburg always depicted even the most devastating chaos with elegantly precise style.

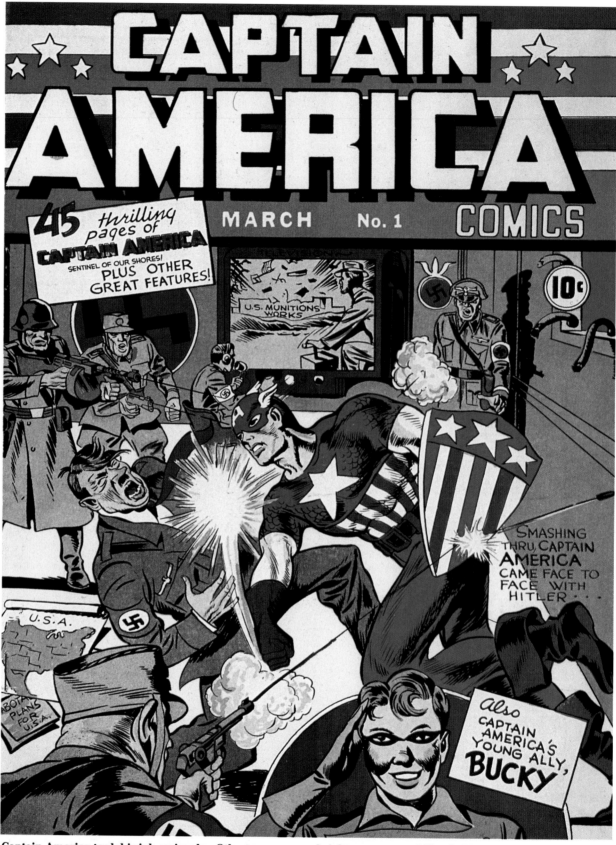

Captain America took his job seriously. Other super heroes might fight fascist foot soldiers, but he headed straight for the high command. This provocative cover, which provided wish fulfillment for countless readers, set Captain America off on one of the brightest careers of The Golden Age. Cap's shield, which may have inspired the Timely Comics logo, soon underwent a modification in design, but either way it came in handy for a character who wasn't bulletproof himself. Cover: Joe Simon and Jack Kirby.

The formula that turned skinny Steve Rogers into the brawny Captain America may smack of steroids to today's audiences, but things were simpler in 1941, and chemicals that built muscles in moments were strictly science fiction. The avuncular scientist who created the concoction was called Professor Reinstein, a clear reference to Albert Einstein, the physicist whose equations did indeed play a part in putting an end to World War II. Story and art by Joe Simon and Jack Kirby.

THE SENTINELS OF LIBERTY: MARVEL'S FIRST FAN CLUB

Combining patriotism with promotion, the first issue of Captain America Comics offered kids the opportunity to join the Sentinels of Liberty. For a dime, Cap or one of his assistants would mail out a membership card and a badge. Signing the card meant promising "to uphold the principles of the Sentinels of Liberty and assist Captain America in his fight upon the enemies who attempt treason against the United States of America."

Joe Simon invented the club and its card and badge. "We were stirring up the population," says Simon today. "We weren't making any money on it, but the kids were taking an oath to defend the Constitution."

The club was dropped in the middle of the war with the explanation that the metal in the badges was needed for ammunition. "That's a good story," says Simon, "but I think the club was just becoming a bother." Either way, the club had made readers feel involved, a key to the company's success.

enough nerve to imagine themselves as the hero could at least identify with the eager young assistant and imagine themselves tagging along.

Cap's inspiring image also carried implicit intimations of President Franklin D. Roosevelt, crippled by polio and yet a charismatic leader during the Depression and World War II. But there was more to Captain America than the simple patriotic ideal; dozens of other super heroes would wrap themselves in the American flag without making an equivalent impression on the reading public. Cap was a very special hero destined to appeal to readers for a very long time.

The Sensational Simon and Kirby

It was the extraordinary skill of his creators that made Captain America special. Simon and Kirby were becoming consummate comic book collaborators, and their style took full advantage of the medium. Their pages had more punch than any others in the business, and their techniques were based on an intelligent division of labor. The day of the lone creator was passing, and these two artists learned to combine their talents in a way that maximized the results. Too busy for ego clashes, they worked together without much regard for who did what or who got credit. "We didn't even think of that," says Simon. "We just wanted to get the stuff out. I wanted to make more money, and Kirby felt exactly the same way. In those days, everything we did was for a sale."

"The usual practice," Simon recalls, "was that I would do the writing right on the page in pencil, in the balloons, and do the layouts. Then Kirby would tighten them up, and then most of the inking was mine. Not all, but a lot of it. We turned out so much work." Sometime after the first issue of *Captain America* was published, a young artist named Syd Shores came in to help with the inking, and thus became the third member of the Timely staff. Also about this time, Jack Kirby acquired the title of art director.

The new system of separating writing and penciling and inking would become standard, but it worked best when the collaborators had the talent and boldness of Simon and Kirby. Simon's layouts and Kirby's figures leapt off the page when contrasted with the static grids and stiff poses of many early comic books. As panels grew to fill a page, and then a two-page spread, "wide-screen" comics were born. "I was producing at a furious rate," says Kirby, explaining that his very speed was responsible for the dramatic distortions that made his work stand out. The results were similar to the "squash and stretch" techniques he had used in animation, where exaggerated actions were employed to create impact. Kirby's dynamic fight scenes were based on his own boyhood experiences on the streets of New York's Lower East Side. "I was in fights almost every day," he says. "Believe me, it was all reality."

A Teenage Sidekick Named Stan

In late 1940, with the runaway hit *Captain America* scheduled monthly, Simon and Kirby needed a young assistant of their own, and Stanley Martin Lieber, the teenage cousin of Martin Goodman's wife, was hired. Lieber was not a kid who liked the comic book concept of the adolescent subordinate; he readily imagined himself able to fill an adult hero's shoes, and he had enough ambition to match his imagination. Under the name Stan Lee he would become the most famous writer and editor in the history of comic books.

"He was a nice kid," says Simon. "Actually, he wasn't that much younger than we were. At first, he got us coffee."

Lee was seventeen at the time, a recent high school graduate, and not the only family member involved in Timely. In fact, the small company was very much a family business. "Martin had a brother named Artie, who did a lot of technical stuff," Lee recalls. "There was another brother named Abe, who was treasurer. And he had another brother named Dave, who did photography for the picture magazines Martin published."

Lee worked hard: "I did proofreading, I'd run errands, I'd erase the penciling from the inked pages, but then very quickly they let me do writing and I got into it. I mean, I hadn't taken the job to be a gofer, and I thought of myself as a writer. I don't think I had to press too hard because they needed somebody to help them with the writing." Like most of his contemporaries, he did not expect to remain in this strange new business for very long. "In those days the comic book business was the absolute bottom of the cultural totem pole," says Lee, "and if I wanted to be a writer, I wanted to write books."

Among his favorite writers were Edgar Rice Burroughs, Arthur Conan Doyle and Robert Louis Stevenson. Lee was also fascinated by the sonority of Shakespeare and the Bible. And of course he read comic strips, paying special attention to the futuristic "Flash Gordon" and to detective strips like "Dick Tracy" and "Secret Agent X-9."

Lee's first writing for the company was a two-page text filler in *Captain America #3*, a prose piece that qualified comic books for inexpensive magazine mailing rates. Entitled "Captain America Foils the Traitor's Revenge," it includes such breathless passages as: "Captain America suddenly picked up Bucky by his arms and swung him right into the two thugs, knocking their guns out of reach. 'All right, Bucky, m'lad,' he cried, 'see how brave they are without their toys!'" A certain lack of respect for the apprentice hero is apparent, but, as Simon says, "Nobody read those things anyway."

Stanley Martin Lieber signed that story with the name "Stan Lee." Whether it was his first name divided in two, or the first syllables of his first and last names, the pen name stuck, and eventually he adopted it legally. "I changed it because I felt someday I'd be writing The Great American Novel and I didn't want to use my real name on these silly little comics. I'm sorry I did it, because Stan Lee is a dumb name. Well, I guess in the long run it hasn't hurt."

If he was skeptical about using his real name, Stan Lee was not shy about promoting his alias. His first comic book story, stuck in the back of *Captain America #5*, recounts an adventure of "Headline" Hunter, Foreign Correspondent. The big opening illustration, known as the splash panel, reads "Story by Stan Lee," at a time when

Young Stan Lee, who in the early 1940's went from gofer to writer to editor almost overnight, recuperates with his British actress/novelist bride, Joan.

▲ This prose piece, Stan Lee's first published comic book work, appeared in *Captain America #3* (May 1941).

◄ The Sentinels of Liberty badge, a premium offered to Captain America fans for one thin dime. It's worth lots more today.

▲ The first of the innovative two-page spreads that helped make *Captain America* a pioneer in the art of comic book storytelling. Can you guess the killer? From *Captain America* #6 (September 1941). Story and art: Joe Simon and Jack Kirby.

▼ Another "wide-screen" spectacular from Simon and Kirby, this one from October 1941. Even back in the days when it was classical musicians who were called "longhairs," there was something suspicious about people who shunned barbers.

CAPTAIN AMERICA

Marvel's biggest success during The Golden Age, and one of the top-selling super heroes of all time, Captain America is, first and foremost, a manifestation of patriotism. His debut preceded his country's entry into World War II, and he rode the wave of public spirit that followed Pearl Harbor; thus he identified himself forever with a period that may have been The Golden Age of the United States as much as it was The Golden Age of comic books. Sentimentally, a certain nostalgia for the period remains, even among those who are too young to have experienced its triumphs and tragedies firsthand.

Cap's March 1941 debut.

When the war ended, Captain America seemed to lose his purpose. Within a few years he was retired, and a short-lived revival in the 1950s seemed to confirm fears that he had become irrelevant. His successful return in the 1960s, however, ingeniously took advantage of the problem: Captain America was portrayed as a relic of a less complicated era awakened like Rip Van Winkle. Now his quest for identity and direction are the themes of his adventures; he seeks the meaning of freedom in a time where patriotism may not be quite the same thing as unquestioning loyalty to political leaders.

Of course Cap has always been wrapped in the American flag, yet he is best symbolized by the shield he carries. Creators Joe Simon and Jack Kirby originally designed it to be triangular, but soon after made it round instead. It represents both defense and a target, and when thrown like a discus, it also functions as a surprisingly effective weapon. A safeguard that draws fire and then fights back, the shield is the perfect emblem for Captain America.

THE VILLAIN TO BEAT: THE RED SKULL

The Red Skull, who had a face to match his name, was the greatest Marvel villain of The Golden Age. Created by Joe Simon and Jack Kirby for the first issue of *Captain America,* he was originally a Nazi spy who was killed, unmasked and revealed to be a corrupt American industrialist named George Maxon. Like many villains, however, The Red Skull found death merely a temporary affliction, and returned again and again, a figure of endless ingenuity and evil. The details of his first appearance were forgotten and he was transformed into an icon of Nazi cruelty, who, after one of his many demises, actually succeeded in dragging Cap down to hell with him for a fight. No wonder kids forgot the mask and assumed The Red Skull was as ugly as he looked.

When Captain America was revived in 1964 by Kirby and Stan Lee, could The Red Skull have been far behind? Hardly. In a new story explaining his origin, The Red Skull was given a new background. The resurrected villain started out this time as a German criminal who was hand-picked to be Hitler's protégé, and embarked on his campaign of brutality and terror at the führer's command. The sinister Skull thrives even today as the embodiment of the most terrible scourge of the twentieth century, and as a warning that the spirit of Nazism might rise again. He continues to be declared dead from time to time, but nobody really expects him to rest in peace for long.

writers were rarely credited and the artists only occasionally signed their work. In the next issue Lee created a scythe-wielding hero named Father Time, but signed that story with the name "Neel Nats" so readers wouldn't know that he had written two stories in the same comic book. Even Stan Lee's alias needed an alias.

An Expanding Empire

Timely's fortunes were on the upswing; more writers and artists came into the company to constitute the in-house staff that became known both within the company and to readers as "the bullpen." More titles were inaugurated, four in the middle of 1941 alone. Timely's original hero finally got his own book with the publication of *The Sub-Mariner* (Spring 1941). *USA Comics* was a mixture of minor heroes who didn't last long, so *All Winners Comics* (Summer 1941), which included Timely's top three characters, was simply common sense. Captain America, The Human Torch and The Sub-Mariner appeared in separate stories in each issue of this book.

The company pushed its crusade against the Nazis about as far as it would go with *Young Allies Comics* (Summer 1941), which portrayed a gang of boys fighting World War II at a time when the United States was still deciding whether or not to join up. Led by moonlighting sidekicks Bucky and Toro, the kids were Jeff, Tubby, Knuckles and Whitewash. Although he was a deplorable stereotype, Whitewash was nonetheless Marvel's first black hero. Simon and Kirby actually provided only the concept and the cover for *Young Allies*; most of the remaining creative work was done by other writers and artists.

The war was fast approaching, and much of Timely's top talent would eventually be caught up in it. Stan Lee captured the feeling of growing grimness when his first important character, The Destroyer, appeared in the sixth issue of *Mystic Comics* (October 1941). This forbidding figure, drawn by Jack Binder, wore a pale mask and had a skull emblazoned on his chest. He worked behind enemy lines as a resistance fighter, and he was out for blood. "I tried to do heroes who wouldn't be the obvious cliché type," says Lee. "Maybe that's why I liked The Destroyer, because I did try to make him a real, flesh-and-blood, angry guy." He was a hit, and soon moved into other books.

The Big Battle

Challenged by so much activity and so many new titles and heroes, Bill Everett and Carl Burgos outdid themselves when they produced their wildest epic ever, a 60-page Torch versus Sub-Mariner battle that ran in *Human Torch* #5 (Fall 1941). The coming war was shunted aside for one last, great, just-for-the-hell-of-it fight. After the traditional taunts, traps and attempted fish-fries, the story

climaxed when The Sub-Mariner wiped out the entire city of New York with a flood of cataclysmic proportions. The story was spectacular, its length and scope unprecedented. No comic book had ever topped this one in sheer audacity and exuberance, and for many readers it still remains the pinnacle of Timely's Golden Age.

As Everett described it later, the creation of this spectacular special issue on short notice was something of an epic undertaking in itself: "There were quite a few of us that got together and went to my apartment and did the whole thing. We just stayed there the entire weekend. Nobody left except to go out and get food or more liquor and come back to work. We had four or five writers, and we had at least six artists including Carl and myself. Oh, anything up to a dozen people, in and

▼ **The Torch and The Sub-Mariner back at each other's throats in Fall 1941. This was the big one. Cover: Alex Schomburg.**

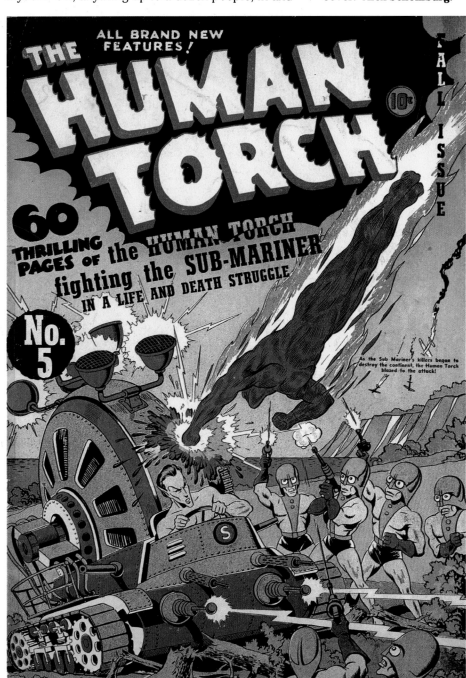

This was what the fans paid to see: two super heroes going head-to-head. The Sub-Mariner played the villain, of course, but when he was on a rampage, nobody was more fun. He started by kidnapping The Human Torch's annoying assistant Toro, just so the fight would be fair, then set out to wreck the planet From the sixty-page epic "The World Faces Destruction," in *The Human Torch* #5 (Fall 1941). Story and art: Bill Everett, Carl Burgos and others.

The big battle between The Sub-Mariner and The Human Torch raged all over the globe, with settings from London to the Arctic, but the climax was the ever-popular trashing of New York. The Torch cleaned up the mess, but clearly he was a little late. The art, by a team of exhausted artists who labored over a weekend to do the whole issue, looks a trifle tired itself, but in the early days of comic books it was the thought that counted.

The three greatest heroes of The Golden Age at Timely Comics, grown to giant size just because they were big stars, go into action on yet another of Alex Schomburg's wild covers (left). The terrific triumvirate weren't really oversize on the pages inside, and in fact never appeared in the same story until World War II was over, but this cover (Winter 1943–44) epitomizes the action and exuberance that typified Marvel before it was Marvel.

Publisher Martin Goodman (above) is seen holding the cover for *Captain America* #11 (February 1942). He watched his minor pulp publishing concern turn into a comic book bonanza. Goodman shrewdly guided the business for four decades, from the first western pulp in 1932 until he relinquished his hold on the company (which he had already sold) in 1972. Goodman, only in his early thirties when this picture was taken, was prematurely gray, but apparently that happened before he became involved with comic books.

Cap had a new foe in the first issue prepared after Pearl Harbor (April 1942).

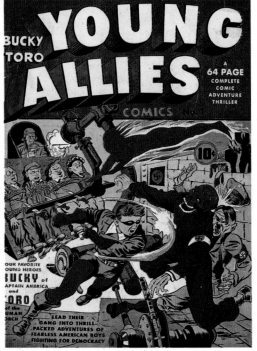

Kids v. Hitler and The Red Skull in the first *Young Allies*. Cover: Simon and Kirby.

Patriotic fervor on an unusual "book" cover. Story: Stan Lee. Art: Al Gabriele.

out constantly, working on this thing. It was a pretty wild weekend."

Exit Simon and Kirby

A major shake-up occurred at the end of 1941 when the team of Joe Simon and Jack Kirby left the company. Martin Goodman had dismissed Simon, citing the conflict of the work he continued to do for other publishers. "That's roughly right," says Simon, "but there's more to it." From his viewpoint, there were questions about fair compensation regarding the immensely lucrative Captain America. "We had a royalty arrangement with Goodman, but it was never in writing," Simon says, "and it never worked out to our advantage." Whatever the details of the matter, it was symptomatic of conditions in the industry, where publishers generally retained rights to the characters created by the artists they employed. To cite a now-famous example, it was DC Comics and not Jerry Siegel and Joe Shuster who owned all the rights to Superman.

Simon and Kirby left the shield-wielding Captain America behind and took their considerable talents to rival DC, where they created new characters like The Boy Commandos and The Newsboy Legion. Oddly enough, they had their biggest later success as a team when they invented the extremely popular genre of romance comic books for Prize Publications in 1947. Simon never again worked for Marvel after the break in 1941, but Jack Kirby would be back.

Meanwhile, Stan Lee was left as the sole member of the creative department that had just lost its editor and art director. He had come a long way from the day when his cousin-in-law Martin Goodman had spotted him in the office and asked absent-mindedly, "What are you doing here?" Lee says he was delighted at his new opportunity, and, at the same time paradoxically saddened to see his bosses go. "Jack never had much to say. He was just drawing and Joe did most of the talking. He taught me a lot."

Marvel's third editor, Vince Fago.

Lee the Leader

Vince Fago, who became a top artist at Timely doing humor books, recalls Lee at the time: "He was a young kid, and to him writing was like talking, and he used to love to talk. He was absolutely nonconformist, but a very wonderful guy. And it was unreal, because jobs were usually such grim things. He used to write a page and then call the free-lance artists and dictate it to them, a page at a time, over the phone. He'd work with about three or four people, giving them parts of stories. He was very good."

While a hard worker, Lee was nevertheless a high-spirited eighteen-year-old. "I was so young, I know I must have acted silly. In those days I played the ocarina. And people have told me—I had sort of forgotten it—that I used to hop up on top of the filing cabinets and sit there playing my

MARVEL'S WEIRDEST HERO

Of the countless heroes created during The Golden Age, none was weirder than The Whizzer. His special power was uncanny speed, acquired through a method unconvincing even by comic book standards: an injection of mongoose blood. The treatment was prescribed by one Dr. Frank for his son Bob, who lay dying of a jungle fever in Africa. "That's it," Dr. Frank says to a fast-moving fur ball. "I'll use your blood! I'll inject the blood of a mongoose into Bob!" What he hoped to gain is anybody's guess, but what he got was an exceptionally silly super hero. Dressed in yellow tights with a "W" on the chest and wearing a hat with clumsy-looking wings, Bob Frank became the quick-as-a-mongoose Whizzer in the first issue of

USA Comics (August 1941).

The Whizzer's original adventure was illustrated by Al Avison, but the name of his inventor is shrouded in mystery. Joe Simon, who was editor at the time, denies all knowledge of The Whizzer, and Stan Lee says, "I don't know if I made that up, but I remember writing it, because I wrote them all." Nobody wants credit. Yet The Whizzer was too fast to stop until 1947, when he bowed out after solving "The Riddle of the Demented Dwarf." He was briefly revived three decades later, but only so that he could be killed off for good. And yet, even today, half a century after his crazy creation, Marvel's mongoose-man is remembered with affection whenever mongeese meet.

Stan Lee, who went from
gofer to writer to editor of
the entire comic book line
in little over a year,
contributed his share of
characters in the
company's early days.

Stan Lee's first script for a comic book story, in *Captain
America* #5 (August 1941). Characters without
costumes were common before super heroes took over.

Lee's most successful 1940s hero, The Destroyer, made
his debut in *Mystic Comics* #6 (October 1941), three
decades ahead of The Punisher. Art: Jack Binder.

Father Time, another early Lee creation, lasted for
only seven stories. Note Lee's alias.
Art: Mike Sekowsky.

Another Stan Lee alias, "S. T. Anley," took the credit
for the adventures of The Witness, a vigilante whose
career was brief. From *Mystic Comics* #8 (March 1942).

Super Rabbit spoofed super heroes successfully in
Animated Movie-Tunes #1 (Fall 1945). Cover: Vince Fago.

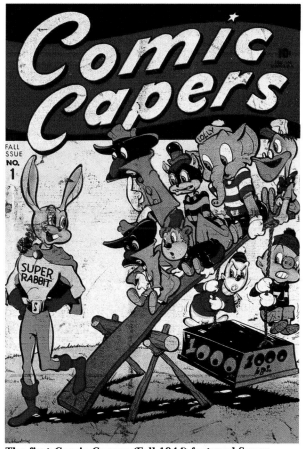

The first *Comic Capers* (Fall 1944) featured Super
Rabbit and several animal teams. Cover: Vince Fago.

Vince Fago, Marvel's third
editor, was a former
animator who specialized
in funny animal characters.
He oversaw development
of new genres that
eventually eclipsed the
company's super heroes.

Ziggy Pig and Silly Seal showed up everywhere, even
in their own title. Cover: Vince Fago.

Ziggy Pig appeared without Silly Seal on this Vince
Fago cover for *Komic Kartoons* #1 (Fall 1945).

The company's first attempts at humor featured funny people, not animals. *Comedy Comics* (April 1942) replaced *Daring Mystery*.

Joker Comics, which started simultaneously with *Comedy Comics,* presented the adventures of a goofy hero who called himself Stuporman.

Super Rabbit fought Nazis just like his human counterparts; here he foils a fascist pig in March 1944. Cover: Mike Sekowsky.

ocarina. I kidded around a lot, and it must have been a crazy place. But I had fun."

Another Timely writer with a bright future ahead of him was Mickey Spillane. While he didn't work on much except the obligatory text fillers, everyone who worked at Timely remembers him today because he became famous for his Mike Hammer detective novels. Actually, Spillane had plans for starting his own comic book company, with Hammer as the star attraction, but when financing for that project fell through he turned to prose—and made a fortune.

Remember Pearl Harbor

By the end of 1941 when the United States actually entered the war, many of Timely's characters had already been fighting it for so long that at first the change in the comics wasn't easy to discern. But soon there was a new emphasis on Japanese villains rather than Germans. Racial prejudice and resentment over the attack on Pearl Harbor created a climate in which it didn't seem out of line to depict Orientals as subhuman monsters. In 1942 a patriotic new insignia, a shield colored red, white and blue, was adopted to proclaim the books as Timely titles. But of course the biggest change came when many of the comic book artists and writers ended up in the service. Among them were Joe Simon, Jack Kirby, Bill Everett and Carl Burgos. Young Stan Lee patriotically volunteered for the army and after various assignments ended up writing training films.

Ironically, by the time the war really came the fighting super heroes no longer had the comic book stage all to themselves. Beginning in April 1942, Timely expanded into humor with *Comedy Comics* and *Joker Comics*, and *Krazy Komics* was not far behind. Timely's move was a response to the success of adaptations of Walt Disney's animated cartoon characters from Dell Publishing. Most of Timely's "crazy critters" were in-house creations, but in October came *Terry-Toons Comics,* featuring Mighty Mouse, Gandy Goose and other characters created by the Paul Terry animation studio. This was the company's first attempt at licensing characters from outside; it led in 1946 to *Mighty Mouse Comics.*

"It Was Always Rabbits"

The artist Vince Fago became Timely's third editor in 1942. As Stan Lee recalls it, "When I went into the army, the trend was funny animal books, and Vince was very good at that. That's why he became editor when I left."

Like Jack Kirby before him, Fago had worked at the Max Fleischer studio, which produced cartoons starring Popeye and Betty Boop. "Stan liked my work," Fago says, "because I was really a professional compared to most of the people who were drawing comics, excepting the great ones like

Simon and Kirby." Fago and Lee had collaborated on some early animal comics, including Ziggy Pig, Silly Seal and Frenchy Rabbit. "That was the thing in my life," says Fago. "It was always rabbits."

Things changed dramatically for Fago when he became editor and took responsibility for supervising the more melodramatic world of the super heroes. "It was an overwhelming job because we did maybe five books a week. The heaviness of the adventure stuff was a little overwhelming but I liked it because it was new." Martin Goodman encouraged Fago to produce covers for the super hero books that emphasized wartime violence. "I didn't like the blood too much," Fago recalls, "but I'd do it so I could do the nice stuff."

After a while, Fago began to sense that the super heroes scripts could take care of themselves. "I used to have to figure out what it was going to be with *Captain America* or whatever, what the hell do you do with it, what's a good plot. The writers would come up and we'd spend hours talking about what would make a good story, and I'd always agree because I felt these guys knew what they were doing."

Mighty Mouse was the company's most famous funny animal, an adaptation of the animated cartoons produced by Paul Terry and shown in theaters all over the world. The words "A Marvel Magazine" appear in the upper left corner of this Vince Fago cover (Spring 1947); the company had found its name, but inexplicably lost it again, and did not officially and permanently become Marvel Comics until 1963.

The Funny Animal Phenomenon

At the same time, the tide of funny animals reached full flood. The titles included *All Surprise, Funny Tunes, Comic Capers, Krazy Krow, Komic Kartoons, Silly Tunes, Ziggy Pig, Silly Seal Comics* and more and more and more. Fago had fun making up the titles, which today seem virtually indistinguishable, especially since the same characters were likely to pop up in any of them. Martin Goodman's policy of mastering the market by overwhelming it was in full swing.

Super Rabbit was the biggest hit. He got his start in *All Surprise* (Fall 1943), and his own book in the same season, achieving ultimately a run of five full years. "He was fun," says Fago. "I had ideas like having him come in on an aircraft carrier, the guys flagging him in. I liked doing him. I drew a little and wrote a little, and I used to rough in the covers."

Although these animal comics have little connection to what eventually became the adventure mainstream of Marvel Comics, many of them are charming and clever, and they have devoted fans even today. More of the Timely funny animals might have survived longer with the benefit of publicity from film tie-ins, a supporting benefit that characters like Donald Duck and Bugs Bunny always enjoyed.

The war years were boom years for comics. The books were still a novelty and a fad, and the animal comics expanded the readership to younger children while their older brothers in the service snapped up the super heroes. For a while, Timely's animals were actually selling as well as the super heroes. The only problem for publishers was getting rationed paper, but Goodman maintained a generous paper supply through the efforts of his attorney Jerry Perles, who managed to convince the authorities that the firm needed just as much paper as it had been using before the war. Once Timely had the paper, most of the pulps were dropped and the paper allotted for them was used to print comic books.

The Timely staff continued to expand, and the company moved into bigger offices in the Empire State Building. "Everything was selling," says Fago. "There were about fifteen people on the staff penciling and inking." One outstanding artist was Mike Sekowsky, who, Fago says, "drew as if it just rolled out of his fingers. He would almost not look while doing backgrounds on animated figures, and he did adventure stuff, too."

One factor about the humor books that doubtless appealed to Goodman was the pay rate. "If you penciled the animal cartoons," says Fago, "which were supposed to be easy, they would pay you less." If humor was cheaper to produce and sold just as well, there was no reason not to push it. A versatile artist like Sekowsky could be more profitably employed on funny animals. In any case, Timely was slowly drifting away from the

CAPTAIN AMERICA GOES TO THE MOVIES

A Marvel hero made the first leap into another medium in 1944 with the release of the motion picture serial *Captain America*. The producing studio, Republic Pictures, was regarded as the top purveyor of Saturday afternoon serials because of its skillful, enthusiastic staging of action scenes.

Of course, Hollywood made major changes in the material. In the film, Cap carried a gun instead of a shield, had a female assistant instead of the boy hero Bucky, and worked as a district attorney instead of a soldier. Even his name was changed for the movie version, from Steve Rogers to Grant Gardner.

Dick Purcell played *Captain America* acceptably, but the cast's main asset was veteran villain Lionel Atwill who showed melodramatic flair as the evil Dr. Maldor, a murderous archaeologist whose alias was "The Scarab."

Briskly directed by John English and Elmer Clifton, the 1944 *Captain America* is most notable as proof that the comic book character had become a hot property who could even sell tickets at the box office. Meanwhile, creators Joe Simon and Jack Kirby were away at war and didn't get a chance to see the serial.

With super heroes fading, Marvel put its strongest characters in one long story and unleashed it in Fall 1946.

The second appearance of The All Winners Squad (Winter 1946–47) was also its last. An era was ending.

Sun Girl, The Human Torch's new sidekick, got her own comic book in 1948 when Marvel tried female heroes.

super hero genre; during the greatest popularity of comedy comics, in fact, few new hero books were published.

There She Is, Miss America

And then, almost accidentally, Timely tapped into a new audience: teenage girls. The inadvertent cause of it all was a female character who made her debut in the back pages of *Marvel Mystery Comics* in 1943. Miss America, created by Otto Binder, was dressed in stars and stripes and was clearly a female version of Captain America. She got her own title in 1944, and very soon it turned Timely toward a new audience. "I hired a friend from the animation business, Pauline Loth, and she did the art for the first *Miss America* book," Fago recalls. "She could draw very well, no problem, and they had an ad in the book for a buck subscription. And in about two weeks, I guess, they had 20,000 answers to it. I had to take the artwork out of the filing cabinets and put the money in there. There was a lot of money in that."

Almost immediately the title character was dropped and *Miss America Comics* began to focus on the activities of average American female adolescents. Features were added on clothes, makeup and cooking, and a whole new division of comic

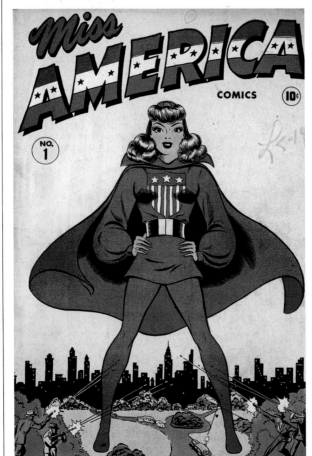

Miss America, the most popular of Marvel's women in tights, became the star of her own title in 1944, but lost control of it in the next issue. Cover: Pauline Loth.

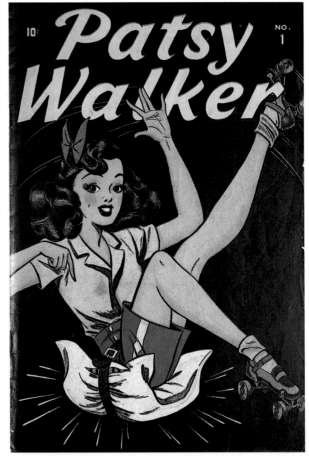

Adolescent antics on display in *Patsy Walker* #1 (1945, no month designated). Cover: Mike Sekowsky.

books came into being. *Patsy Walker*, whose adventures involved dates and dances, became a virtual industry after its first appearance in 1945, spawning several other titles. Patsy eventually became the star of the revamped *Miss America* as well. Altogether, the Patsy Walker phenomenon continued to thrive for twenty years.

Meanwhile, sales of the super heroes continued to decline. In the fall of 1945, *USA Comics* was canceled, even though Captain America had become the featured character.

The war was over, and when Stan Lee and Bill Everett and the others came back to comics they found things changed. Adolescent girls were in the driver's seat, and the Axis villains who had provided the motive for so many adventures were a thing of the past.

Lee took up the Timely reins again, even though he had to adjust to books like *Miss America*. In fact, he created *Millie the Model, Nellie the Nurse* and *Tessie the Typist.* Fago went on to other companies and other char-

Miss America #2 turned to teen topics and scored heavily.

acters, including Supermouse; he later created a long-running newspaper strip, the hero of which was Peter Rabbit, one of that long-eared breed that seemed to follow Fago everywhere.

The Postwar Blues

Lee made several attempts to boost up the sagging super heroes. The three old reliables, Captain America, The Human Torch and The Sub-Mariner, had been featured together on some of Alex Schomburg's wartime covers, but the trio had never been in the same story. Now, in 1946, Lee created The All Winners Squad for the nineteenth issue of *All Winners Comics*: he put the big three into the same story along with Miss America and Timely's resident speed demon, The Whizzer. A few years earlier such a move might have created a sensation, but now the public didn't seem to care. The book-length super-crossovers lasted two issues; then *All Winners* was canceled.

Next, several women took up heroics for Timely, which obviously hoped to capitalize on its pool of female readers. *Blonde Phantom Comics* appeared in 1946. Clad in a floor-length red evening gown and a tiny black mask, an outfit even less suited to adventuring than leotards, Louise Mason was able to solve the crimes that her boss, a male private eye, could not. Created by writer Otto Binder, The Blonde Phantom enjoyed a respectable run. So three more titles of the same ilk were added in

◄ The Blonde Phantom, Marvel's glamorous masked crime-fighter, got her own comic book (formerly *All Select*) in Winter 1946–47. Cover: Syd Shores.

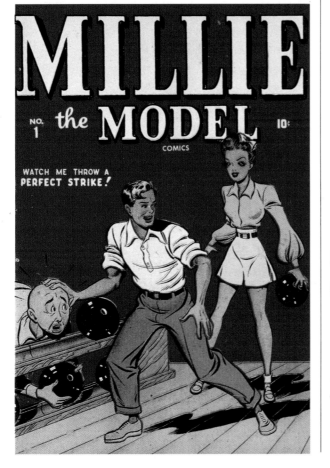

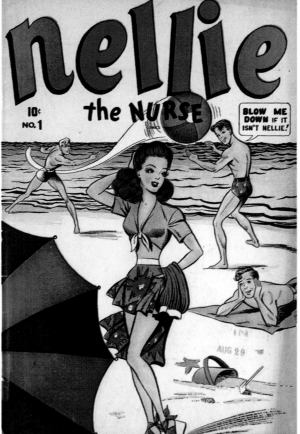

◄ Adolescent girls evidently preferred humor to women with super powers, so newly returned editor Stan Lee gave them what they wanted. The first issues of *Millie the Model* and *Nellie the Nurse* appeared in 1945. Covers: Mike Sekowsky.

This Marvel logo appeared and disappeared during the late 1940s.

August 1948 saw the debut of three female super hero comic books, including *Sun Girl*.

Namora #1 (August 1948) presented the amphibious companion of Prince Namor, The Sub-Mariner.

Venus was nobody's sidekick, but she had the powers of a goddess and lasted the longest.

▶ Boy companion Bucky bites the bullet, leaving Captain America free to work with a girlfriend instead.

August 1948: *Namora, Sun Girl* and *Venus.* The latter, featuring the exploits of the Roman goddess working among mortals as a reporter, was drawn by Bill Everett. The title managed to last nineteen issues, while *Namora* and *Sun Girl,* featuring the female counterparts of The Sub-Mariner and The Human Torch, were able to stay afloat for only three issues apiece.

These shapelier versions of the super heroes were evidently part of an effort to attract adolescent boys as well as girls. In the process, the long-standing tradition of boy companions finally came to an end. In *Captain America* #66 (April 1948) the unthinkable happened when Bucky was shot, sent to the hospital and never came out. As a result, Cap got a glamorous new partner called Golden Girl. Stan Lee today admits with a chuckle that this was probably his idea: "I have always hated teenage sidekicks."

Lee also says that these stunts were part of an effort to stir up flagging interest in what were becoming well-worn characters: "You never want to drop a title you have years invested in. You're always trying to find a way to shore it up before you drop it." Somehow the once invulnerable super heroes had become feeble indeed. The encouraging sales of the funny animal comics and the teenage comics had prompted the company to diversify its offerings, and the latest trends were sweethearts, cowboys and gangsters. Fan taste was fickle and consequently everything was subject to change.

There was even an effort to change the firm's name. The old Timely insignia had vanished from the covers and was replaced first by the words "A Marvel Magazine," and then by a "Marvel" logo reminiscent of the "Red Circle" from the old days of the pulps. The company toyed with the Marvel name that would eventually become world famous, but then unceremoniously dropped it. Timely, or Marvel, or whatever it was called, was in danger of losing its identity.

"Martin Goodman was a very successful publisher," says Lee, "because he kept his ear to the ground, and he would try to detect the trends. He would notice what was selling, and we'd put out a lot of books of that type." The short term results were lucrative; but while other publishers took the long view and kept their stables of heroes solid, Goodman let his slide. Still, he was publishing more titles than ever before, and his continued success seemed sure.

Crime comics, featuring crooks but not the costumed crime-fighters, and purportedly based on actual cases, had been growing in popularity since the 1942 debut of *Crime Does Not Pay* from Lev Gleason Publications. Timely jumped on that bandwagon in 1947 with *Justice Comics,* then added *Crimefighters, All True Crime, Official True Crime Cases, Lawbreakers Always Lose, True Complete Mystery* and many more. Some of the stories may even have been true.

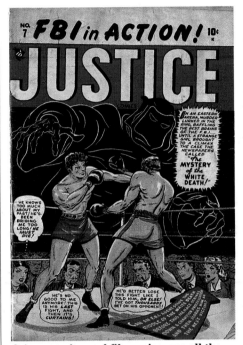

Crime comics and film noir were all the rage in the postwar period. Marvel jumped on the bandwagon in Fall 1947, with *Justice* and *Official True Crime Cases.*

These crime comics were the start of Marvel's involvement in a controversial genre that featured violence, cheesecake and disrespect for authority. Cover: Syd Shores.

Many crime comics claimed to be fact-based, but it wasn't a claim to take to the bank. Early work by Gene Colan from *All True Crime* #27 (April 1948).

Guns and Roses

A whole slew of cowboy comics was next. "I enjoyed the change," says Stan Lee. "I always felt that if you're a writer, you can write anything. Instead of saying 'Follow that car,' you say 'Follow that stagecoach.'" The first to follow the stagecoach for Marvel was *The Two-Gun Kid* (March 1948); others in the posse were *Annie Oakley, Blaze Carson, Tex Morgan, Tex Taylor* and *Kid Colt, Outlaw.* This genre proved to be exceptionally solid, especially in the next few years. Several of the western characters flourished for decades, establishing endurance records that put The Golden Age super heroes to shame. Martin Goodman had come full circle, returning to the

Two-Gun Kid #1 (March 1948) brought the western hero to Marvel comics for the first time. *Kid Colt* started in August 1948 and didn't stop shooting until April 1979.

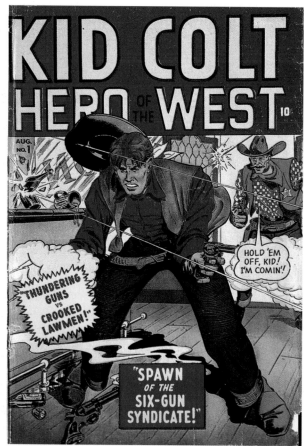

sagebrush setting of his first pulp magazines.

Stan Lee pressed on like a good soldier. "When we did westerns, I wrote more westerns than anybody; when we did romances, I wrote more romances. You could always tell what was selling by what we were publishing."

"Love" comics had suddenly become popular, and so Marvel introduced *My Romance* in September 1948. Close behind it were *Love Romances, Love Adventures, Love Tales, Love Dramas* and a load of others, including *My Love* and *Our Love.* Again, Marvel was playing follow the leader, and again, some of the titles in the new genre would enjoy unusually long runs. The redundantly titled *Love Romances,* for example, kept on chronicling the trials of the heartbroken until July 1963.

Brutally, shamelessly, the company next merged heartthrobs with hoofbeats and unleashed *Romances of the West* in November 1949. Four examples of the hybrid followed simultaneously in the following month: *Love Trails, Rangeland Love, Western Life Romances* and *Cowboy Romances. Cowgirl Romances* was not far behind. Asked to assign the blame for this concept, Stan Lee says, "It must have been me. We were trying."

Things had come to a pretty pass. Trends were transient things, and even Vince Fago's favorite Super Rabbit got the ax when his book, the last animal title, was canceled in 1948. At about this time, two new artists, Gene Colan and John Buscema, both of whom would later make superior contributions to the super hero genre, were put to

Love, love, love. Long a staple of pulp magazines, tales of romance took comic books by storm in the late 1940s, and Marvel followed suit. *My Romance* (September 1948) was the first of maybe too many.

work on crime comics. Colan recalls that when he met Stan Lee for the first time, the editor was wearing a propeller beanie on his head. "That little propeller was spinning around, and it made him look a little goofy," Colan says. "I'd never seen anything like it. It made me feel I was in the right place, to tell you the truth, because I was just as goofy myself."

An End to Heroes

By 1949 there was no place for the amazing if occasionally absurd super heroes who had defined The Golden Age. The old heroes who had gone to war before the country did just faded away while everyone was busy reading cowboys, crime and love. There was even room in the 1949 publication schedule for a comic book called *Blaze the Wonder Collie.*

Marvel's first super heroes went out fighting. *The Human Torch* **quit undefeated in March 1949, and** *The Sub-Mariner* **followed in June with a cover by Bill Everett.**

Gene Colan drew the cover of the final issue of *Captain America* (February 1950), but by then it was a horror comic called *Captain America's Weird Tales* and the old shield-wielder didn't even appear in it. *The Human Torch* had burned out in March 1949, and his former sparring partner *The Sub-Mariner* sank three months later. *Marvel Mystery Comics,* the title that had started it all, disappeared in June 1949. It had run for a very successful ninety-two issues, just under ten years.

Stan Lee is philosophical about the day the heroes died. "I never felt sentimental about them, because when something isn't selling you don't feel sentimental about it, you just wonder what you did wrong, and you're kind of glad to walk away from it. And then, there was always something else to do."

Bill Everett was not quite so willing to roll with the punches. His brainchild Namor had been somewhat domesticated after the war, and later the grandiose rebel had been reduced to slugging thugs. "I was annoyed that a lot of synopses of story ideas that I submitted weren't accepted, or were changed," he said. "I didn't like it much; therefore I don't think I did my best work."

And then the water was drained out of the pool, and Namor was no more. "I felt a slap to my pride, I guess," said Everett. "What the heck! You mean The Sub-Mariner, it's not selling? I don't believe you. It's impossible! My character—my baby— he's not selling? This is ridiculous! This just doesn't happen!"

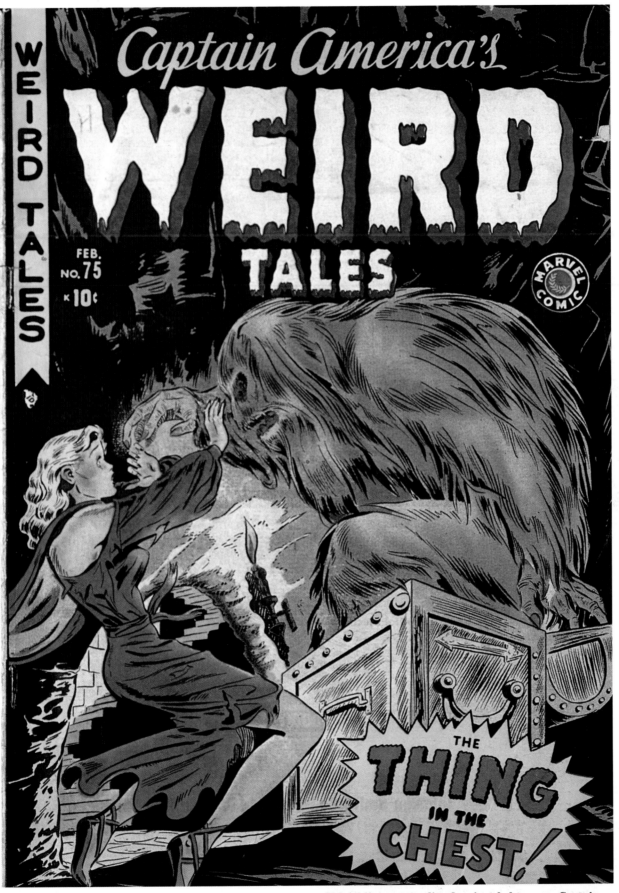

Old soldiers never die; they just fade away. Captain America was the last Marvel super hero to give up the ghost, lending his name but not his presence to this final issue (February 1950). Cover: Gene Colan.

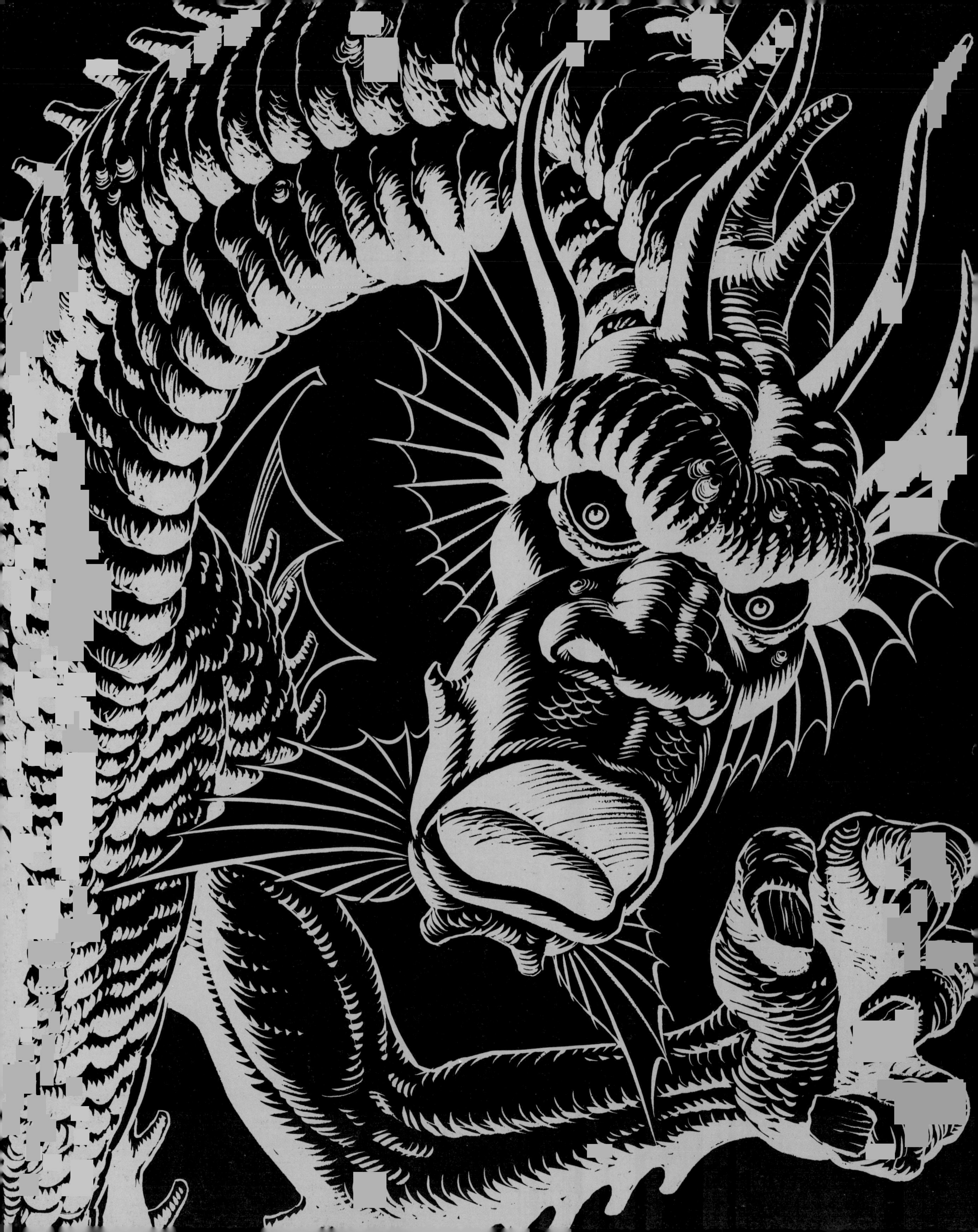

CHAPTER THREE

Comics in Crisis
(1950–1961)

Marvel tries every kind of comic book imaginable,
from humor to horror, and for a while sales
are strong. But boom turns to bust as the medium
comes under fire for presenting images of crime and
violence. Congressional hearings investigate the
link between comics and juvenile delinquency.
The future looks dark.

Often sentimentalized as complacent, happy days, the 1950s were actually a time of considerable tension in the United States. On the surface, things could hardly have been better. The country had come through the ordeal of World War II comparatively unscathed, and the economy was strong enough to allow generous foreign aid around the world. The atomic bomb in the American arsenal stood guard over the collective dream of the nuclear family in its neat suburban home. The United States called itself a "superpower," a super hero among nations, and saw itself playing the role of Captain America on the vast stage of global politics.

Yet there were undercurrents of fear, guilt and anxiety throughout the land. Conventional wisdom asserted that dropping atomic bombs on Hiroshima and Nagasaki in 1945 had saved lives by shortening the war; nonetheless, over 100,000 people had died in those two blasts. Humanity had acquired the power to eradicate itself. Americans felt a sense of betrayal as our former allies became our enemies; the Russians were perceived as thieves who had stolen our atomic secrets. We built underground shelters to protect ourselves, and saw flying saucers in the sky. The alien beings inside these ships might be enemies, or perhaps they were saviors come to relieve us from the awesome responsibility of policing the planet. In short, the country had the jitters.

Communists from Outer Space

Out of this uneasy atmosphere came *Marvel Boy* (December 1950), Marvel's first and only new super hero of the decade. Drawn first by Russ Heath and then Bill Everett, the new character shared only his name with the old Marvel Boy created by Simon and Kirby in 1940. The 1950 version was Bob Grayson, an American lad of seventeen raised on the planet Uranus by his father, who had ended up there when his rocket made an unexpected "right-angle turn." Blessed with the powers of strength, speed and mental telepathy, Bob returns to the land of his birth upon learning that "Earth is in a bad way," then trades in his Uranian flying saucer for a properly phallic American spaceship.

Everett's Marvel Boy stories are a rich stew of the symbols that made up the nation's nightmares. In one of them, evil aliens from a flying saucer kidnap a scientist who had invented an "anti-radioactivity ray" as protection against nuclear weapons. Although the bad guys are from outer space, Marvel Boy calls them "comrade" while he punches them. Their base on Earth is in Arizona, and despite his super powers Marvel Boy decides the best plan is to drop an atomic bomb on them: "WHOOM!!!" He then announces, even though it makes nonsense of the plot, that the kidnapped scientist was actually the leader of the Communists from outer space, and that the antinuke ray was a plot to weaken our defenses. The story sug-

Marvel Boy, the only new Marvel super hero of the 1950s, had a short career, but his adventures epitomized the era. The covers of the only two issues produced are full of the symbols of American anxiety: flying saucers and aliens launching attacks on democracy's sacred shrines. Covers: Russ Heath.

gested to its audience that radiation was desirable, flying saucers were full of Russians, and the bomb was our only friend.

All things considered, it's no surprise that the *Marvel Boy* comic book lasted only two issues. Yet in 1950, Marvel couldn't have cared less. Like the country, the company seemed strong and fat and happy; nobody felt the turbulence beneath the surface. Financial reverses for Marvel might have been considered a possibility at some point, but not even the wildest imaginations in the business could have dreamed that comic book creators would soon join the Reds and the Martians on the roster of America's enemies, and that the whole industry would soon be teetering on the brink of doom.

The Big Bullpen

By 1950, Marvel had become the consummate comic book factory, producing an incredible total of eighty-two separate titles on a monthly schedule. The turnover of titles was also impressive: many didn't last any longer than *Marvel Boy*. But the office in the Empire State Building was cranking out pages at a furious rate, and the center of activity was known as the bullpen.

In the nineteenth century, the term "bullpen" was used to describe a holding cell for prisoners; later it came to denote an area where baseball pitchers warmed up. At Marvel, the bullpen was a big room where close to twenty artists worked on salary, penciling and inking pages that were handed from one man to another until the job was done. Artists like Carl Burgos, Syd Shores, Gene Colan and John Buscema toiled side by side, trad-

ing tips and quips while they created tales of love and crime and cowboys.

"The bullpen was great," says John Buscema. "I loved working that way and being exposed to all those fantastic talents." Buscema was especially fascinated by the creator of The Human Torch. "I watched Carl Burgos and saw that something strange was going on; he was drawing with his left hand and then his right hand. He was ambidextrous. And he could write with both hands *simultaneously*, with his left hand backwards and his right forwards. It was unbelievable.

"When we worked, we worked," Buscema says, "but if something interesting came up, we might stop for a discussion, especially during the baseball season. We had a radio, and there was always a big to-do about whether we'd listen to the Yankee game or the Brooklyn Dodgers. We'd bring our own lunches, and there was usually a poker game at lunchtime."

Gene Colan, who had been hired by editor Stan Lee during one of those card games, recalls veteran staffer Syd Shores, the man who supervised the bullpen: "Syd had the experience and seniority, and he was good. He was the overseer of all the other artists and he gave quick lessons on how to make the work better if they ran into trouble. I learned a lot from Syd."

The Undeclared War

In 1950 Colan and his colleagues suddenly found themselves working in a new genre: war comics inspired by the outbreak of the Korean War. Dur-

▲ The atomic bomb's mushroom cloud was the emblem of the age. From *Marvel Boy* #2 (February 1951). Art: Bill Everett.

Caricature of Syd Shores, who started at Marvel in 1940. By 1950 he was running the legendary Bullpen, offering advice and encouragement to its artists.

▶ War comics of the 1950s emphasized the horror of battle, not its glory. *War Adventures* #1 (January 1952). Cover: George Tuska.

▶ This bizarre true crime tale (far right) featured the first Marvel work by John Buscema, who has since become one of the company's premier pencilers.

The tersely titled *War Comics* #1 (December 1950) was the company's first offering in the genre.

Battle #1 (March 1951) depicted the symptoms of stress under fire.

ing this conflict, which was like no other America had experienced, Marvel began to produce comic books very different from the ones that had been published throughout World War II. The battles depicted were no longer a matter of super heroes bashing bad guys; comics now began to show the pain, misery and fear of ordinary soldiers. Perhaps the change stemmed from the experience of writers and artists who had seen combat themselves, but the new war they portrayed was different too.

Technically, our troops were engaged in what was called a "police action," and officially the United States never declared war. Our soldiers fought under the banner of the United Nations, helping South Korea resist the 1950 invasion by North Korean and Red Chinese troops. By the time an armistice was declared in July 1953, more than 50,000 American soldiers were dead. Perhaps because of the unusual nature of the American involvement, the Korean conflict did not produce a great burst of pride and patriotism in the United States. Rather, the public response to the conflict fluctuated between skepticism and grudging support.

Marvel offered generically titled books like *War Comics, Battle, Combat, War Combat, War Action* and *Battlefront*. A few macho heroes were created, notably *Combat Kelly* (November 1951), but the majority of Marvel's comics in the genre emphasized the fact that war was a brutal and bloody business.

The Cutting Edge

Marvel's most innovative competitor during this period was a company called EC, an acronym for Entertaining Comics. EC's war comic books, generally regarded as the best in the business, were edited, written and sometimes drawn by Harvey Kurtzman, who went to EC in 1950 after a few years of free-lance humor work at Marvel.

"I was trying to keep Kurtzman busy," says Stan Lee. "I didn't want to lose him and we really didn't have anything for him at the time, so I gave him some gag pages to do and they were wonderful." These comedy pieces, which were occasionally published by Marvel under the title "Hey Look," foreshadowed Kurtzman's ground-breaking satirical EC comic book *Mad* (October 1952). EC's other editor, Al Feldstein, handled unusually intelligent science fiction comic books like *Weird Science* (May 1950) and well-crafted and extremely gruesome horror comics like the notorious *Tales from the Crypt* (October 1950). With its product clearly aimed at comparatively sophisticated readers, EC was at the cutting edge of the industry in the early 1950s. Interestingly, EC's publisher, William Gaines, is the son of M. C. Gaines, the man who had first thought of selling comic books on newsstands way back in 1933.

The success of EC had a definite influence on Marvel. As Stan Lee recalls, "Martin Goodman would say, 'Stan, let's do a different kind of book,' and it was usually based on how the competition

The first issue of *Mad*, EC's
most famous comic book.
Cover: Harvey Kurtzman.

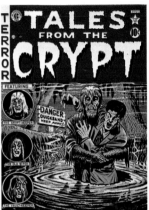

The wild and wonderful
Tales from the Crypt was
EC's leading horror comic.
Cover: Al Feldstein.

Weird Science was one of
EC's lurid but thoughtful
science fiction titles.
Cover: Wallace Wood.

◄ Harvey Kurtzman created
satirical gag pages like this
for Marvel before starting
Mad for a rival publisher.
From *Gay Comics* #37
(April 1949).

In January 1954, Atlas made this contribution to the brief 3-D craze. Cardboard glasses with red and blue lenses were included.

was doing. When we found that EC's horror books were doing well, for instance, we published a lot of horror books."

Bye-Bye, Bullpen

War was good for comics, as it had been in the 1940s, and business was booming. In fact, Marvel's large creative staff was working at such a clip that its very productivity resulted in a dramatic and ironic change in the lives of the artists.

Without any warning, the bullpen closed down for good. John Buscema recalls what happened: "One day somebody opened up a closet and found tons of completed artwork, penciled and inked and lettered and just tossed aside into this closet. I don't know how many thousands of dollars' worth of inventory was stockpiled there, and none of it had been published. So overnight, everyone was told that from then on we would work free-lance." The comfortable days of the salaried artist were over, and after the early 1950s the company's top talent would never again work together in one room.

This mass layoff was the first of a series of jolts that would punctuate the decade, a string of reversals that Stan Lee calls the "black days." Yet the end of the bullpen was really only a warning of what was to come. "The company didn't fold," says Gene Colan, "but they felt they could save some money by not having a staff of artists. But there was lots of free-lance work there—I picked up plenty, and I know the other guys did too."

The legend of the bullpen continues to live on. Twenty years after its demise, fans believed, and were still encouraged to believe, that all their favorite artists and writers were members of some kind of crazy club that met regularly every day. And for a while, it was true.

Alias Atlas

Publisher Martin Goodman's decision to cut back on office overhead and artists' salaries had a specific purpose. With comic book production at an all-time high, Goodman decided to maximize profits by breaking with his distributor, Kable News, and by setting up his own national distribution organization, the Atlas News Company.

The elimination of the middleman meant a chance to increase profits, but was initially a costly venture, and so the bullpen was sacrificed to make the new company possible. In one of Goodman's typically complex business arrangements, Atlas News became part of Atlas Publishing, which also included twenty-five separate corporations to publish the comic books and

Goodman's line of general interest magazines. By the end of 1951 the Atlas logo, a black-and-white globe, was appearing on all of Goodman's comic books. Marvel had become Atlas.

Adventures into Weird Worlds

Atlas branched out aggressively into the newly popular genre of horror, leading off with *Strange Tales* in June 1951 and following up with such titles as *Mystic, Spellbound, Journey into Mystery* and *Adventures into Weird Worlds*. The horror comic books of the day, following the example set by EC, featured an unprecedented level of graphic violence. The brief tales appearing in each issue were savage little morality plays in which evil and greed received their comeuppance in some spectacularly gruesome fashion. A typically cruel and unusual punishment appeared in a story that also incorporated the era's rampant anticommunism, Stan Lee's "Throw Another Coal on the Fire!" from *Adventures into Weird Worlds*. When the miserly janitor of a Moscow tenement hoards coal while the tenants freeze, they respond by tossing the man into the furnace.

The brutal irony of the horror comics was matched by the dark imagery of the best war comics and the corruption on display in the crime comics. The writers and artists, many of them cynical about conditions in the booming postwar world, portrayed a seamy side of life that many mainstream Americans had no wish to see. Comic books had in a strange way become part of the critical, alienated avant-garde. And when somebody finally noticed, there would be hell to pay.

The Super Heroes Return

With the Atlas distribution operation up and running, Martin Goodman suggested that Stan Lee, who had survived the layoff, try a revival of the three top characters from Timely's Golden Age. Super hero stories, once the mainstay of the company, had become virtually the only type of comics that Atlas wasn't publishing. So an experimental comeback was launched in the twenty-fourth issue of an unimportant book called *Young Men* (December 1953). Harking back to the triumph of *Marvel Comics* in 1939, Good-

Super hero revival (May 1954). Cover: Carl Burgos.

Three top heroes of The Golden Age were revived simultaneously, with suitable explanations, in *Young Men* #24 (December 1953).

The new Sub-Mariner comic book, with art by Bill Everett, made its debut with this issue in April 1954.

The Torch got his own comic book again in April 1954; it lasted only three issues. Cover: Carl Burgos.

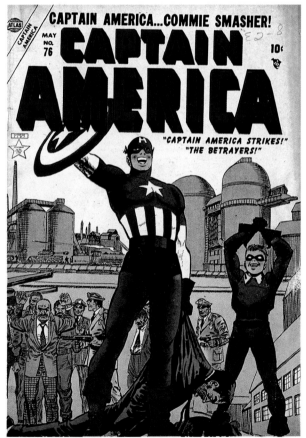

Captain America's comeback began in May 1954, but it didn't last long. Cover: Syd Shores.

SHOOTING STAR: JOE MANEELY

During the hectic days of the 1950s, no artist contributed more to Marvel than a young man named Joe Maneely. "He was the best," says Stan Lee. "Joe became a close friend, and he was the most versatile guy: romance, western, war, comedy, funny animals, horror— you name it, he drew it." But Maneely's specialty was illustrating the past. His countless westerns had an authentically dusty, rumpled look, and his greatest moment may have been the medieval saga, *The Black Knight*, that he created with Lee in 1955.

"He was also the fastest artist we've ever had," says Lee. "He could do seven pages a day, pencil and ink, if he had to. He would just do a stick figure and then he'd put the drawing down in ink." Maneely produced hundreds of covers, and in his spare time collaborated with Lee on a newspaper strip about scouting called "Mrs. Lyon's Cubs."

In 1958, at the age of thirty-two, Maneely was killed when he accidentally fell between the cars of a moving commuter train. "He was an intelligent, versatile artist, blessed with tremendous speed and an uncanny gift for characterization," says Maneely's colleague, John Romita. "It was a revelation to watch him work. If Joe Maneely hadn't died at an early age, he would have been Stan's mainstay."

A caricature of Stan Lee by Joe Maneely, who is sobbing in the background.

Covers by the prolific and talented Joe Maneely. *The Black Knight* #1 (May 1955) presented an unusual historical setting. Some western characters fared better: *The Rawhide Kid* first drew his gun in March 1955 and didn't hang it up again until May 1979.

man put The Human Torch on the cover of *Young Men*, with tiny panels at the bottom to assure the faithful that The Sub-Mariner and Captain America were "also in this issue." Later, each of the trio had separate stories in *Men's Adventures*, and again The Torch got top billing.

Carl Burgos did a couple of covers, but the artist who drew the first new Torch story was Russ Heath. Perhaps inevitably, nuclear fission was the cause of the character's reappearance. The story explained that criminals had doused his flame with chemicals and buried him in the Nevada desert, where a convenient atomic bomb test set him free with his powers enhanced. Most of the subsequent Torch tales were drawn by free-lancer Dick Ayers, who in typical adventures depicted the fiery hero fighting assorted criminals armed with nuclear devices, and characters like the menace from space who called himself "Comrade X" of the "Red Planet."

The highlight of the Atlas super hero revival was Bill Everett's work on his character The Sub-Mariner. The artist's style had evolved; he combined cartooning with conventional illustration to give Namor a sleek, streamlined appearance that epitomized the characteristic comic book look of the 1950s. A few of Everett's stories featured ordinary plots about Communist spies masquerading as aliens to steal atomic secrets, but most were zany, off-the-wall offerings with strong elements of self-parody. In one group of brief tales, Everett amusingly explored his fish-man's childhood as the half-human prince of an underwater race. The quality of Everett's improved technique was reflected in the fact that the new *Sub-Mariner* (April 1954) lasted for ten issues, while *The Human Torch* and *Captain America* managed to survive for only three issues each.

A New Recruit

The artist who revived Captain America was John Romita, who had begun moonlighting for Marvel in 1951 while he was still serving in the army. Assigned to Governor's Island in New York harbor, where it was his job to create recruiting posters, the twenty-one-year-old Romita took the ferry to the Marvel office in Manhattan and picked up free-lance assignments that quadrupled his army pay. Lee encouraged him to experiment with new techniques. Romita says, "Stan was very good at introducing new artists to the business. In those days it was easier to get a break." By 1953, Romita was out of uniform and ready to take on the challenge of illustrating Captain America's new incarnation as a hero for the 1950s.

"*Captain America* just didn't work," says Romita. "I was conscious of Jack Kirby's legacy and tried to keep that flavor. I guess I wasn't really that good, but Stan said it had nothing to do with the artwork." Lee, who wrote the scripts, may have been right. The book was weighed down with heavy propaganda; on every cover was the slogan "Captain America–Commie Smasher!" Meanwhile, Jack Kirby and his partner Joe Simon were spoofing such attitudes with *Fighting American* for Prize Publications. And in fact the gung-ho posture of the new Cap was an example of "too little, too late." Identifying foreign foes was going out of

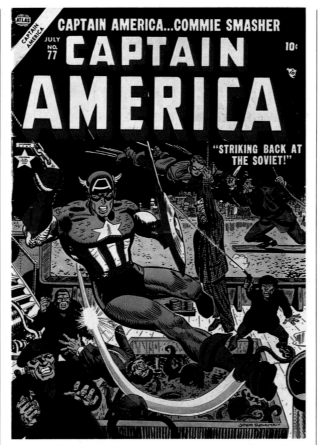

▲John Romita's original pencil sketch for the cover of *Captain America* #77, with the finished product as it appeared on the newsstand in July 1954.

style. Encouraged by politicians like Joseph McCarthy and Richard Nixon, the country had turned its search for enemies inward. Americans had begun calling each other un-American, and comics were about to take the fall.

Seduction of the Innocent

Dr. Fredric Wertham, a New York psychiatrist, was mad at comic books, and he had been for years. With his long, narrow, bespectacled face and his high, thin voice with a slight Teutonic accent, he did not seem the kind to inspire a mass political movement. But Wertham was driven by the desire to warn the public about the evils he saw around him, and he was implacably persistent and extraordinarily, shockingly successful with his one-man campaign.

A specialist in the treatment of disturbed children and juvenile delinquents, Wertham observed that most of his patients read comic books (as, of course, most kids without problems did as well). He claimed to have determined that comic books were surely detrimental to "mental hygiene," and that they encouraged children to commit crimes. Armed with a cause, Wertham embarked on a campaign of lectures, public statements and magazine articles that cul-

SEDUCTION OF THE INNOCENT

the author of THE SHOW OF VIOLENCE and Dark Legend

Fredric Wertham, M. D.

the influence of comic books on today's youth

The cover of the book that crippled the comic book.

minated in 1954 with the publication of a provocative and sensationalistic book. *Seduction of the Innocent*, Wertham's compendium of rabble-rousing half-truths, scared the hell out of a lot of parents. Today, comic book fans with a sense of irony consider this diatribe to be a classic of wrong thinking and unintentional humor.

Wertham's major targets were the violent horror and crime comic books that in fact were not appropriate reading matter for younger kids, but to Wertham every comic was a crime comic. "Western comic books are crime comic books," he wrote, "they describe all kinds of crime." War comic books, he claimed, were "just another setting for comic book violence," as if the books had inspired the war rather than the other way around. Even funny animal comics might corrupt toddlers: "Ducks shoot atomic rays and threaten to kill rabbits."

Wertham found super heroes especially objectionable, as he told the Senate Subcommittee to Investigate Juvenile Delinquency during his testimony in April 1954. "They arouse in children phantasies of sadistic joy in seeing other people punished over and over again while you yourself remain immune. We have called it the Superman complex." Wertham also preyed on the

AP/WIDE WORLD PHOTOS

Wertham, who nearly destroyed an art form.

Stylish artwork by Russ Heath recounts the resurrection of The Human Torch, complete with atomic explosion, in the first story from *Young Men* #24. The return of the super heroes in 1954 was cut short when sales plummeted as a result of Dr. Wertham's attack. *The Sub-Mariner,* containing some of the best work of Bill Everett's career, struggled on until the last issue (right) appeared in October 1955; then the super heroes were put back into cold storage. Cover: Joe Maneely.

public's prejudice against homosexuality by suggesting that certain super heroes were sexually involved with their teenage sidekicks: "If Batman were in the State Department he would be dismissed."

Not even love comics escaped Wertham's wrath. He warned that they might lead to child prostitution, and that perverts congregated around stores that sold comic books, looking for kids to corrupt. *Seduction of the Innocent* repeatedly emphasizes sexual depravity, probably because Wertham knew the topic would inflame his readers. He complained about comic book drawings of "protruding breasts" and condemned Atlas characters like Millie the Model and Nellie the Nurse, asserting that they inspired girls to stuff their blouse fronts with tissue paper. Wertham's most absurd moment came when he reprinted a greatly enlarged portion of a comic book panel to emphasize a shaded area of one male character's shoulder. To Wertham, the triangular patch of ink depicted a woman's genitalia: "There are pictures within pictures for children who know how to look." How many days and nights did Dr. Wertham spend, alone in his office, poring over his collection of lurid comic books and searching for the hidden drawings that were positive proof of corrupting secret sin?

Wertham's motives and goals remain inscrutable. His assertion that comics led to crime was disputed by educators, law enforcement officials and by other psychiatrists. He claimed the dissenting experts were either misinformed or paid off by comic book publishers. Like many censors, he vacillated by announcing, "I detest censorship," and then advocating "a law or ordinance against crime comic books." Whatever he might have intended, he set off a furor that nearly killed comic books completely.

Strange Tales in the Senate

When Wertham's charges brought comic books to the attention of the Senate subcommittee in 1954, the chairman, Senator William Langer of South Dakota, announced that "more than a billion comic books are sold in the United States each year." The committee's executive director, Richard Clendenen, gave the Senators a description of the industry and its publications which echoed Wertham's position.

For one of his displays, Clendenen held up an Atlas comic: "The next comic book is entitled *Strange Tales*, and has five stories in which thirteen people die violently," he said. He retold one of the stories in some detail: "When the girl is placed upon the operating table, the doctor discovers that the criminal's girlfriend is none other than his own wife." Afterwards, Clendenen described Martin Goodman's labyrinthine corporate structure and tried to suggest that Goodman's many companies had been created to conceal the owner's identity

Venus started out in 1948 as a glamorous goddess, but her tales grew grim. By November 1950 (left) she was caught up in a science fiction apocalypse, and her last two issues in 1952 (with covers by Bill Everett) were sheer horror.

With the first issues of *Strange Tales* (June 1951) and *Journey into Mystery* (June 1951), Atlas began to move decisively into horror . In the 1960s, these titles introduced new heroes like Thor and Dr. Strange.

Images like this probably gave more nightmares to worried parents than they did to their kids. This first issue of *Menace* (March 1953) is a good example of what got comics into trouble. Cover: Bill Everett.

rather than merely to protect his profits. Associate Chief Counsel Herbert Beaser sensibly pointed out that all Goodman's comics carried the Atlas trademark, a very public acknowledgment of ownership with no hint of subterfuge. The matter was immediately dropped.

The subcommittee hearings were scheduled to resume after the *Strange Tales* session ended, but in fact they never did. Evidently more important business intervened. The Senate was apparently willing to forget all about comic books, but fear of an imminent government crackdown caused most of the industry to panic. Customers boycotted some retailers. Books were publicly burned. Sales dropped drastically. Companies went bankrupt. For one hysterical moment, citizens had

▼ **The melancholy figure of The Zombie proved to be a memorable one: he returned in his own comic in 1973. From *Menace* #5 (July 1953). Script: Stan Lee. Art: Bill Everett.**

Who was that masked man? Stan Lee, disguised as a western hero for *Black Rider* #8 (March 1950).

been convinced that comics were a serious menace to youth. Soon the public would find new scapegoats in rock and roll or television, but by then the comics industry had been seriously and apparently irreparably hurt by the furor.

"I used to hide the fact that I was in comics," says John Romita. "We used to say we were in commercial illustration rather than admit to being comic book artists. It wasn't until the 1960s that I started telling people how proud I was of my comics industry."

Words to Live By

In 1955 the handful of comic book publishers who were still in business responded to their troubles by creating a trade association, the Comics Magazine Association of America, which in turn created an administrative body, the Comics Code Authority, to censor the publishers' comic books. The effect of this self-censorship was to homogenize the books dramatically in deference to the youth and innocence of potential readers. Comic books declared themselves an infantile medium not entitled to the freedom enjoyed by literature, drama or film. Words like "horror" were not allowed in titles. The Comics Code seal became a guarantee of blandness, but most of the comic book companies folded anyway. EC dropped all its titles except *Mad*, which it converted to a black-

When the company flagship *Marvel Mystery Comics* sank, it was converted to horror in August 1949.

Watered-down horror with Code approval didn't sell, and *Marvel Tales* folded (August 1957).

MARVEL'S ODDEST EXPERIMENT: WORLD'S GREATEST SONGS

Editor Stan Lee tried every conceivable comic book genre during the 1950s, and even invented a new one. "People in those days loved lyrics and music," he explains, "so we published something called *World's Greatest Songs*. I thought it would be great. We illustrated the lyrics." Artists drew pictures for popular songs of the day in comic book form.

The experiment lasted only one issue (September 1954), but it is something of a collector's item today because the results were just so strange.

"We didn't know what to do with it," says Lee about this oddball effort. "We just stuck it on the newsstand and it got lost in the shuffle." Perhaps it was just as well. If *World's Greatest Songs* had lasted a little longer, it would have run head-on into the rock and roll era, and a few artists might have lost their minds trying to illustrate the nonsense syllables that were fundamental to songs like "Sh-Boom" and "Tutti-Frutti."

▶ The bizarre and uniquely memorable style of Basil Wolverton was effective for both humor and horror. His heroes here are men deformed by their trip to a distant dimension. From *Adventures Into Terror* (December 1951).

The concept of the "white goddess," the voluptuous female version of Tarzan, was commonplace in comic books for decades. Marvel published many like *Lorna, The Jungle Queen* (July 1953).

During the 1950s, when comic book sales were at an all-time high, publishers searched everywhere for new ideas. Marvel ranged from *Spaceman* (September 1953) to *Bible Tales for Young Folk* (August 1953).

Imitations of *Mad* briefly ran riot. This one was actually called *Riot* (April 1954). Cover: Carl Burgos.

Wild #1 (February 1954) had a parody of the wildly popular Charlie Chan. Cover: Joe Maneely.

Like many comics in this vein, *Crazy* #1 (December 1953) spoofed horror. Cover: Bill Everett.

and-white magazine exempt from Code censorship. Atlas hung on by a thread.

Atlas Shrugged

For a while, Atlas was able to stave off the worst effects of the general disaster. Because Goodman was his own distributor, he was independent of the nervous businessmen who kept some other comic book companies from getting their books to the newsstands. As a result, many of the industry's top talents drifted over to Atlas, but most of them didn't stay long. Declining sales meant fewer books and lower rates for free-lancers. "Every time I took another job I took another cut in pay," says

▼ Artist Don Heck's early work at Marvel included this series of well-crafted maritime adventures. From *Navy Combat* #1 (June 1955).

▲ Science fiction and fantasy art by Jack Kirby (above) and Steve Ditko (below) were Marvel mainstays during the late 1950s.

Christmas cards presented to editor Stan Lee by the Marvel staff during the early 1950s. Some good-natured mockery of the boss is in evidence. Among the signatories are artists Carl Burgos, John Buscema, Gene Colan, Bill Everett, Russ Heath, Mike Sekowsky, Syd Shores and longtime letterer Artie Simek.

THE VILLAIN TO BEAT: THE YELLOW CLAW

To capitalize on the specter of a Communist conspiracy haunting American minds during the 1950s, Stan Lee decided to go all the way and create a comic book named after a Commie: *The Yellow Claw*. "We fashioned him after Fu Manchu," admits Stan Lee, referring to the famous villain created in 1913 by British author Sax Rohmer. (In fact, Rohmer also wrote a novel called *Yellow Claw*, but Fu Manchu wasn't in it.) Like his literary predecessor, the comic book Yellow Claw was a brilliant scientist; he also dabbled in the occult and had created an elixir that extended his life abnormally.

After the Korean war, the Red Chinese were disliked perhaps even more than the Russians, but *The Yellow Claw* avoided blatant racism by making its hero Chinese too. This evenhandedness may have been one reason why the comic book lasted only four issues, but then again, very few bad guys ever got their own comic books in the first place.

Revived in the 1960s, the Claw abandoned Marxism and set out to rule the world himself. If he hasn't succeeded yet, credit must go to Marvel heroes like Nick Fury, Captain America and Iron Man, who in recent years have struggled to thwart his nefarious schemes.

Top two covers by John Severin; bottom cover by Bill Everett. Clutching Claw by Joe Maneely.

John Romita.

Many artists were forced out of the field by economic pressures. Bill Everett took a job with a greeting card company. John Buscema, and then Gene Colan, drifted into advertising. "It was a very bad time," says Colan. "I had the full catastrophe. I had a house and a family and I just had to do whatever else I could." Romita held on as long as possible and then moved over to DC, where longstanding conservative fiscal and artistic policies had kept the company in comparatively good shape. He stayed at DC "doing really dreadful, mindless romance comics for about eight years." By 1955 it looked like Atlas might be nearing the end of the line.

Oddly enough, it was a group of recent arrivals at Atlas who eventually turned things around. Artist Don Heck had arrived in 1954 and was soon enhancing the war books with his vigorous work on characters like "Torpedo" Taylor. In 1956, artist Steve Ditko brought his unusual drawing style to the toned-down horror books and turned out a series of atmospheric fantasies. Most important of all, in 1956 Jack Kirby came back.

Recently separated from his longtime partner Joe Simon, Kirby was one of the most creative forces in the business and he needed the outlet that Atlas could provide. "When I got back they were practically taking the furniture out of the place," he says, "and I had to stop them. I had to have a place to work."

But before things got better, they got worse. Atlas, Goodman's distribution arm, was gradually becoming a liability. By 1957, because there weren't many comics to distribute and expenses were high, Goodman closed down Atlas and arranged for a deal with the American News Company, one of the country's largest magazine distributors. To Goodman it seemed like a good idea at the time. He didn't realize how far Dr. Wertham's poison had spread, and he never suspected that American News was itself on the verge of collapse until suddenly it fell. Catastrophe turned to cataclysm, and suddenly there seemed to be no way at all for Goodman to get the comic books to the customers.

Stan Lee was left alone in a small office with a backlog of finished art. There was no work for anyone, not even on a free-lance basis. "It was very tough," says Lee. "These were all people that I'd worked with. I knew their families. And I was asked to let everybody go. I don't know why Goodman kept me on. I guess he just felt that if there was any chance at all he wouldn't give up the comics completely."

The Thing that Lived

Somehow the company survived, even though it was now nameless since the Atlas trademark was gone for good. Ingeniously, Goodman made a deal with rival publisher DC to get his few remaining comics to the stands via DC's own distribution system, which usually carried a few other lines. However, DC agreed to handle only eight Goodman comic books a month—a rather uninteresting mix of war, western, romance and teenage titles.

By 1958, however, Lee could offer gainful employment once again to free-lancers like Jack Kirby, Steve Ditko and Don Heck. He had replaced some of his more shopworn titles with a line of science fiction books bearing recycled names like *Strange Tales* and new ones like *Tales to Astonish*. Heck describes the comics as crammed full of "buildings tumbling down all over the place— Japanese monster movie stuff." The highlight of every issue was a gigantic creature drawn dramatically by Kirby and named outrageously by Lee: Torr, Zzutak or Fin Fang Foom, The Thing that Lived or The Thing that Shouldn't Exist. "They were fun to do," says Lee. "I loved making up those crazy names."

In 1961, however, Lee knew that these wild yet essentially nonthreatening monsters had run their course and that something new was called for. He wasn't sure he wanted to make the effort. He was pushing forty now, and had spent his entire adult life in a business that was widely believed to have no future. Recurrent reversals had left him discouraged and disillusioned: "I felt I'd been there too long," Lee says, "and I wanted to leave. I figured I could always get a writing job of some kind. I was ready to quit."

He was only a dragon in purple pants, but Fin Fang Foom's silly name made him famous. Art: Jack Kirby.

Monsters like Torr were almost all that Marvel offered as the 1960s dawned, and even they were running out of steam. Jack Kirby drew the cover for *Amazing Adventures* #1 (June 1961), which lasted six issues and then became *Amazing Adult Fantasy* #7 (December 1961). Steve Ditko was the principal artist for its eight issues. Things looked bleak, but during 1961, editor Stan Lee was working with Kirby and Ditko to create a new line of super heroes.

CHAPTER FOUR

The Marvel Age (1961–1970)

Marvel ushers in a comic book renaissance
by humanizing super heroes. Creators introduce
a new generation of troubled characters
ambivalent about their powers, including
Spider-Man, The Fantastic Four
and The Incredible Hulk.
Readers respond and sales soar.

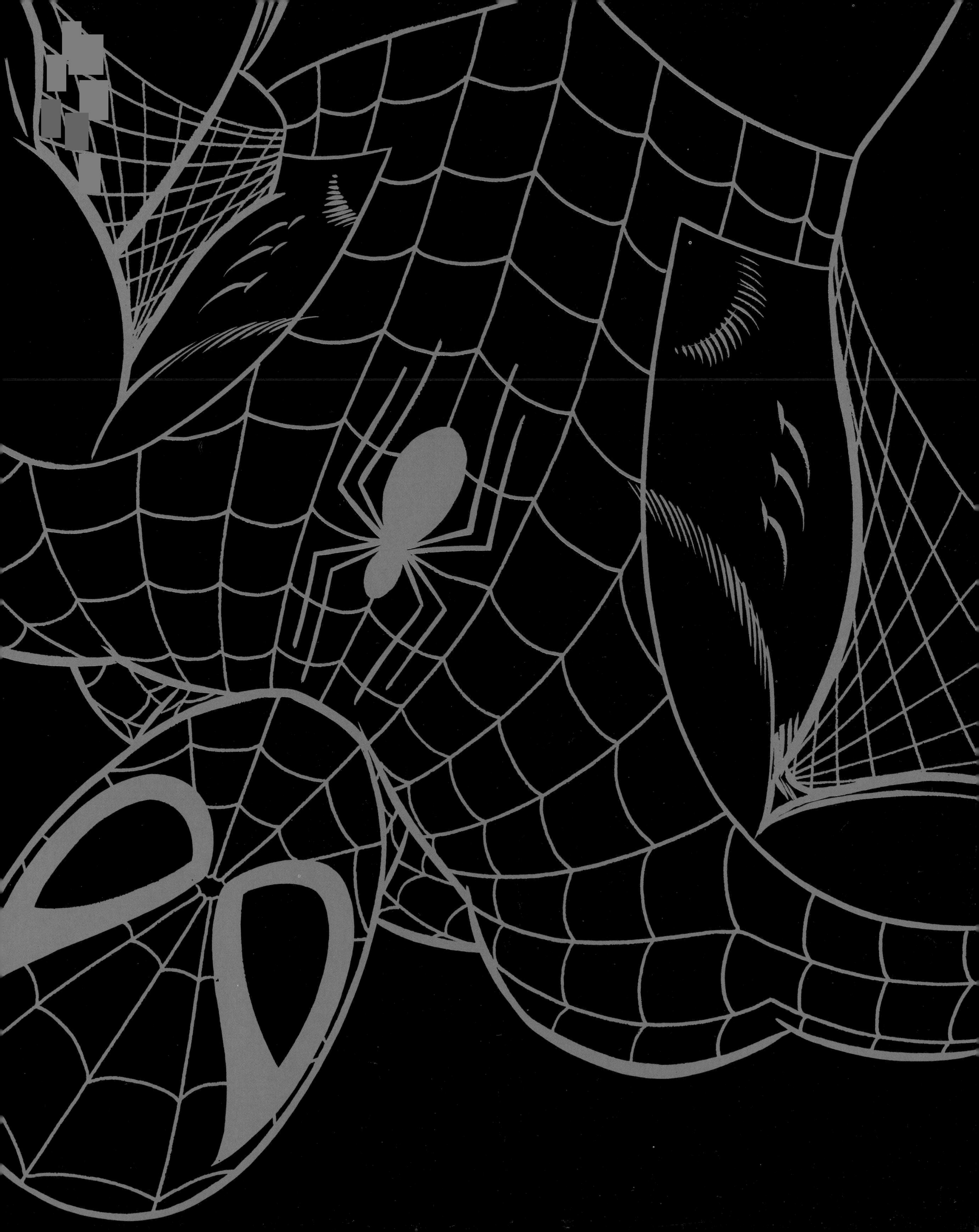

The burst of creativity that led to modern Marvel Comics began in 1961. A torrent of ideas seemed to rush through the pages of the company's publications as the concept of the super hero was reworked and revised, reshaped and revitalized. Ultimately, a veritable renaissance was achieved. A virtual army of new characters sprang up in the 1960s and became giants in the field; their combined strength turned a moribund industry around. With characteristic hyperbole, but also considerable accuracy, editor Stan Lee dubbed this period "The Marvel Age of Comics." In fact, the term has been adopted by comic book fans all over the world and is still used today to describe the 1960s.

At the start, it looked like an uphill battle for the forces seeking to create a new kind of comic book. Jack Kirby, the artist whose style and vision defined the look of the new Marvel, had begun to wonder if there was any hope for the industry by the end of the 1950s. "It was just a losing field," he says. "But working on comics was the only profession I knew. I was a married man and I had to make a living." Already one of the top talents in the business, he determined to make an extra effort to keep himself and even comic books themselves afloat. "I worked feverishly," he says.

If Jack Kirby felt weighed down by responsibility, Stan Lee was suddenly reckless. A skilled professional with twenty years of experience behind him, Lee, at thirty-eight, saw little future for himself in comics, and even less opportunity for self-expression. "It was always a case of what the publisher wanted," he explains. "It was never what I was interested in." He was planning to start a new career, but his wife Joan convinced him to go out in a blaze of glory. "She said to me, 'If you're planning to leave anyway, why don't you just turn out a couple of books the way you think they should be done, and get it out of your system before you actually quit?'"

Ironically, it was publisher Martin Goodman who provided the impetus to start Lee and Kirby on the most fruitful collaboration in the history of comic books. Goodman had recently heard about an idea that was generating sales for the competition, and he directed his editor to come up with something similar. As it turned out, Goodman got more than he bargained for.

Par for the Course

It was business as usual for Goodman, who always kept an eye out for the coming trend. While playing a game of golf, Goodman got a tip from Jack Liebowitz, who was then publisher of DC Comics. The industry leader at the time and also the distributor of Goodman's small line of comics, DC had recently been having considerable success with *Justice League of America*, a new series that featured a team of several well-known heroes, including Superman, Batman and Wonder

Woman. Goodman left the golf course planning to publish a super group of his own, despite that fact that his current lineup of characters included nobody more powerful than Millie the Model.

As Lee recalls it, "Martin Goodman said, 'Gee, maybe we ought to do a team of super heroes.' And when he said, 'Gee, maybe we ought to,' that was a command. I went home and wrote a two-page outline and sent it to Kirby. We talked about it, and he went home and drew it. We didn't know we were doing something that was going to be almost historic. It was just another story."

It was a story, however, in which Lee threw caution to the wind and Kirby applied all the years of expertise he had acquired developing best-selling comics with his former partner Joe Simon. The result was dynamite. With its debut in November 1961, *The Fantastic Four* marked the beginning of the Marvel renaissance, even though the word "Marvel" was not yet appearing on any of the company's covers.

Fantastic Four: Personality Plus

In creating *The Fantastic Four* and the ground-breaking books that followed it, Lee and Kirby established that the personalities of the heroes, rather than the plots, should be of paramount importance. "I was really interested in the charac-

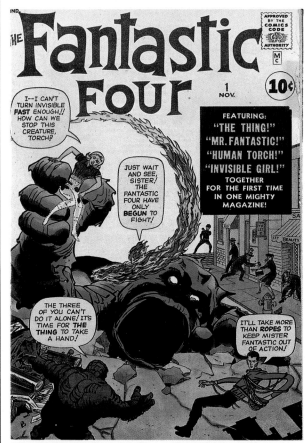

The Fantastic Four **#1 (November 1961) set Marvel on the path to the top of the industry. Pencils: Jack Kirby. Inks: Dick Ayers.**

◄ Inundated with cosmic rays, Reed Richards, Sue Storm, Ben Grimm and Johnny Storm are transformed into The Fantastic Four. Script: Stan Lee. Pencils: Jack Kirby. Inks: Dick Ayers.

ters as people," Kirby says. "I have a genuine feeling for real people and what I do is recreate them in a fantastic formula."

"Characterization is the most important thing in any story," says Lee. "First I thought of the kind of character I wanted, then I figured out what kind of super power he'd have." In a field where gimmicks were usually considered to be most important, the approach was revolutionary.

The Fantastic Four acquired their amazing powers after their experimental rocket passed through a storm of cosmic rays. For their leader, Lee envisioned "the world's greatest scientist, who is also a little bit of a bore. He talks too much, he's too ponderous and he drives the others crazy." This was Reed Richards, who took the name Mr. Fantastic after he acquired the somewhat absurd ability to stretch his body into any conceivable shape. There had been other "stretch" characters in comics before—notably Jack Cole's Plastic Man from Quality Comics—and Timely had published a few tales about Flexo the Rubber Man in 1940. Yet the contrast between the flexibility gimmick and the rigid stuffiness of Richards made Mr. Fantastic fresh and interesting.

"I thought we also had to have a girl," continues Lee, "but with a new twist: she's not just a girlfriend who doesn't know what the hero does." (In fact, The Fantastic Four didn't bother with secret identities; all the other characters knew about their powers.) Sue Storm, a full-fledged member of the team and Richards' fiancée, was able to transform herself into The Invisible Girl (later The Invisible Woman). She also learned to project a force field as a defensive weapon.

The third member of the group was Johnny Storm, Sue's kid brother. He was a teenager, but quite different from the stereotyped worshipful sidekick. Instead, Johnny was a show-off and a bit of a troublemaker; he used his powers to attract attention, and often displayed more interest in girls and fast cars than in fighting the forces of evil. "I thought it was a shame that we didn't have The Human Torch anymore," says Lee, "and this was a good chance to bring him back." So Johnny Storm was given the name and the incendiary powers of the fiery hero Carl Burgos had created in 1939 for the original issue of *Marvel Comics.*

The individual in the group who represented the greatest degree of innovation also became the most popular—with his creators as well as with the fans. The cosmic rays turned Ben Grimm, a tough test pilot, into an ape-shaped, orange-skinned, craggy monster known as The Thing. Ben's tragic plight was dramatized by the occasions when he temporarily reverted to human form, but his belligerent sense of humor was his most endearing trait. "I wanted something really different," says Lee, "and I realized there was no monster, no funny, ugly guy who's a hero. All these characters have powers they like, but when *this* guy becomes very powerful, he also becomes

Fantastic Four

The Fantastic Four are a group of super heroes who have experienced some of the wildest adventures ever depicted in comic books, but perhaps the root of their appeal is the extent to which they embody the idea of a family, warts and all. Bound together by the strange powers that each acquired while manning an experimental rocket, they are also joined by legal and blood relationships. Reed Richards and Sue Storm were engaged when the series began in 1961 and married a few years later; Johnny Storm is Sue's younger brother. The odd man out is Ben Grimm, ostensibly just a friend of the family, but really the heart and soul of the team.

Reed Richards developed a flexible, elastic body and became Mr. Fantastic, but remained a brilliant and aloof scientist, more at home with his work than with people. Sue Storm, transformed into The Invisible Girl (later Woman), maintained the air of a middle-class matron. These two rather restrained characters were the symbolic parents of the group, while the adolescent Johnny, an updated version of The Human Torch, functioned as their spoiled son. Ben Grimm, who turned into the hideous but powerful Thing, appeared to be the family's gruff but lovable uncle, one who came from a distinctly less privileged background.

In the original synopsis that writer-editor Stan Lee gave artist Jack Kirby, Lee proposed making The Thing into "the heavy." Deformed, underprivileged and argumentative, Ben actually became the most lovable group member: honest, direct and free of pretension. He brought humor and pathos to the stories, while his emotional responses and frequent tantrums suggested that he might really be the baby of the household. The others sported spiffy uniforms, he wore a big blue diaper. The perfect balance of this original family unit, with its staid parents, privileged older son and squalling, uninhibited infant, has made The Fantastic Four a uniquely appealing team.

Over the years, the balance of The Fantastic Four has shifted on several occasions. More than one member has walked out in a huff, and even been apparently replaced, but with the passage of time, the status quo has always reasserted itself. The ties of blood and loyalty are as strong for misfits as they are for mortals.

grotesque. It had a touch of pathos." The Thing, who griped and bickered continuously, became the prototype for a number of Marvel's later heroes who were irritable roughnecks.

The Marvel Method

The Fantastic Four dazzled readers with their oddball personalities, but the manner in which they were brought to life was even more of a breakthrough. One of Stan Lee's greatest achievements as an editor was to introduce a new technique for creating stories that is now known throughout the comics industry as "The Marvel Method." Born of expediency as much as inspiration, it enabled the artists to achieve their full potential by emphasizing the visual elements that are at the heart of the medium's appeal.

Most comic books had been created from scripts prepared by writers and editors. The words came first, and usually the artists were given instructions on how to divide the stories into pages and panels. Sometimes they were even handed pages with the panels established and written balloons already in place; the artist's job was to fill in the empty spaces with artwork. This system worked for companies with large staffs, but it was very tough on Lee, who was his company's most prolific writer, as well as the editor and the art director. "I feel it's impossible to be an accomplished editor," says Lee, "without being an art director as well." In an attempt to keep a number of artists working at the same time, Lee gradually abandoned the idea of such fully scripted stories.

With an accomplished professional like Jack Kirby, Lee knew that he would receive powerful pages even if he gave the artist nothing more than a synopsis, which was all he provided for the first issue of *The Fantastic Four.* When the drawings came back, Lee added dialogue and captions. The results were so splendid that Kirby and Lee never worked any other way again. Gradually, Lee tried the technique with other artists, and in little more than a year every comic book the company produced was being done the "Marvel" way.

"The best thing about this method of working," says Lee, "was that the artists could use their creativity. I never restricted them or said they had to follow what I gave them to the letter. Once in a while I wanted something very specific and I would take great pains with the synopsis, but usually I just gave them the broad outlines and a description of how I wanted the problem solved at the end. How the artists arrived at it was their business."

Lee feels that the method produced stronger writing as well as more effective art. "I'd look at Jack's pictures and the words just came into my mind because the expressions and poses of the characters were so dramatic. I would tailor the writing to the art." Lee wrote as much or as little dialogue as the scene seemed to require, placing and spacing the speech balloons so they would not obscure interesting images.

The Fantastic Soar

The first issue of *The Fantastic Four*—which was supposed to be Lee's swan song—had an impact that took him by surprise. "I never realized it would sell that well," he says. Fan mail began to arrive, and by the third issue Lee was printing it in a letters column. Readers were taken with the humanized heroes, and seemed to enjoy every aspect of the new team except the absence of traditional comic book costumes, a drawback that was soon overcome with the introduction of simple blue uniforms. Exhilarated by the response, Lee created a slogan for the third issue: "The Greatest Comic Magazine in the World!!" Soon altered to "The World's Greatest Comic Magazine," it has appeared on *Fantastic Four* covers ever since. "The slogan was tongue in cheek in the beginning," says Lee, but it certainly drew attention to the upstart little company with big ideas. More importantly, the claim would soon become difficult to deny.

The third issue also startled readers with a new price of twelve cents, a move that symbolized a break with the past quarter century. Comic books had cost a dime since their inception, but the inflation of production costs had caused the number of pages to shrink from a high of sixty-four, until, by the early 1960s, there were little more than twenty editorial pages in each issue. The traditional comic book had featured several short stories in each issue, but diminishing space and growing confidence dictated that one long story featuring The Fantastic Four would be the best way to fill the available pages. An expansive, epic quality resulted.

The Human Torch revives The Sub-Mariner in March 1962. Script: Stan Lee. Pencils: Jack Kirby. Inks: Sol Brodsky.

▶ When The Sub-Mariner returned, he was up to his old tricks. Pencils: Jack Kirby. Inks: Sol Brodsky.

▶ Introducing Doctor Doom, one of the great villains (far right). Pencils: Jack Kirby. Inks: Joe Sinnott.

Fantastic Foes

When The Fantastic Four weren't fighting among themselves—which they did quite often—they needed enemies, and Stan Lee provided one of the best when he revived Bill Everett's classic character from 1939, The Sub-Mariner. This time around, Namor's hostility was caused by a nuclear test that had destroyed his underwater kingdom, and he complicated matters by developing a not entirely unrequited passion for the Invisible Girl. The triangular relationship among Sue Storm, Reed Richards and the vengeful but noble Namor would continue for years. More significantly, in *The Fantastic Four* #4, Lee and Kirby set the stage for a reenactment of one of the company's great successes, and soon The Sub-Mariner and The Human Torch were at each other's throats, just as they had been twenty years before. A sense of continuity had been established: "I always loved the old characters," explains Lee.

The fifth issue's encounter, "Meet Dr. Doom," introduced The Fantastic Four's most frequent future foe, a crazed scientific genius who hid his scarred face behind a metal mask. Formerly one of Reed Richards' college classmates, Victor von Doom had become the ruthless ruler of a small country who used his diplomatic immunity to cloak his plans for world conquest. He was perhaps the ultimate refinement of Marvel's many megalomaniacal villains, and in issue six he even

teamed up with The Sub-Mariner to take on our heroes. Namor, who ultimately rejected his more corrupt cohort, was back again in issue nine, gloating as The Fantastic Four went bankrupt due to bad investments—a kind of misfortune that had never happened to ordinary super heroes. And Dr. Doom returned again in issues ten, sixteen and seventeen. Although each tale was complete in itself, Lee and Kirby were also clearly establishing a super story that extended over months. Before long, only narratives that ran to several issues would be able to contain their increasingly complex ideas.

Very soon, The Fantastic Four were not alone in the stable of new Marvel super heroes. A whole crew of innovative characters had been created, and Stan Lee's career plans had changed. "I never left," he says, "because The Fantastic Four sold well, and next The Hulk sold well, and then Thor, and then Spider-Man...."

The Green Giant

For their second super hero, Lee and Kirby came up with another monstrous figure, who was inspired by the success of The Thing, and also by the numerous creatures they had been devising for comic books like *Tales to Astonish*. The result was *The Incredible Hulk* (May 1962).

Clearly, The Hulk was derived in part from

literary figures: Mary Shelley's monster from *Frankenstein* and Robert Louis Stevenson's shape-shifting scientist from *The Strange Case of Dr. Jekyll and Mr. Hyde.* Kirby's drawings of The Hulk were loosely based on the makeup created by Jack Pierce for Boris Karloff's role in the 1931 film version of *Frankenstein.* "I always felt that the monster was really the good guy," says Lee.

The fear of radiation was a theme that recurred throughout the early 1960s, and again, radiation was the gimmick that provided the protagonist with his uncanny powers. Overt anxiety about the unleashed atom had diminished somewhat since the 1950s, even if only due to familiarity with the idea. However, a strong undercurrent of concern remained, and many of the super heroes of The Marvel Age owed their existence to the dreaded new technology. For Jack Kirby, the concept was more than just an easy way to set a story line in motion: "As long as we're experimenting with radioactivity," he explains, "there's no telling what may happen, or how much our advancements in science may cost us." The Hulk became Marvel's most disturbing embodiment of the perils inherent in the atomic age.

The original Hulk story depicted the first test of a new "gamma-bomb" invented by a scientist named Bruce Banner, who was exposed to the blast through the machinations of a Communist spy working under the transparent alias "Igor." The spy was a throwback to bygone days; eventually such conventional devices were abandoned in favor of more imaginative plot developments, but Igor was tolerated because his presence served to turn Banner into The Hulk.

A massive figure of tremendous strength, The Hulk was gray in his initial adventure. However, the printer had trouble maintaining a consistent tone with this color, and in the second issue The Hulk became green. In either shade he was an antisocial brute who was constantly harried because of his appearance. Like Greta Garbo, he only wanted to be alone: "Have to get away—to hide." The Hulk's plight made him a sympathetic menace, and his alter ego Bruce Banner was one of the first comic book protagonists to hate his constant transformations into a super hero.

The Baby Boom

Stan Lee first realized how much of an impact the new heroes were having when a contingent of Columbia University students showed up at the office to announce that they had made The Hulk their mascot. Marvel's revolutionary style of story-telling was still in its embryonic stages, but already it was attracting an older and more sophisticated audience than comic books were conventionally expected to reach. Apparently the concept of a studious scientist who periodically went berserk had considerable appeal for the Ivy League scholars, who presumably longed for such extraor-

dinary powers and opportunities themselves.

Despite condescending conventional wisdom, the imaginative world of comic books has always attracted the most intelligent kids: the introverted readers and dreamers who have fantasies of acquiring brawn to match their brains. And the Marvel heroes, with their sudden physical transformations and endless personal problems, spoke to the hopes and fears of troubled adolescents everywhere. Hordes of readers who had not looked at a comic book in years were suddenly being drawn back into the fold by Marvel's new approach.

And the hordes were there. Marvel had fortuitously tapped into a demographic gold mine:

▼ Doctor Doom invades the Marvel office in *Fantastic Four* #10 (January 1963). Script: Stan Lee. Pencils: Jack Kirby. Inks: Dick Ayers.

► In his first issue, The Hulk was gray. Pencils: Jack Kirby. Inks: George Roussos. By the second he was green and fighting Toad Men. Pencils: Jack Kirby. Inks: Steve Ditko.

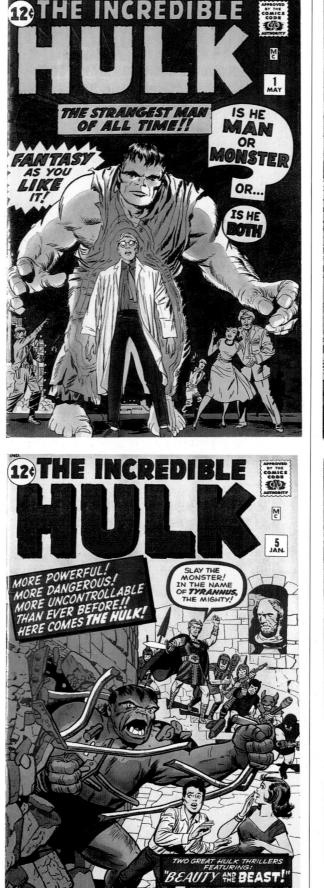

► The Hulk never grasped the principle of the door. Pencils: Jack Kirby. Inks: Dick Ayers. At far right, the final cover of The Hulk's short initial run (March 1963), drawn by Steve Ditko.

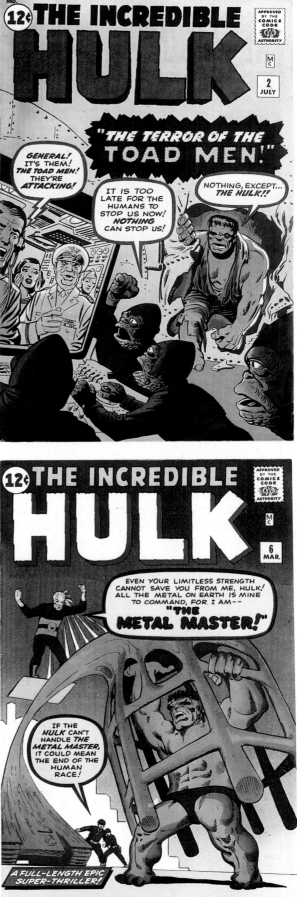

PROFILE

THE INCREDIBLE HULK

The Hulk, a character with immense power and limited intelligence, has proven to be one of Marvel's most memorable heroes. His overt appeal lies in his embodiment of ferocious brute force. Yet there is more to The Hulk than meets the eye.

Like The Sub-Mariner before him, The Hulk sometimes appears to be a villain, and his destructive rages allow readers to blow off steam of their own. At the same time, however, The Hulk's ugliness and limited intellect make him a pathetic figure. When he first appeared in 1962, writer Stan Lee and artist Jack Kirby depicted The Hulk as a crafty monster, but the early decision to diminish his brain power somehow made him more attractive. For one thing, it provided a greater contrast with the creature's alter ego, Bruce Banner.

Another early change was also significant: at first The Hulk was a nocturnal being, summoned by the sunset, but before long, Banner's emotions became the trigger that transformed him into a rampaging beast. In short, symbolically The Hulk became force guided by feeling.

Bruce Banner, however, is almost pure intellect. He represents science in the service of the military, an alliance symbolized by his romance with a general's daughter. A researcher employed to create weapons for the government, Banner was out of touch with his feelings and unaware of his power; only when his "gamma bomb" turned him into The Hulk was he forced to confront his deeper emotions. And he needs his crude, embarrassing other self more than it needs him: when an experiment temporarily divided man and monster into separate entities with independent existences, Banner began to waste away.

On the surface, The Hulk may suggest the dangers of anti-intellectualism, but when he lashes out mindlessly, he frequently finds the right target. His instinctive impulses serve as a reminder that our physical and emotional lives are not to be despised. And the ultimate irony, of course, is that brilliant Bruce Banner, builder of nuclear bombs, is actually far more dangerous than the brutish Hulk.

The Hulk was gray on his first appearance, and recently wore the same shade again, but as a rule he's green.

THE MIGHTY THOR

Thor, who represents Marvel's deliberate effort to transcend all other super heroes, is nothing less than a god. Writer Stan Lee worked with artist Jack Kirby to interpret an ancient legend through a new medium, but in the process they produced a concept that would gradually take on a meaning different from the original myth.

Thor's powers allow him to operate on a grandiose, cosmic scale, yet the old Norse tales that Marvel adapted demanded that he be subordinate to an even greater force. Odin, the virtually omnipotent leader of the legendary gods, is Thor's father, and he rules with an iron hand. Many comic book heroes are orphans, inspired to fight crime because of the death of their parents, so Thor's somewhat awkward position as a dutiful son sets him apart. None of this seemed especially significant when the series began in 1962, but over the years the relationship between father and son has developed some interesting twists.

The first Thor stories followed a common pattern of wish fulfillment. Frail Dr. Don Blake discovered Thor's magic hammer hidden in a cave, and used it to transform himself into a being of incalculable might. Over the years, however, Blake failed to develop as a character, and Thor took centerstage. Eventually it was revealed that Blake was a fraud with no real existence at all. Odin explained that years before he had punished his son Thor's arrogance by clouding his memory and placing his spirit in a mortal body. When "Blake" found the hammer and its power, he was only following his father's unspoken orders. Armed with this knowledge, Thor dropped the Blake persona, yet could not bring himself to abandon the human race that he had come to cherish. Marvel's reworking of Thor's story had taken on overtones of a more exalted ancient tale, one in which God sent his only son to earth to serve mankind.

◄ Thor's debut in August 1962 was only one of the stories in *Journey into Mystery*. Loki, Thor's adopted brother, was a constant threat. Covers by Jack Kirby and Dick Ayers.

◄ In the origin story, Don Blake is granted the magic of Thor's hammer, even though he thinks Thursday is the fourth day of the week. Plot: Stan Lee. Script: Larry Lieber. Pencils: Jack Kirby. Inks: Dick Ayers.

the gigantic generation of baby boom children and teenagers who had been born in the years following World War II. This group, one of the largest, best-educated and most affluent generations in American history, was ready and waiting for The Marvel Age.

The Golden God

By 1962, Marvel was on a roll. "It's as if we were hit by lightning," says Stan Lee. "What amazes me is that all the characters worked. The success fed on itself." The little company was bursting at the seams, and was beginning to feel constrained

The birth of Marvel's most famous character in a dying comic book. Steve Ditko drew the original cover (right), then collaborated with Jack Kirby on the final version (below) when Stan Lee asked for another angle.

by the deal with DC that allowed only eight Marvel comic books to be distributed per month. As a result, the next round of super heroes made their first appearances not in new publications, but as features in the already existing "monster" comics, which had now outlived their popularity.

In August 1962, The Mighty Thor took the stage in *Journey Into Mystery* #83. "Nobody had ever done anything with the Norse legends," Lee says, although the company had enjoyed some success with the Roman goddess Venus in the late 1940s. "We already had The Hulk, the strongest man on earth," says Lee, "so the next logical step was a character who was a god." Jack Kirby was also fascinated by the idea of a mythological deity as the ultimate super hero, and by "the chance to use this concept with characters from our own day."

A typically flawed modern Marvel hero, Dr. Don Blake walked with a limp and used a cane until he discovered the long-lost hammer of the ancient god Thor. Its power changed Blake into the virtually omnipotent Thor, complete with armor, helmet and flowing golden locks—a haircut that seems prescient, since in a few years such coiffures would become fashionable among young men.

In fact, in 1962, Thor was in other ways a little ahead of his time. The character was moderately successful at once because the switches between Earth and the mythical Norse realm of Asgard were intriguing, but Thor did not achieve his full potential until the mid-1960s, when Lee and Kirby went to work and turned him into one of their indisputable classics. In the meantime, Thor was a solid addition to Marvel's growing stable of super heroes.

In the early 1960s the super heroes were popular, but they were coming out only once every two months, interspersed among the regular monsters, westerns and teenage humor titles. Lee had enough time to work on the plots, but he turned the detailed scripting of Thor over to his brother Larry Lieber, who had previously spent most of his time as a free-lance artist. The results were good, but to some extent Thor remained untapped because the tiny Marvel crew was just too busy to give him the attention he deserved. More effort was being expended on another new super hero, one who would eventually become the company's best-known creation, and ultimately its informal corporate mascot as well.

Caught in the Web

The first Spider-Man story was originally intended as no more than a one-shot experiment, and almost didn't get into print at all. "Martin Good-

◄ Peter Parker experiences the power of a radioactive spider bite in the first Spider-Man story. By the end of the story, he experiences revenge and regret. Script: Stan Lee. Art: Steve Ditko.

man didn't want to publish it," recalls Stan Lee. Goodman was convinced that readers would find the subject of spiders distasteful.

Fortunately for all concerned, a comic book called *Amazing Adult Fantasy* was about to be canceled due to faltering sales. "Nobody cares what you put in a book that's going to die," says Lee, "so I threw in Spider-Man. I featured him on the cover and then forgot about him." For the occasion, the comic book reverted to its original title of *Amazing Fantasy*, an appropriate amendment since Spider-Man was to be the most important adolescent super hero in comics.

Spider-Man was the hero and the teenage helper rolled into one; he was his own sidekick. Marvel's first editor, Joe Simon, theorized that kid companions like Captain America's Bucky were important because they gave the protagonist someone to talk to; Spider-Man talked to himself. In fact, he has delivered more soliloquies than Hamlet. In his first appearance he mused aloud, but subsequently Lee adopted the device of the thought balloon with its characteristic bubbles. "I used those thought balloons to help the exposition," says Lee. "I could put interesting thoughts there that weren't necessarily about what was happening in that particular panel—something to hold the reader's interest."

Spider-Man, despite the fact that he was not originally intended to star in a series, became the epitome of the radical innovations that charac-

terized The Marvel Age. Lee used him to challenge the very concept of the super hero. Spider-Man was neurotic, compulsive and profoundly skeptical about the whole idea of becoming a costumed savior. The Fantastic Four argued with each other, and The Hulk and Thor had problems with their alter egos, but Spider-Man had to struggle with himself.

In the origin story (August 1962), Peter Parker is a bookish, bespectacled high school student, isolated and unpopular. An orphan, he lives with his elderly relatives, Aunt May and Uncle Ben. While attending a science exhibit, Peter is bitten by a spider that has accidentally received a dose of radioactivity. As a result, Peter acquires the agility and proportionate strength of an arachnid. He sews his own super hero uniform and uses his scientific knowledge to build mechanical devices that eject sticky webbing, but he is less interested in fighting crime than in making a buck. Disguised as Spider-Man, he becomes a professional wrestler and then demonstrates his abilities on television. He blithely ignores the chance to stop a fleeing thief, but his indifference ironically catches up with him when the same criminal later robs and kills his Uncle Ben. Eventually, Spider-Man subdues the murderer, but for a tearful Peter Parker, there is no peace. He wanders remorsefully off into the night to the accompaniment of Lee's now-famous caption: "With great power there must also come—great responsibility!"

SPIDER-MAN

Spider-Man is the quintessential Marvel character. Although a super hero, he is spared none of the slings and arrows of ordinary life; he experiences difficulties with friends, family, sweethearts and employers. His powers enable him to do good, but not to improve his own lot in life, and it is his simple humanity, rather than his exotic talent, that has won him millions of enthusiastic fans. He is one super-hero who has not lost the common touch, and in fact he is frequently described as "your friendly neighborhood Spider-Man."

It's a secret identity we have here, not a split personality.

In his 1962 debut, Spider-Man took to fighting crime for a reason commonplace in comic books: he was motivated by the murder of a father figure, his Uncle Ben. Yet Spidey's driving force is guilt, not revenge; he must live forever with the knowledge that he could have prevented the killing if he had not been so self-absorbed. Perhaps he suffers from a classic Oedipus complex; in any case he is certainly neurotic, forever agonizing over the choices that confront him when he attempts to do the right thing. Despite his best efforts, he is viewed with a touch of suspicion by those in authority, and is sometimes considered little more than a criminal himself.

Although nobody seems to understand him, Spider-Man has the spirit to be a joker as well as a tragic figure. He is quick with a quip, appreciates the irony of his endless predicaments, and relishes the chance to play tricks on people who never suspect that he and Peter Parker are one and the same.

As originally depicted by writer Stan Lee and artist Steve Ditko, Peter Parker was just a bit of a wimp. Bright, imaginative, but nonetheless an alienated adolescent, he might well have been a typical comic book reader. Although he has matured and gained in confidence over the years, Spidey is still all too human. He misses appointments, catches the flu when he needs to fight, forgets to put film in his camera and has trouble paying the rent. In short, Spider-Man remains Everyman, "the super hero who could be you."

From 1982 to 1988, Spider-Man was seen around town in this black costume, but now he has returned to his true colors.

This story, with its challenge to comic book clichés, created an unexpected sensation. "A few months later," Lee recalls, "we got the sales figures, and that Spider-Man issue of *Amazing Fantasy* was one of the best-selling books we ever had. There were no flies on us, so we put him out in his own title." However the usual months of creative and production work leading to publication kept *The Amazing Spider-Man* #1 from appearing until March 1963.

A Talent for Weaving Webs

Until this time, Jack Kirby had been drawing all of the company's new characters, but Spider-Man ended up in the hands of another artist. Kirby drew several pages of a version of Spider-Man, but he never completed a story. Kirby's version was as bold and dynamic as the rest of his work, but Lee wanted something a bit more offbeat and edgy. Steve Ditko was the artist to provide it, and Lee asked him to illustrate the initial Spider-Man adventure. The now famous cover for the first story was drawn by Kirby and Ditko together. "Steve Ditko was a fine artist," says Kirby, "and he did a fine job on Spider-Man."

Born in 1927 in Johnstown, Pennsylvania, Ditko had already won a cult following with the dark, moody tales he had illustrated for comic books like *Amazing Adult Fantasy.* An intensely private individual who shuns personal publicity and consistently refuses interviews, Ditko has always preferred to let his work speak for itself. The analogy to Peter Parker working behind the mask of Spider-Man may not be entirely inappropriate. Ditko was the perfect choice to depict the new anti-hero, a skinny kid who just didn't know what to do with the extraordinary gift that had unexpectedly come his way. "Steve was every bit as inventive as Jack Kirby was," says Lee. "He always added so much." As time went on, Ditko also began to contribute significantly to the plotting of the stories. From the very start, Ditko's sensitive, humanistic portrayal of the beleaguered Peter Parker was enough to alter the look of the medium forever: he brought a touch of realism into a world of fantasy.

Bugs in the System

Before Spider-Man received his own comic book, another super hero with bugs in his system got a regular series, starting in *Tales to Astonish* #35 (September 1962). Henry Pym discovered a formula for shrinking himself down to become the insect-size Ant-Man. He also invented a helmet with antennae that allowed him to communicate with his insect friends. The value of such accomplishments was dubious, and Pym did not have much of a personality; Stan Lee and Jack Kirby were beginning to spread themselves a little too thin. They launched Ant-Man, then turned him over almost immediately to writer Larry Lieber and

MARVEL'S NUTTIEST NEMESIS: THE LIVING ERASER

"In the comic book business," says Stan Lee, "you're always trying to think of a new villain." Over the years, Marvel created some splendid menaces, and also one that was primarily an in-joke: The Living Eraser, the ultimate threat to heroes who were really only lines on paper. This was a bad guy who could cause people to vanish with just a few swipes of his hand. "I got a big kick out of it when I dreamed up that idea," Lee says with a smile.

The Living Eraser showed up in *Tales to Astonish* #49 (November 1963), and attempted to wipe out the faltering hero Ant-Man, who was in the process of becoming Giant-Man. Unfortunately, plot demands obliged Lee to explain the erasing as a method of traveling from one dimension to another, but this rationale did little to negate the arresting images of Giant-Man and his friends being rubbed off the page and into comic book oblivion. Embodying an almost surreal use of the medium, The Living Eraser was definitely one of a kind.

▶ **The new Human Torch, a hit in *The Fantastic Four*, gets a solo series in *Strange Tales* #101 (October 1962). Pencils: Jack Kirby. Inks: Dick Ayers.**

artist Don Heck, who realized that Ant-Man's talents were not the stuff of which heroes are made: "He was being carried around by ants all the time," says Heck.

Don Heck, who had started with the company in 1954, describes himself as "the utility man" of The Marvel Age. "Whenever anything suddenly came up, they would say, 'Don't worry, Don can handle that.'" Frequently shunted about from one series to another, Heck would eventually be given his chance to shine, but all he could do with Ant-Man was lavish attention on the hero's female assistant, The Wasp, who showed up in the tenth story. The Wasp was never depicted as a deep thinker, but Heck's drawings made her lively and attractive. "I was married to a good-looking woman at the time," says Heck, "so that was a big help."

After five more issues, an attempt was made to save the faltering Ant-Man by changing him into Giant-Man. Even with his new size, this was one hero who never really made the grade and who never seemed to be touched by the Marvel magic.

Torch Song

To bolster another of the flagging "monster" books, The Human Torch was given a solo series in *Strange Tales* #101 (October 1962). This was the new Human Torch, teenager Johnny Storm, a team player who worked most effectively as part of The Fantastic Four. As an individual performer he never really caught fire, and before long The Thing was brought in to strengthen the act's appeal. Nonetheless, this feature, like Ant-Man, was not really up to the new standards the company had attained, and its run was not very long. Lee and Kirby soon relinquished the character to writer Larry Lieber and artist Dick Ayers, who had drawn the original Torch during his 1950s incarnation.

The Torch and Ant-Man served principally to establish new beachheads in old titles, indicating that the company had committed itself to super heroes. Yet so much was happening so fast that the old standby genres sometimes looked safest:

the two oversize twenty-five-cent annuals for 1962 were devoted not to Marvel's new breed of innovative super heroes but to reprints from *Millie the Model* and the prehero *Strange Tales*.

A Hero with a Heart

Seeming to pluck ideas out of the air as major new characters appeared, Stan Lee showed something like vision when he chose the country of Vietnam as the setting for the origin of Iron Man (*Tales of Suspense* #39, March 1963). In 1963 comparatively few Americans were interested in Vietnam, but before long the war being waged there would become the most crucial and controversial event of the 1960s. For Lee, the setting may have been merely expedient, enabling him to introduce the Communist villains he still employed with some regularity. Later, he had second thoughts about his somewhat simplistic treatment of the Asian nation's problems. Yet Iron Man was a character whose very premise demanded political intrigue.

The protagonist of the tale, Tony Stark, is a millionaire inventor and arms manufacturer who leads a seemingly charmed life, but who soon develops a problem, as did all of Marvel's best characters. While testing experimental transistor-powered weapons in the jungles of Vietnam, Stark is injured by an exploding booby trap and is captured by the enemy. Fatally injured by a piece of

Ant-Man's January 1962 debut. Pencils: Jack Kirby. Inks: Dick Ayers.

Ant-Man acquires a costume. Pencils: Jack Kirby. Inks: Dick Ayers.

Ant-Man meets the Wasp. Pencils: Jack Kirby. Inks: Don Heck.

shrapnel that is working its way toward his heart, Stark is ordered to spend his last days inventing new armaments for the Communists; instead he constructs a suit of transistorized armor that also serves as a pacemaker to keep his heart beating. As Iron Man, he conquers his foes and manages to escape, but he is doomed to remain at least partially encased in metal until the day he dies. Life as a Marvel hero was never a bed of roses.

Don Heck had the honor of drawing the initial Iron Man story, a rare opportunity in the days when Jack Kirby seemed to get first crack at just about everything. And, in fact, Kirby did have a hand in Iron Man. "He designed the costume," says Heck, "because he was doing the cover. The covers were always done first. But I created the look of the characters, like Tony Stark and his secretary Pepper Potts." Over all, it was Heck's solid craftsmanship that set Iron Man on the road to success.

Meanwhile, Heck was introduced to the intricacies of The Marvel Method of comic book creation. When he was first handed a story synopsis, Heck told editor Lee: "You've got to be kidding. I'm not used to that. I'm used to a full script." Eventually Heck adjusted, and gradually came to enjoy the chance to contribute to the stories, but he remembers that some artists "said the hell with it and left." Some top talents in the field passed in and out of the company quickly because they never adapted to Lee's revolutionary method. "Stan would call me up," says Heck, "and he'd give me the first couple of pages over the phone, and the last page. I'd say, 'What about the stuff in between?' and he'd say, 'Fill it in.'"

Heck's solid background in war comics helped him get Iron Man off to a good start, but he wasn't entirely pleased with the character's armor despite his boundless admiration for Jack Kirby. "He was terrific," says Heck. "He was always willing to help somebody or tell you how to do something. And as for the super heroes, the main reason they existed was Jack Kirby. He used to call them 'the guys in the long underwear.'"

Kirby's original Iron Man suit, realistically bulky given the circumstances under which Tony Stark had to build it, soon changed from forbidding gray to gold. Later, it was streamlined into a red-and-gold design by Steve Ditko. Perhaps because the suit is a machine, many artists have been tempted to tinker with it, and over the years, Iron Man's costumed appearance has changed more often than that of any other Marvel super hero.

Iron Man, a wealthy patriot with a war injury, might have reminded some readers of President

John F. Kennedy, whose inauguration in 1961 had infused the United States with a feeling of adventurous optimism. Stan Lee has never compared J.F.K. to Iron Man, but he has speculated that the Kennedy era's spirit provided the ideal atmosphere for the introduction of new super heroes. Kennedy's assassination in 1963 ended the era all too quickly, and signaled the advent of the turmoil that would characterize the rest of the decade. Kennedy had encouraged the buildup of American troops in Vietnam, and as the war there became more deadly and more divisive, Iron Man began to look even more like a symbol of The United States: he went halfway around the world to fight for what

Iron Man clanks his way into *Tales of Suspense* #39 (March 1962) (below). By issue #44 (left), Iron Man had acquired a golden glow. Covers by Jack Kirby and Don Heck.

he thought was right, and he came home with a wound that seemed as if it would never heal.

The Marvel Universe Evolves

The surprise success of Spider-Man brought him his own comic book, *The Amazing Spider-Man,* in the same month that Iron Man was launched (March 1963). Spidey's first adventure in the new comic book showed how the troubled hero was mistakenly reviled after he had risked his life to save a U.S. astronaut. Manned space flights had been in the news since the initial triumphs of Russian Yuri Gagarin and American Alan Shepard in 1961, and such feats were just as useful and appropriate to comic books as were nuclear weapons. And clearly, these stories were no longer science fiction—they were coming true.

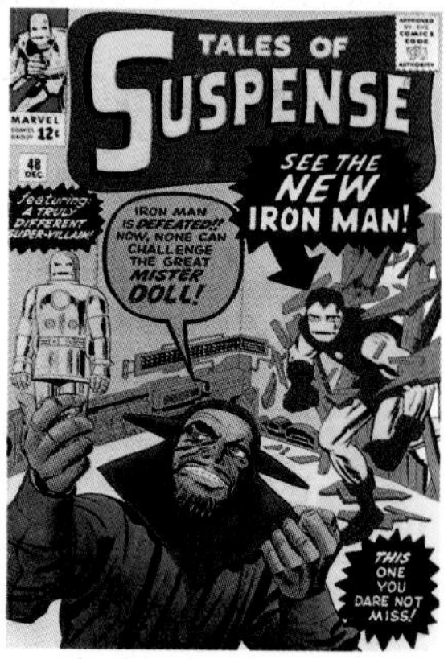
TALES OF
SUSPENSE
SEE THE NEW IRON MAN!
IRON MAN IS DEFEATED!! NOW, NONE CAN CHALLENGE THE GREAT MISTER DOLL!
THIS ONE YOU DARE NOT MISS!

► Steve Ditko designed the streamlined armor that first appeared in December 1963. Cover by Jack Kirby and Dick Ayers.

The Fantastic Four, who had gained their super powers during an experiment in outer space, put in a guest appearance in *The Amazing Spider-Man* #1, helping to introduce the new hero and set him on the path to a popularity that would eventually rival and then surpass their own. In the story, Spider-Man broke into The Fantastic Four headquarters looking for a well-paying job, but ended up frustrated and forlorn as usual.

In the same month, The Hulk appeared as a guest in *Fantastic Four* #12, but simultaneously his own comic book was canceled. The former event was ultimately more significant than the latter. There has been speculation that *The Incredible Hulk* was in artistic or financial difficulty, but Jack Kirby insists that "The Hulk worked all the time, really. The lapse had something to do with the publishing business." In fact, Marvel seethed with more creativity than Martin Goodman's company could contain, and the limited opportunities for distribution were beginning to take their toll. Apparently The Hulk lost his own comic book temporarily to enable Spider-Man to get his.

The appearance of The Hulk in *Fantastic Four* while The Fantastic Four were in *Amazing Spider-Man* represented another of the innovations that made Stan Lee a great comic book editor. The crossovers were cross-fertilizing one title after another, introducing fans of one hero to all of the company's other characters while simultaneously creating a richly populated cosmos that would soon be known as "The Marvel Universe." "I used to love doing that," says Lee. "I felt that having the characters meet each other and get involved in each other's stories made the whole thing realistic. And of course the readers loved it when there was a fight."

Battles between good guys were set in motion by elaborate misunderstandings, made plausible because the characters were so full of quirks. Jack Kirby's fight scenes grew wilder than ever—they were exuberant wrestling matches staged by mighty titans. Even the villains loved a brawl, and often eschewed loot for the chance to go head-to-head with a super hero.

The center of The Marvel Universe was New York, New York. Everyone connected with the company lived in the city or nearby, and the decision was made early on that the super heroes would live there too. Fictionalized cities like Superman's Metropolis or Batman's Gotham City gave way to the real thing. The Fantastic Four had

▼ Artist Don Heck shines as Iron Man walks for the first time. Plot: Stan Lee. Script: Larry Lieber.

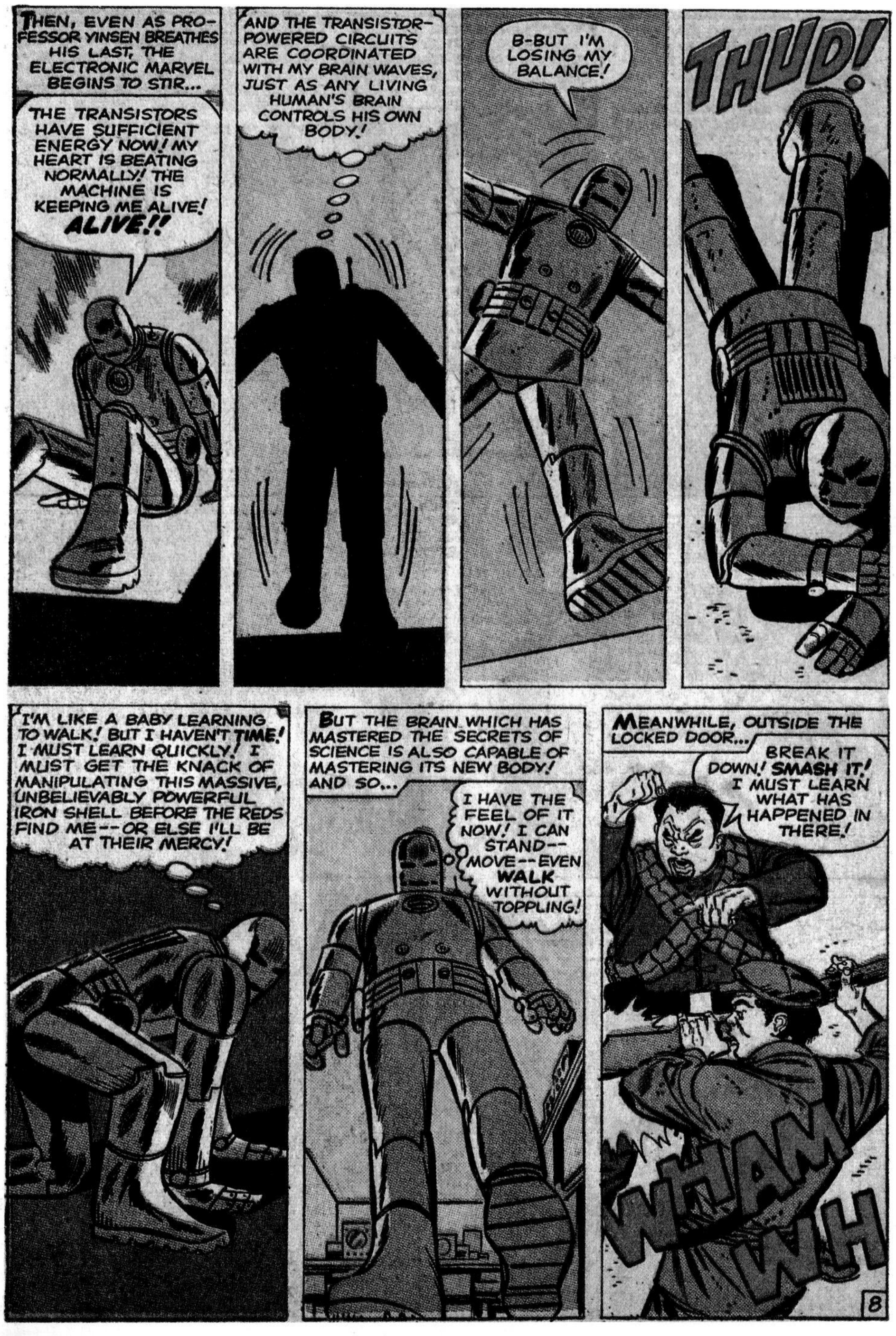
THEN, EVEN AS PROFESSOR YINSEN BREATHES HIS LAST, THE ELECTRONIC MARVEL BEGINS TO STIR...
THE TRANSISTORS HAVE SUFFICIENT ENERGY NOW! MY HEART IS BEATING NORMALLY! THE MACHINE IS KEEPING ME ALIVE! ALIVE!!
AND THE TRANSISTOR-POWERED CIRCUITS ARE COORDINATED WITH MY BRAIN WAVES, JUST AS ANY LIVING HUMAN'S BRAIN CONTROLS HIS OWN BODY!
B-BUT I'M LOSING MY BALANCE!
THUD!
I'M LIKE A BABY LEARNING TO WALK! BUT I HAVEN'T TIME! I MUST LEARN QUICKLY! I MUST GET THE KNACK OF MANIPULATING THIS MASSIVE, UNBELIEVABLY POWERFUL IRON SHELL BEFORE THE REDS FIND ME--OR ELSE I'LL BE AT THEIR MERCY!
BUT THE BRAIN WHICH HAS MASTERED THE SECRETS OF SCIENCE IS ALSO CAPABLE OF MASTERING ITS NEW BODY! AND SO...
I HAVE THE FEEL OF IT NOW! I CAN STAND--MOVE--EVEN WALK WITHOUT TOPPLING!
MEANWHILE, OUTSIDE THE LOCKED DOOR...
BREAK IT DOWN! SMASH IT! I MUST LEARN WHAT HAS HAPPENED IN THERE!
WHAM
WH
8

Stark publicly proclaims that Iron Man is his bodyguard, and to avoid prosecution for his own violence he once announced that the man in the suit had died and been replaced. He might have been talking about himself, since he is empowered by machinery and sustained by another man's heart. Beneath his polished veneer, Iron Man may be the most troubled of Marvel's heroes, forever fighting to prove that his armor is not hollow.

Iron Man, like knights of old, is identified by the armor he wears. The best-dressed of the Marvel heroes, he has changed his look frequently since his debut in 1963, but he can afford to: the man who wears the suits (and designs them) is wealthy inventor Tony Stark. So the man makes the clothes, but do the clothes make the man?

Not only does Tony Stark have no super powers of his own, but the armor that gives him strength was also created to keep his damaged heart beating; he could not survive without his iron shell. Eventually his cardiac condition was corrected by a heart transplant, and a later injury that left him paralyzed was repaired with a microchip. So even without his high-tech costume, Tony Stark is a mixture of man and machine, what science fiction writers call a cyborg.

This bulky prototype was soon abandoned.

Exactly who Stark might be without his armor is difficult to say. Writer Stan Lee and artist Don Heck initially presented him as a suave playboy, part of a long tradition of rich men who have become masked heroes. Yet unlike most of his predecessors, Stark got his income from a specific source: he manufactured and sold weapons. This was a slightly sinister occupation, despite its undoubted utility, and there were hints that Stark was ambivalent about his role. When his business was menaced by a hostile takeover in a 1979 storyline, he collapsed into alcoholism, and a friend was obliged to take over temporarily the job of Iron Man. So the suit can function without Stark, but can Stark function without the suit?

▶ The Marvel Universe takes shape as Spider-Man gets his own title and immediately confronts The Fantastic Four. Cover: Steve Ditko.

their headquarters atop a midtown skyscraper; Spider-Man stayed with his widowed aunt in Forest Hills, in the outer borough of Queens; Iron Man owned a mansion in Manhattan. In fact, New York City itself became a major character in The Marvel Universe, and its citizens were usually depicted with their eyes on the skies, watching costumed characters cavorting overhead.

Small World

The fans who relished all this wild activity would have been shocked if they had realized what a small piece of New York was actually occupied by their favorite comic book company. "The Marvel office was at 655 Madison Avenue," says Flo Steinberg, who was hired as Stan Lee's gal Friday in March 1963. "It was a teeny little two-room office, and Stan was the only person working there besides me. We had two little cubbyholes with a head-high partition between them." This was the same office Stan Lee had occupied since the slump of 1954, stuck in a back corner of the floor occupied by Martin Goodman's large magazine publishing company.

"Stan was very good-natured," says Steinberg.

▲ The second meeting of The Hulk and The Fantastic Four led to their wildest fight.

◄ Hulk and Thing clash, but New York suffers most. *Fantastic Four #25* (April 1964). Pencils: Jack Kirby. Inks: George Roussos.

◄ Spider-Man villains included a doctor with metal arms, a scientist with reptilian tendencies and a special-effects expert who drove Spidey to a psychiatrist's couch. Covers: Steve Ditko.

Marvel finally became
Marvel in May 1963; Steve
Ditko designed the cover
element that made it official.

► In March 1963, the
same month that Spider-
Man met The Fantastic
Four, The Fantastic Four
also met The Hulk.
Crossovers were good for
business. Pencils: Jack
Kirby. Inks: Dick Ayers.

"A really great person. He was the best boss I ever had. I was in charge of the mail, which wasn't that much back then. I would pick out the letters that seemed important and he would choose the ones that got printed—if they were typewritten they had a better chance. I think everybody got sent some kind of answer, but sometimes I would sign Stan's name, and sometimes he did. He was busy typing out plot synopses in the office; later on he started just talking them over with the artists.

"The artists used to come up and chat with Stan; they liked to hang out. It was a break for them from working at home all the time. Jack Kirby always smoked a cigar and he was very funny. It was something like a team; everybody liked each other. They had a skill and this place was paying them to use it. Nobody acted like a star."

Artist Sol Brodsky, who often came into the Marvel office, had organizational skills that eventually earned him the post of production manager. He also did the lettering on some of the character logos that have remained in use for decades. "Sol was really my right-hand man for years," says Stan Lee.

Kids who came for a peek at the heart of The Marvel Universe were doomed to disappointment, but it didn't stop them from coming. "They always wanted to have tours of the office," says Steinberg, "so I'd go out and they'd have to be satisfied with me. There was just nothing back there to see." Occasionally, enthusiasts tried to bulldoze past Steinberg, and "I'd have to body-block 'em or trip 'em or something. Kids used to come up who became important in comics later, people like Marv Wolfman and Len Wein. They were all just little fans at the time. I'd wish them well and tell them to finish high school. It was in that office that Stan got the idea to start a fan club."

Marvel Mania

Amazingly enough, it was not until May 1963 that the company inspiring so much enthusiasm finally gave itself a name: Marvel Comics. The tiny letters "MC" had been appearing in the upper right corner of the comic book covers for some time—right under the Comics Code seal—but readers didn't really know what they meant. Finally, Steve Ditko created a design element that is still employed today, a vertical box placed in the extreme upper left corner of each cover. A picture of the title's leading character was placed inside, along with the words "Marvel Comics Group."

After twenty-four years of groping, Marvel Comics finally had a name; it was the title of the first comic book the company had published, way back in 1939.

"Martin Goodman and I were looking for a good name," Stan Lee recalls, "and he said, 'You know,

the first thing we did was Marvel.' And I knew Marvel was a word we could play with. There was a lot I could do with that." Editor Lee had already established The Marvel Method and The Marvel Universe, even though nobody was using those terms in 1963. Now he embarked on a campaign that could have been called Marvel Mania.

"I think I really treated the whole line as a gigantic advertising campaign," says Lee. "I don't mean that we tried to put anything over on anyone, but I felt we had good stories, and we were all very excited about what we were doing. I wanted the readers to feel the same way, to feel that we were all part of an 'in' thing that the outside world wasn't even aware of. We were all sharing a big joke together and having a lot of fun with this crazy Marvel Universe."

Lee began to engage in wild hyperbole, coining slogans like "Welcome to the Marvel Age of Comics," or "Make Mine Marvel," or "Marvel Marches On." Every cover was emblazoned with endorsements like "Another Spectacular Smash Hit from The House of Ideas!" There were even pleas like this one: "Have we got a tale for you!! Please don't frustrate us . . . You've got to read it!!" Only the most unsophisticated readers took this sort of

◄ Letters to Marvel were answered with these cards, personalized with Flo Steinberg's handwriting.

▼ Jack Kirby depicts the core Marvel staff of the 1960s as The Fantastic Four: Stan Lee, Kirby, Flo Steinberg, Sol Brodsky. From *What If?* #11 (October 1978).

THE MERRY MARVEL MARCHING SOCIETY

In January 1965, Stan Lee announced the creation of The Merry Marvel Marching Society, "an honest-to-gosh far-out fan club in the mixed-up Marvel manner." Lee had been dropping the mysterious initials M.M.M.S. into the comic books for months to whet the curiosity of the fans, who responded in enthusiastic droves when membership application forms were finally published. "Nobody ever expected it to be so big," says Lee's gal Friday, Flo Steinberg. "There were thousands of letters and dollar bills flying all over the place. We were throwing them at each other."

For a dollar, each member received a package of "nutty gizmos," including a membership card, stickers and a big button. The most unusual item was a flexi-disc recording featuring the voices of Lee and a group of writers and artists cracking corny jokes like this:

Stan Lee: Say a few words to the fans.
Jack Kirby: Okay—"a few words."

For this, people paid money. In fact, branches of the M.M.M.S. sprang up at hundreds of colleges and universities, including such august institutions as Oxford and Cambridge. Lee never presented the M.M.M.S. as anything more than a lot of foolishness, but apparently this very quality made it a big success. And significantly, this fan club was not for just one character, but for an entire line of comics.

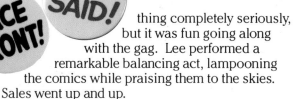

thing completely seriously, but it was fun going along with the gag. Lee performed a remarkable balancing act, lampooning the comics while praising them to the skies. Sales went up and up.

Even the titles of the books were part of the campaign. Characters came complete with their own publicity, like *The Incredible Hulk* and *The Amazing Spider-Man.* Some of the adjectives were left over from the old "monster" books, but Lee came up with new ones as well. "I don't know," he says, "I'm corny."

And fair too. For the first time in the history of the industry, almost everyone who worked on the comics was given public credit, even the unsung heroes who lettered the speech balloons. A typical box on the opening page of a story might read as follows: "Incredible Story by Stan Lee! Incomparable Penciling by Jack Kirby! Invincible Inking by Joe Sinnott! Inevitable Lettering by Artie Simek!" Lee tried to make a celebrity out of everyone who worked for Marvel, while simultaneously making them members of the family. Even Flo Steinberg, Lee's secretary, acquired fans.

Stan's Soapbox

"I answered every letter we printed in the comic books," says Lee. "I tried to keep it warm and friendly, not stiff. Instead of writing 'Dear Editor,' people wrote 'Dear Stan and Jack,' or just 'Hey, you two crazy nuts,' and that was just the feeling that I really wanted."

By 1965, Lee had inaugurated the Marvel Bullpen Bulletins page, which appeared in every issue of every comic book. Along with news about the artists and the characters, the page eventually included a feature called "Stan's Soapbox," in which the editor held forth on both comics and social issues. His message, if it can be distilled, was one of good-natured tolerance. Somehow Lee managed to convey his feeling that while fights between super heroes might be entertaining fantasies, real people in real life were expected to exhibit more restrained behavior.

Sometimes Lee seemed like a lovable sergeant giving his green recruits the wisdom they needed to survive. Some of his catchphrases, like "Face Front!" and "Hang Loose!" and "Nuff Said!" were admittedly inspired by his army service during World War II. "The attitude slipped in," he says, "but most of the expressions I made up." He took a generation under his wing, and his advice was good. "I tried to write," says Lee, "as if the readers were friends of mine and I was talking specifically to them."

Gambling on The Sarge

While Lee promoted the Marvel style with his unique mixture of humor and enthusiasm, new heroes continued to emerge from "The House of Ideas." A surprising level of success was achieved by *Sgt. Fury and His Howling Commandos* (May 1963). Set in World War II, a less controversial war than the Vietnam conflict, the series was born out of a bet between Lee and publisher Martin Goodman. Puzzling over the company's growing popularity, Goodman reacted with skepticism to Lee's claim that a new style had been developed that would work with any genre. To prove his point, Lee bet that he could make a hit out of a comic with the apparently outdated war theme and "a horrible title." Lee won, but he had forgotten to name the stakes.

Jack Kirby was the obvious choice to illustrate the adventures of the cigar-chomping Nick Fury and his mismatched men. Although the Comics Code prohibited brutality in either language or action, Kirby feels that "there was reality in the stories because of my own war experiences. *Sgt. Fury* had the essence of military life in it."

The six soldiers who accompanied Sgt. Fury were ethnically mixed,

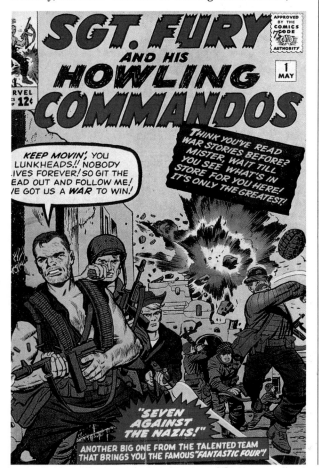

MEMORABILIA COURTESY OF JOE FRANK

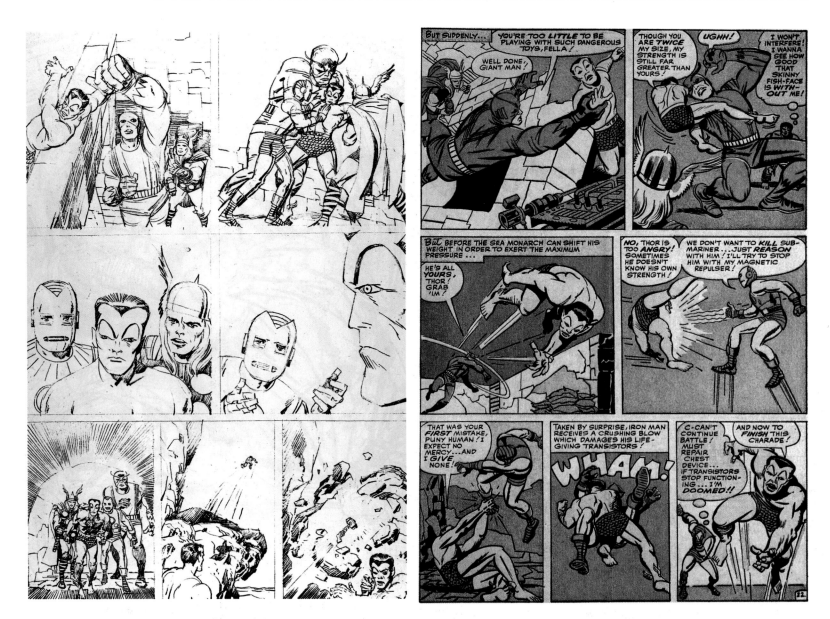

▲ The elegant simplicity of Jack Kirby's work is evident in this penciled page, which was nevertheless rejected in favor of a different approach to the action, inked by Paul Reinman. From *Avengers* #3.

and one of them was a black man named Gabe Jones. The visual stereotypes once common in comics were no longer acceptable at Marvel, and eventually Stan Lee was obliged to send a detailed memo to the company that did the color separations to make it absolutely clear that Gabe was a black man.

Marvel's progressive attitude delighted most readers, but annoyed at least one. Flo Steinberg recalls opening a letter addressed to the Sgt. Fury staff that read, "You pinko commies! What have you got against the Nazis? I'm going to come to the office and shoot you all!" The FBI was called in, but nothing ever came of the threat. Clearly, however, the new Marvel style was making an impact on the reading public.

The Super Group

By September 1963 it was easy enough for Marvel to fulfill Martin Goodman's 1961 wish that his company could publish a comic book as jam-packed with popular super heroes as DC's *Justice League.* By late 1963, Marvel had super hero stars to spare, and some of them were joined together to form a new super hero group called *The Avengers.*

The original Avengers were Iron Man, Thor, The Hulk and Ant-Man, along with his female partner, The Wasp. Including the antisocial Hulk in the group was an odd choice, even for a company that made a specialty of character conflict. He quit in the second issue, but returned in the third to battle the remaining Avengers with the help of the traditionally testy Sub-Mariner. Jack Kirby handled the penciling for the first eight issues—exactly as long as he had stuck with *Sgt. Fury*—and then Lee turned the series over to "utility man" Don Heck. *The Avengers* often had a crowded look as multiple villains showed up to fight the many heroes. "It was easy enough for the writers," Heck notes, "to say that six guys come in from the left and six guys come in from the right, but the artist had to draw them all."

Given the rambunctious nature of Marvel's super heroes, it's not surprising that over the years The Avengers proved to be a singularly unstable super

The first Avengers: Iron Man, The Hulk, Thor, Ant-Man and Wasp.
Cover: Kirby and Ayers.

▲ Captain America, frozen since World War II, is thawed out in *Avengers* #4 (March 1964). Script: Stan Lee. Pencils: Jack Kirby. Inks: Paul Reinman.

▼ The original Avengers are replaced in May 1965. Cap takes charge, and Hawkeye is resentful. Script: Stan Lee. Pencils: Jack Kirby. Inks: Dick Ayers.

In *Avengers* #3, Hulk joins Sub-Mariner to battle the good guys. Cover: Kirby and Reinman.

Captain America comes back to life and joins The Avengers. Cover: Kirby and Reinman.

► Captain America, his brief 1950s incarnation forgotten, returned from World War II to lead the super group The Avengers. Early members and a few enemies are pictured behind him. Cover: Jack Kirby and Don Heck.

group. Kirby, who often set the visual style for new books and then moved on, did stay long enough to draw once again the member who proved to be the heart of the group: Captain America. The great Golden Age hero created by Kirby and Joe Simon in 1941 was revived in 1964 when The Avengers discovered him frozen in the Arctic and thawed him out. He soon took command of the whole team, and by the sixteenth issue (May 1965), he was the only big star left.

Stan Lee has admitted that by this period the intertwined tales of The Marvel Universe were beginning to confuse even him. Keeping top heroes like Thor active in *The Avengers* without contradicting the information in Thor's own series was becoming a chore. A changing of the guard was the result for *The Avengers* and Captain America was soon leading a motley crew of reformed villains like Hawkeye, Quicksilver and The Scarlet Witch. "It was difficult in the beginning," says Don Heck, "like losing old friends." There were eventual compensations, however. Hawkeye, an arrogant, sarcastic archer for whom Heck had done the original drawings in 1964, was named the most popular hero of *The Avengers* in a 1989 fan poll. Considering the competition—almost every Marvel hero has been a member of the group—this was quite a tribute.

Teenage Mutants

The X-Men, a comic book series featuring a very different sort of super hero group, made its debut simultaneously with *The Avengers* in September 1963. Stan Lee had originally wanted to call the team of teenagers The Mutants, but Martin Goodman felt the name might baffle young readers, so Lee came up with X-Men, which had a nice hint of the unknown about it. The leader of the team was Professor Xavier, a wheelchair-bound telepath who ran a school for gifted youngsters who were all secretly mutants. Feared by ordinary people, The X-Men were nonetheless in training to protect humanity from a gang of evil mutants headed by the sinister Magneto.

The notion of mutants whose powers originated in their genes was new to Marvel, although the concept of the misunderstood adolescent was reminiscent of Spider-Man, and the idea of bickering malcontents inevitably suggested The Fantastic Four. At first, The X-Men seemed too busy to develop fully rounded personalities, especially when the six of them were battling five Avengers, as they did in *X-Men* #9. In addition to Professor X, the mutants were Cyclops, whose eyes emitted deadly rays; The Angel, who flew on huge feathered wings; Marvel Girl, who moved objects through telekinesis; Iceman, a reverse Human Torch who could freeze anything, including himself; and The Beast, whose erudition was masked by the strength and contours of a gorilla.

Once again, Jack Kirby joined Lee as cocreator of the comic book. "Jack was the best guy to work with you can imagine," says Lee. "Any idea I would give him, he could make it better. When Jack brought in the first story, it opened with all

▲ Fighting perennial foe Magneto in *X-Men* #1 (September 1963). Pencils: Jack Kirby. Inks: Sol Brodsky.

◄ In *X-Men* #1 the teenage mutants work out in The Danger Room while their leader Professor X welcomes a new recruit. Script: Stan Lee. Pencils: Jack Kirby. Inks: Paul Reinman.

▲ **Unpublished covers by Werner Roth, who followed Jack Kirby on** *The X-Men.* **Editor Stan Lee, who also served as Marvel's art director, often requested several versions of covers as they were vital to sales.**

The X-Men fighting in the place they called The Danger Room, where they were trained. That was Jack's idea. And it was the most brilliant opening because it started with action and showed all their abilities immediately." Yet Kirby, who was working simultaneously on almost everything, drifted away from the series fairly soon, and Lee eventually turned the writing over to other hands as well. "I think maybe Jack and I should have stayed with it a little longer, to give it more push," Lee admits. *The X-Men* drifted along, erratic and occasionally brilliant, but a decade passed before the series began to achieve its full potential.

Soap Opera

As the Marvel style continued to develop, the characters and stories became more and more complex, until not even an entire comic book had enough pages to contain a single adventure. For example, *X-Men* #4 concluded with a cliff-hanger that went unresolved for two months. "To get a really good story going," says Lee, "you have to make it long. And I had to dream up so many plots that it was easier for me if I could continue them over two or three issues." Some readers wrote in to complain, suggesting that the serials were merely an artificial marketing device, but the majority found extended narratives to their liking. Gradually, cliff-hangers became the norm. It was yet another Marvel innovation that has become standard in the industry.

With tongue in cheek, Lee began to describe the comic books as "soap operas," a reference not only to the serial stories but also to the portrayal of suffering individuals that was one of his main strengths as a writer. The unresolved romantic triangle among Cyclops, Marvel Girl and The Angel of The X-Men was a perfect example. Like soap operas, Marvel sagas prompted a tremendous loyalty in their audience. The tiny office where Stan Lee had stuck it out for so many years was expanded and then moved twice to accommodate a growing production staff. Marvel was pulling itself up by its bootstraps to become one of the giants of the comic book industry.

PROFILE

the Original X-MEN

Angel

Iceman

The original X-Men embodied every youngster's greatest hope and fear: to be different from everyone else. They were teenage mutants, gifted with latent powers that usually did not manifest themselves until the onset of puberty, and the metaphor that equated adolescents with budding super heroes was a masterstroke. The notion that mutants were fated to be hated and feared by ordinary people emphasized the adolescent sense of isolation, and the mutants had to conceal their powers so they could remain at large to aid their ignorant persecutors. Hidden talents, however, created ethical dilemmas. Should the mutant Angel, for example, choose safety and conformity by keeping his wings hidden beneath his clothing, or should he risk self-expression and fly free?

The wheelchair-bound Professor X was leader of the teenage mutants.

All in all, Stan Lee and Jack Kirby had come up with something special when they introduced this super hero group in 1963, but somehow it didn't quite take flight. Gifted teenagers struggling in an uncomprehending world seemed a natural concept, but it was weakened by the decision to make The X-Men students. They were enrolled at Professor Xavier's School for Gifted Youngsters, and it was the older and wiser Professor X who called the shots. If kids with built-in death rays still had to attend classes, what use were super powers after all? The X-Men were ordered around like ordinary teenagers, forced to wear the school uniform, and put through grueling training exercises that actually endangered their lives. The idea of sending kids into deadly combat struck an uneasy note, and minor rewards like praise and individually designed costumes didn't seem quite good enough.

The only way The X-Men could express their natural rebelliousness was to drop out of school. Most of them waited only until a new roster of adult mutants had been introduced. Subsequently, the original members were regrouped, and achieved solid success on their own as X-Factor, but by then they weren't being presented as kids anymore.

Marvel Girl

Cyclops

Beast

Dr. Strange (above) appeared suddenly to share *Strange Tales* with The Human Torch (right). Cover: Bob Powell.

THE NO-PRIZE

Only Stan Lee could have come up with a way to turn an empty envelope into a collector's item treasured by fans all over the world: The No-Prize. It began simply enough with a few of Lee's jocular responses to published fan mail. If a letter particularly struck his fancy, he would award the correspondent a "no-prize," which meant exactly nothing. Before long he hit on the idea of actually mailing out the nonexistent awards in specially designed envelopes.

At first, any clever letter might be enough to win a No-Prize, but before long the standards grew stricter: the only way to win was to spot an error in one of the Marvel stories.

Today, the rules are even more rigid. The reader must not only find a mistake but invent a plausible, if farfetched, excuse for it. After almost thirty years, people are still trying to acquire this thing that never was. Rarely have so many done so much for so little.

A Doctor in the House

Dr. Strange, an unusual hero who soon developed an enthusiastic cult following, achieved prominence by creeping up on it. Initially conceived as a one-shot in the back of *Strange Tales* #110 (July 1963), Dr. Strange subsequently appeared and disappeared from the pages of the comic book that had given him his name. This seemed only proper since, after all, he was a magician. By 1964 his adventures had begun to show up on a regular basis, sharing the pages of *Strange Tales* with The Human Torch.

Inspired by the Mutual Network radio show *Chandu the Magician*, which Lee had enjoyed during his childhood, Dr. Strange was in fact a more impressive character than Chandu. Not content with simply casting spells or causing transformations, Dr. Strange was forever journeying into weird worlds and uncanny dimensions; his environment was perhaps the most unusual in comic books. Steve Ditko's offbeat style was perfectly suited to the delineation of these nightmarish realms, and Dr. Strange, the oddball magician, became the first Marvel hero other than Spider-Man that Ditko handled on a regular basis.

"When you're looking at artwork that you think is magnificent, it's a privilege to put the words in," said Stan Lee about Ditko's drawing. Ditko was never prolific, in part because he inked his own work instead of having it inked by other artists as Jack Kirby did, yet his style had a dark power that

NICK FURY, AGENT OF... S.H.I.E.L.D.

Nick Fury is an unusual Marvel hero: he has no super powers, inherent or acquired, and for years his adventures occupied two different time frames. Introduced by writer Stan Lee and artist Jack Kirby in *Sgt. Fury and His Howling Commandos* (1963), Fury fought World War II with a gang of colorful misfits, bending the rules to make things hot for the Nazis. Perhaps because he was in a good war against unequivocal evil, Fury's historical exploits were popular with young readers for eighteen years, even though he could not interact with the modern Marvel Universe.

In 1965, Lee and Kirby brought the hero up to date with *Nick Fury, Agent of S.H.I.E.L.D.* Now a colonel, he was recruited by Tony "Iron Man" Stark to take over an international espionage organization. Fury received not super powers but political power, despite his protest that he was "just a bare knuckles kinda guy." His new opponents were elusive and enigmatic; one of them was his own brother.

The high-tech spy began his career as a no-nonsense soldier fighting Nazis on the battlefields of World War II.

The contrast between the simple past and the complex present helped make Fury an interesting character, even though Marvel eventually strained his essential credibility by inventing a youth serum that let him indulge in violent action even after he had become a septuagenarian. Attempting to operate the counterspy organization in his direct, no-nonsense style, Fury was obliged to turn a blind eye on the ambiguous morality inherent in intelligence work; the eye patch he wore served as a symbol of his ethical compromise. Recently, however, Colonel Fury decided to clean house, and in the process discovered so much corruption in S.H.I.E.L.D. that the organization was ultimately disbanded. Yet the need for his services remained, and within a year, Fury was recruited again, this time to organize a smaller and more autonomous version of S.H.I.E.L.D. The biggest battle of Fury's career will be to maintain his integrity and individuality while building a bureaucracy that will almost inevitably subvert him in the end. A rebel who holds office has his work cut out for him.

DR. STRANGE

Dr. Strange is a part of The Marvel Universe, but he has always inhabited his own universe as well. "The Sorcerer Supreme of the Earth," a master of white magic, has experienced many memorable adventures in eerie dimensions that other heroes can only imagine. Yet if Dr. Strange has always been a bit aloof, his journeys into the unknown have served to expand the scope of the comic book landscape for every character who followed in his wake.

Introduced in 1963 by writer Stan Lee and artist Steve Ditko, Dr. Strange was very much a product of his time. The lure of mysticism was strong in the 1960s as a rebellious younger generation forged a counterculture that spurned materialism in favor of more spiritual values. Strange's affinity with bohemian attitudes was evident even in his address: he lived on Bleecker Street in New York's Greenwich Village. Originally a self-centered surgeon, Dr. Strange lost his delicate touch after an automobile accident, and became a wandering derelict. In the Himalayas he sought out a fabled healer called The Ancient One, who ended up repairing Strange's soul instead of his hands. Redeemed from worldliness, the reborn hero also tacitly acknowledged the value of a race and culture other than his own, studying with the old master until he was ready to become a guardian protecting humanity from the intrusion of evil. He encountered wicked wizards, and also abstract entities like Nightmare and Eternity; in each battle his weapon was knowledge rather than force.

Despite its influence, Dr. Strange's initial solo series did not outlast the 1960s. Yet he hung on in sporadic appearances for almost two decades until he was given his own comic book again in 1988. This full-fledged revival may have been tied in to the popularity of New Age occultism, or perhaps to a reaction against a decade devoted to acquisitiveness; in any case, spiritual longings are perennial. Even for those who sometimes find institutionalized religion repressive, a fascination with the supernatural remains.

◄The awesome figure of Eternity confronts Dr. Strange and his enemy Dormammu in artist Steve Ditko's last work on the series, from *Strange Tales* #146 (July 1966). Script: Denny O'Neill.

Daredevil is a super hero with an unusual gimmick: he is blind. His other senses are so acute, however, that his affliction is hardly a handicap, although he initially possessed little of the special insight that popular fiction frequently attributes to the blind. In fact, as originally presented in 1964 by writer Stan Lee and artist Bill Everett, Daredevil was a relatively carefree character who lived up to his name in a reckless secret existence that belied his day job as a responsible attorney. Even the death of his father, which initially inspired his crime-fighting activities, seemed to leave him more or less unscathed. At one point, Daredevil actually created a third identity for himself: he impersonated a nonexistent twin brother and then blithely killed him off when the ruse became inconvenient.

The man who wears Daredevil's mask has hidden depths, however. Over the years the blind lawyer Matt Murdock has sensed the world around him growing darker, and changing conditions have challenged his perception of himself. Committed to an ethical viewpoint and a respect for the law, Murdock could play the role of a vigilante only while serving a higher purpose than revenge. But when the colorfully costumed villains he once fought were replaced by brutal thugs who killed on a whim, Murdock was tempted to retaliate in kind. His beloved secretary became a drug addict, and his law partner an unwitting tool of organized crime. Torn by conflicting emotions and confused by the corruption around him, Murdock spiraled into a devastating depression, from which he emerged a humbler and warier individual.

Perhaps remembering his father, an unsuccessful boxer who lost his life when he refused to throw a fight, Murdock has recently returned to his roots in the slums. The overachiever now serves the underprivileged — as both a lawyer and a super hero. And perhaps the once oblivious Daredevil is at last beginning to understand why, like him, Justice is blind.

DAREDEVIL
THE MAN WITHOUT FEAR!

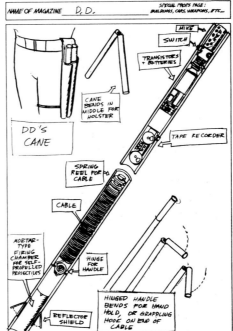

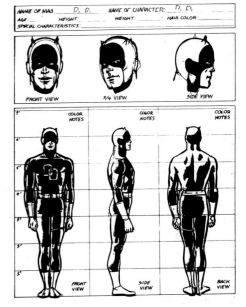

made Dr. Strange unique. Lee rose to the occasion with some of his most colorful dialogue, especially incantations like: "In the name of the dread Dormammu! By the hosts of the hoary Hoggoth! I call upon the mystic realm!" Some gullible fans convinced themselves that Lee was a genuine student of arcane lore, but in fact he was making up nonsense syllables.

◄ Daredevil #1 (April 1964) (top left) introduced the blind super hero in a multi-colored costume. Cover: Bill Everett. Wally Wood's new costume design (bottom left) appeared in April 1965.

Model sheets by Wally Wood for Daredevil's cane and costume.

Taking a Dare

"The ideas just came so easily," Stan Lee says of this period. Casting about for another super hero with a different problem to overcome, Lee hit on the ultimate drawback for a crime-fighter: "I'll make him blind. A blind lawyer." Drawing upon the idea that the blind are compensated by a heightening of their other senses, Lee invented an accident involving radioactive material that left attorney Matt Murdock sightless, but so sensitive in other ways that he could hear heartbeats and read newspapers with his fingertips. This was the only break the character got; his strength and speed were actually no more than those of a trained athlete.

Daredevil #1 (April 1964) presented the debut of the blind hero. The name had been used before, for a character introduced by Lev Gleason Publications but abandoned years earlier, and Lee reasoned that it was particularly appropriate for his new "Man Without Fear." Another name from bygone days became associated with the first issue when Bill Everett came on board to draw the story. The creator of the 1939 Sub-Mariner had been working as a commercial artist in Massachusetts, but Lee managed to lure him back to New York and Marvel; a number of other veterans would return in the months to come.

Everett soon moved on to other characters, and

▶ An updated Sgt. Fury became a super spy in August 1965. Cover: Kirby and Ayers.

▼ Captain America started sharing space with Iron Man in *Tales of Suspense* #59 (November 1964). Cover: Kirby and Ayers.

the complicated red-and-yellow costume that Everett created for the original *Daredevil* cover was changed by artist Wally Wood to simpler red tights. The more devilish new costume is the one that ultimately lasted.

Filling in the Holes

Marvel was bursting at the seams with super heroes. In order to accommodate all the characters clamoring for action, Lee was obliged to put two stars into several of the comic books, each one taking half the pages for his own separate story. The Hulk returned to join Giant-Man in *Tales to*

Astonish #60 (October 1964), and Captain America got his own series next to Iron Man's in *Tales of Suspense* #59 (November 1964). Jack Kirby threw himself enthusiastically into Cap's new adventures, including an action-packed series of stories that flashed back to World War II. Marvel was completely converting the old "monster" books into homes for heroes.

Sgt. Fury, leader of the Howling Commandos, was awarded a second series when letters poured in asking what had become of him after his years battling Nazis. Lee and Kirby answered the questions with "Nick Fury, Agent of S.H.I.E.L.D.," a contemporary series that joined Dr. Strange in *Strange Tales* #135 (August 1965), and replaced the solo Human Torch stories. In his second incarnation, the grizzled veteran Fury was the head of a super-scientific spy system called Supreme Headquarters, International Espionage Law-Enforcement Division. Wearing an eye patch and chewing on a cigar, the hard-bitten hero was hardly as suave as his contemporary cinema counterpart, the wildly popular James Bond, but Jack Kirby was able to create futuristic weapons for him that not even the movies could duplicate, most of them supplied by the laboratories of that wealthy inventor, Tony "Iron Man" Stark.

Simultaneously, The Sub-Mariner replaced the flagging Giant-Man in *Tales to Astonish* #70 (August 1965). With a new series for its oldest hero, Marvel had come full circle. Bill Everett was

◄ Marvel merchandise from the 1960s included T-shirts, sweatshirts, buttons and a Captain America board game.

temporarily too busy to draw Namor, but creator and creature were reunited before too much time had passed.

By 1965, with a whole host of popular and innovative comic books on display, Marvel was in the media spotlight. *The Wall Street Journal* noted the company's growing financial clout; *The Village Voice* analyzed the psychological makeup of the new super heroes; and *Esquire* announced that Marvel's characters had become big men on college campuses.

Marvel had definitely arrived, but the best was yet to come.

Grand Opera

Jack Kirby had brought his talents to almost all of Marvel's new successes, but with so many features firmly established, and additional artists coming in to work on them, the prodigious penciler allowed himself the luxury of concentrating his energies on three favorites: *Captain America* was classic Kirby combat polished to a fine sheen; with *Thor* and *The Fantastic Four* he ventured into uncharted waters. The results possessed a depth and scope of vision virtually unprecedented in comic books.

"Jack is a storyteller in pictures," says Stan Lee. "After a while, I only had to give him a couple of

◄ More Marvel memorabilia from the 1960s: posters, paperbacks, pillows, model kits and a Human Torch ashtray used in the Marvel office.

The Collecting Craze

Kids have always accumulated comic books, but the practice of collecting them as an adult hobby did not really catch on until the 1960s. Intent on recapturing their own youth, the first collectors concentrated on publications from earlier decades, most of which were available for only a few dollars apiece. As the craze grew and came into its own, prices for rare issues skyrocketed until they reached hundreds of dollars, and what had started as fun became a serious business. Meanwhile, the innovative comic books of the 1960s were neglected by many speculators, and thus, in their turn, relatively recent books also became rare. Today, the first appearance of an important title or character from the 40s, 50s, or 60s may command thousands of dollars in the antique comic book market. Adults bemoan the lost possessions and imagined fortunes of their childhoods, usually thrown away by obtuse parents, but of course the resultant scarcity is what makes the existing comics valuable. One drawback is that the old comic books are now too precious to be handled and read for pleasure, but publishers' reprints are beginning to rectify the situation.

Even though collecting, at varying levels of seriousness, is common today, a few very recent publications have caught everyone by surprise and jumped to hundreds of times their face value in a few years. The trick for devoted collectors lies in predicting which new comics will catch the public's fancy. Many speculators hedge their bets and buy double copies of all new comics—one to read and one to save in pristine, mint condition. First issues of all new series are considered particularly promising investments, and publishers invariably record significantly larger sales on their series openers.

With prices for old comics out of reach for the average fan, interest has increased in subsidiary collectibles, notably the toys and games marketed to capitalize on the popularity of certain super heroes. A few Captain America items were produced in the 1940s, but manufacturers did not become really interested in Marvel characters until the comics explosion of the 1960s. Now thousands of collectibles have been produced, from figurines to full-sized costumes, and prices are slowly inching up. Comic book conventions, where enthusiasts buy, sell and trade their treasures, are beginning to feature toys more prominently. Most people continue to collect for their own pleasure, but they are increasingly aware that a smart comic book buy can represent a better investment than almost any stock or bond.

▶ *No Arachnophobia Here*
"I didn't start out as a collector," says Dannee Buck, a computer programmer and Spider-Man fan from Southern California. "I just kept buying stuff." He still buys Spider-Man comic books every month and believes the new ones are better than ever. "I'm a little eccentric," he admits. "My wife says I'm very eccentric, but actually she's my biggest supporter."

▲ *Wall-to-Wall Wall-Crawlers*
This display of Spider-Man toys and paraphernalia represents only part of the huge collection accumulated by Dannee Buck. It's a spin-off of his interest in Marvel comic books that began when he was a youngster in the 1960s. The merchandise collection really began to take shape around 1975, he says, "because that's when they really started making a lot of toys."

◄ *Treasure Trove*
Some of the more unusual items in Dannee Buck's collection include a drinking cup that was printed backwards (lower left), a functioning Spider-Man telephone picked up at a discount store but now worth hundreds of dollars, and the stuffed doll (far right) that was the first piece he acquired. "Collectors have always run in my family," he says, "and I've always liked Spider-Man. Kids could really relate to him."

▲ The Fantastic Four, The X-Men and The Avengers at the engagement party for Mr. Fantastic and The Invisible Girl. Script: Stan Lee. Pencils: Jack Kirby. Inks: Chic Stone.

► Covers by Jack Kirby depict The Fantastic Four in a hostile environment (top), and among the strange beings known as The Inhumans (below).

words on what I thought the plot would be and he would do the whole thing." Of course, Lee's pithy dialogue and obvious affection for the characters assured him a strong presence, and sometimes his role as editor led him to try to hold Kirby back just a bit. "He was so inventive," says Lee. "He kept getting new ideas, and whenever he'd get one he'd put it in the story. And I'd say, 'Jack, save that for the next issue or the one after that. It's too much.'"

On the most basic level, Kirby's fecundity expressed itself in the wild mob scenes that he says were inspired by a lifetime in New York: "I've been used to crowds all my life." The ultimate Kirby crowd undoubtedly appeared in the 1965 *Fantastic Four Annual*, in which Mr. Fantastic finally married The Invisible Girl after a four-year courtship. Older fans had been speculating for some time about the sexual possibilities open to a transparent woman and an infinitely flexible man, but this wedding did not climax in a honeymoon. Instead, in what Lee billed as "The World's Most Colossal Collection of Costumed Characters, Crazily Cavorting and Capering in Continual Combat!," twenty-one invited heroes and twenty-one uninvited villains showed up for a celebratory free-for-all that ended with real-life gate-crashers Lee and Kirby being ejected by Nick Fury. Obviously intended as a romp, the wedding also demonstrated Marvel's commitment to letting its characters change and grow.

On a more serious level, the adventures of Thor were gradually transformed from stories about a strange-looking super hero into a spectacular saga. Vistas of space and time opened up in the dimensions between Earth and Asgard, realms where giants in bizarre armor struggled for supremacy while huge sailing ships soared through the stars. Kirby's figures were as

◄ Odin and Thor launch the ship that sails the skies as comic books strive to reach new heights in *Journey Into Mystery* #120 (September 1965). Script: Stan Lee. Pencils: Jack Kirby. Inks: Vince Colletta.

▲ All hell breaks loose at the wedding of Mr. Fantastic and The Invisible Girl. Script: Stan Lee. Pencils: Jack Kirby. Inks: Vince Colletta.

cosmic overtones, which no one had suspected the medium could achieve, and after five enormously successful years, *The Fantastic Four* was living up to Stan Lee's plucky publicity line: "The World's Greatest Comic Magazine."

By the mid-1960s the rockets and flying saucers so central to the space stories of just a few years earlier were suddenly no more than mundane vehicles used for visiting ordinary planets. Now readers could follow The Fantastic Four to Sub-Space, past Un-Life, into The Negative Zone and through Infinity. "To me," says Jack Kirby, "the images were electrifying. When you're first dreaming them up, that's when they're most interesting. You're reaching for something that truly involves your feelings and you try to get your feelings down on the page."

Kirby's most brilliant brainchild of this period, The Silver Surfer, first appeared in March 1966. He started out as an assistant to an awesome alien named Galactus, and Stan Lee had not originally expected him at all. The plot had been discussed, says Lee, but "when Jack brought back the drawings, I saw a guy on a flying surfboard and I said, 'Who's this?' Jack said that Galactus ought to have a herald who flies ahead of him, and I thought it was a wonderful idea. I loved the way Jack drew him, and I felt there was something so noble about him that I decided I'd get a lot of philosophy in there, letting him deliver remarks about the condition of life on Earth and how we don't appreciate this Garden of Eden we live in."

The Silver Surfer seemed to be part angel, part alien, and the absurd but endearing idea of his surfboard was the perfect comic book touch. He returned again and again, gathering loyal readers and eventually earning his own title.

monumental as statues brought to life, and Lee gave them speech, a mixture of Biblical and Shakespearean styles that was like nothing ever attempted in comic books before. *The Mighty Thor (Journey Into Mystery's* new title as of March 1966) became the equivalent of an endlessly extended Wagnerian opera, played out on sets that no impresario could afford to build.

Cosmic Comics

Perhaps the finest moments of The Marvel Age occurred in the pages of *The Fantastic Four*, where a group of humanized super heroes squabbled with each other, but rose above their conflicts to confront the vast gulfs of an overwhelming universe. The comic book took on mystical and

The Next Generation

In 1965, writer Roy Thomas arrived at Marvel to take some of the work load from Stan Lee. The art-

► The Silver Surfer rides a cosmic wave into The Marvel Universe. From *Fantastic Four* #48 (March 1966). Script: Stan Lee. Pencils: Jack Kirby. Inks: Joe Sinnott.

PROFILE

THE SILVER SURFER

but for his pains he was condemned to spend his life on the planet Earth, denied all access to the endless universe he loved to explore. There are parallels here to the Biblical fall of Adam, who lost paradise in the exercise of his free will and thus was doomed to mortal misery. The Silver Surfer, however, was not tainted by original sin, and remained a detached, bemused observer of human folly. As a symbol of limitless freedom dragged down by mundane reality, The Surfer was indeed a tragic figure, yet he never lost his essential innocence.

The character first appeared in 1966, drawn by Jack Kirby as an afterthought for a story that was already plotted; writer Stan Lee immediately fell in love with The Silver Surfer, and for years would allow nobody else to create his inimitably high-minded dialogue. Eventually Lee and artist John Buscema invented a background for "The Sentinel of the Spaceways," and revealed that he was originally Norrin Radd, a restless inhabitant of a utopian planet. When his race was threatened by the all-consuming Galactus, Norrin Radd saved the day by offering to aid the menace in his endless quest for worlds to devour. In sacrificing himself twice, once for his own people and again for humanity, The Silver Surfer took on Christlike qualities. The selflessness that made him so admired has finally been rewarded, and today he is free to soar among the stars.

The Silver Surfer, who symbolizes the highest aspirations of the spirit, also represents Marvel's most sincere effort to elevate the super hero genre. This noble, contemplative, unselfish character is an anomaly in the slam-bang world of comic books, and as such he has proven to be something of an acquired taste, a character who appeals primarily to older and comparatively sophisticated readers.

Ironically enough, when this benevolent alien first appeared he was working for one of the most terrifying villains in comics, the godlike being known as Galactus. It was the Surfer's courageous decision to defy his master that made him a hero,

Marvel's first black super hero leapt onto the scene in *Fantastic Four* #52 (July 1966). This cover was scrapped and the costume was changed before publication. Pencils: Jack Kirby. Inks: Joe Sinnott.

THE VILLAIN TO BEAT: GALACTUS

Marvel menaces took a quantum leap in 1966 with the introduction of Galactus, a gigantic alien being who feeds on the energy of planets and leaves them as lifeless husks. His approach to Earth in *Fantastic Four* #48 inaugurated a three-issue adventure frequently cited as the finest achievement of the collaboration between Stan Lee and Jack Kirby. Rarely had comic books attempted story-telling on such a scale.

Galactus was more than just an invader from another planet; he was an extraordinary supernatural force beyond all human notions of good and evil, and Kirby consciously designed him to look like a god. The concept grew as the story progressed. Says Lee: "I wasn't thinking about cosmic grandeur—I was just looking for a stronger villain."

The mystical and metaphysical elements that took over the saga were perfectly suited to the tastes of young readers in the 1960s, and Lee soon discovered that "The Galactus Trilogy" was a favorite on college campuses. Both script and art emphasized the awesome size of the universe as The Human Torch soared through endless galaxies on a

rescue mission and returned home almost insane: "We're like ants . . . just ants . . . ants!!"

Galactus was such an impressive character that even his assistant, the rebellious Silver Surfer, had the stature to become a major Marvel hero. Lesser villains had dreams of glory in which they hoped to rule the world, but to Galactus, the planet was mere fast food.

ists were contributing to plots, but in addition to his editorial duties, Lee was still writing the dialogue and captions for almost every story. Lee had tried other writers from time to time, but Thomas was the one who stayed and made his mark. "Roy was wonderful," says Lee. "As I stopped writing various books, he would start doing them, and I found that he did them extremely well."

Born in 1940, Thomas represented a new generation of comic book creators, one that had grown up with the medium. Like countless contemporaries, he had created his own comics as a child—at the age of seven he invented a hero called "Elephant Giant." In theory he had grown to responsible adulthood, graduating from college and becoming a high school teacher. But Thomas also became the publisher of a fan magazine and an active participant in the increasingly organized fan movement that Marvel had helped inspire. He came from Missouri to New York when he was

Roy Thomas & Flo Steinberg.

offered a job with DC, but Thomas wasn't happy working for his DC editor; in less than two weeks he used a lunch break for a meeting with Stan Lee.

"Stan impressed me very much," says Thomas. "He seemed to have a clear picture of what he wanted, plus a lot of enthusiasm for his work. I was flattered when, ten minutes after we met, he invited me to go to work for him, and I accepted almost immediately. I couldn't have been more awestruck if I'd gone to work for a Hollywood studio. Jack Kirby and Bill Everett and people like that were my idols.

"I was very aware that one has to learn one's craft," says Thomas, who started out on *Millie the Model* but was soon handling important super hero groups like *The X-Men* and *The Avengers*. As a combination fan and scholar, Thomas helped to organize and keep track of the expanding Marvel Universe. "It fit what I wanted to do," says Thomas, "and it seemed to fit what Stan wanted to do. I felt he was aiming for a fairly consistent, coherent universe."

Both Lee and Thomas agree that the new writer's age made him valuable to Marvel. "At twenty-five, I wasn't that far away from the typical Marvel reader," says Thomas, "and I sort of knew what they wanted." He had even performed with a rock and roll band, and to millions of readers the new Marvel was part of the burgeoning youth culture represented by musicians like The Beatles and The Rolling Stones.

A Rift in the Web

"Everybody was walking on eggs around Steve Ditko by the time I arrived," Roy Thomas recalls, "because he and Stan had not been speaking for months." Throughout 1965, Lee and Ditko were able to continue their collaboration on the trendsetting *Amazing Spider-Man* by passing the work back and forth through intermediaries, but in 1966 the artist resigned.

"To work with Steve was the greatest pleasure and privilege a writer could have," says Lee. "For instance, there was one scene that became incredibly famous: Spider-Man was trapped in a tunnel

▼ **Artist Steve Ditko squeezes every ounce of anguish out of Spider-Man's predicament, complete with visions of the uncle he failed and the aunt he has sworn to save. From** *Amazing Spider-Man* **#33 (February 1966). Script: Stan Lee.**

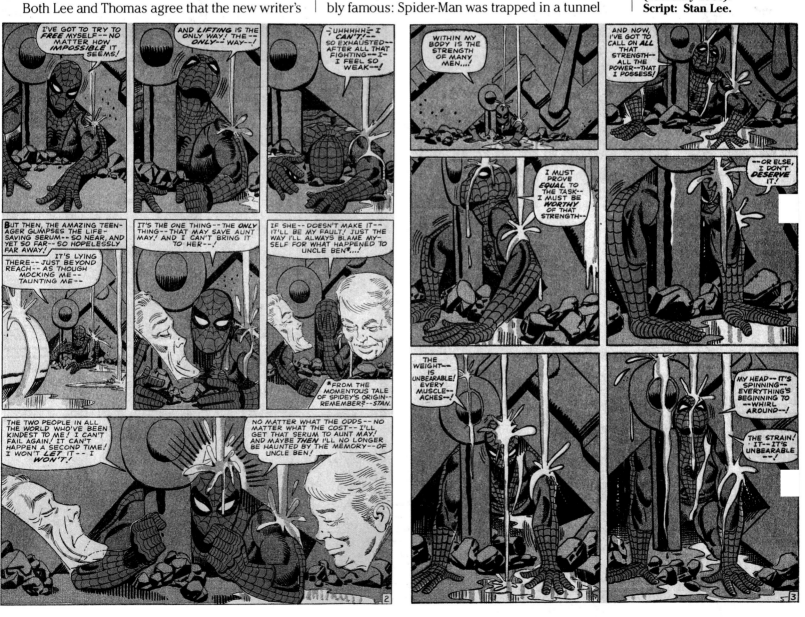

▲ **Self-portrait of artist John Romita surrounded by Spider-Man's friends and foes.**

and had to lift something off himself in order to escape and rescue Aunt May." Most artists would have treated the struggle to escape from under tons of rubble in a few panels, but Ditko drew out the hero's mental and physical anguish for a full eight pages of a two-issue cliff-hanger. "It was something readers have never forgotten," says Lee.

Gradually, however, the two men had begun to disagree. The conflict may have been inherent in The Marvel Method, which allowed artists so much participation in creating the stories. "Steve would sometimes just make up his own plot and bring in all the drawings," Lee recalls. Each man had his own ideas about how to portray the characters most effectively, and when Lee the writer and Ditko the artist had a dispute, Lee the editor was empowered to arbitrate.

The ultimate bone of contention was a recurring villain called The Green Goblin, whose identity had always been hidden. When it became time for the long-awaited unmasking, Lee recalls that Ditko said, "It should be somebody they've never seen before, just some person." Lee, on the other hand, felt that a startling revelation had been promised. "Every reader in America is going to think we're crazy. They'll be angry. It's got to be *somebody*!" Lee said. Ditko left without drawing the story.

Roy Thomas, who saw Ditko quietly resign soon afterwards, feels that he understood both men's positions. Ditko wanted to point up the arbitrariness of life and to show criminals as seedy nonentities; Lee wanted a dramatic climax that would leave readers reeling. The dispute broke up the team that had built Spider-Man into one of the greatest super heroes ever created. "It's hard, partnership," says Thomas.

Hire a Veteran

By the time Steve Ditko left in 1966, a number of talented artists had already joined the Marvel ranks. Three of those who were to stay for long and fruitful associations were no strangers to Marvel, but rather were veterans who had left during the slump caused by the controversies of the 1950s: John Romita, Gene Colan and John Buscema. The seasoned abilities of these three included both superb technique and solid craftsmanship; their contributions were so considerable that Stan Lee groups them with Kirby and Ditko as people who "really transcended ordinary comic book art."

"Some people don't realize how good John Romita is," says Lee, "because his style was never as flashy as

The Green Goblin was an especially dangerous villain. Not only did he menace Spider-Man, but a dispute over his secret identity ended the collaboration between Stan Lee and Steve Ditko.

some others. But he can do anything, and do it superbly." In fact, Romita deliberately cultivated a self-effacing technique, emphasizing clarity and concision rather than razzle-dazzle. "I think comics should be a simple storytelling medium," Romita says. "I want to get past the point where the reader thinks about the artwork to the point where he thinks the characters are really having these experiences."

When Romita returned to Marvel in 1965 he was so demoralized by years of doing love comics at DC that he wanted to confine himself to inking the work of others, but Lee soon convinced him to do penciling for *Daredevil*. Accustomed to working from conventional scripts, Romita got some help in mastering The Marvel Method from Jack Kirby. "It was never easy for me," says Romita. "It was like digging into my insides and pulling it out. But there was a certain satisfaction to it."

In 1966, Romita was given Spider-Man, a plum assignment that was also fraught with pitfalls. A few fans never forgave Romita for replacing Ditko, but sales of *The Amazing Spider-Man* continued to increase until they surpassed *The Fantastic Four* and it became Marvel's most popular title. "I loved the character," Romita says, "the idea of a guy who gets himself tied up in knots because he's trying to consider too many things. When you threw Spider-Man with all his hang-ups into certain situations, the story almost wrote itself."

When ideas didn't come quickly, Romita would discuss the stories with his own kids. "When my son John was eleven, he came up with a character and he got credit for it in the comic book. And now he's in the business and has become one of our top artists. He used to wake up in the morning and find me at the drawing board, still working without having had any sleep. He'd rub my neck

▼ **Steve Ditko portrayed himself as a shadowy figure in an ink bottle, flanked by caricatures of Spider-Man and Dr. Strange.**

◄Peter Parker threatens to renounce his super hero career, and John Romita produces a memorable cover for *Amazing Spider-Man* #50 (July 1967).

First drawn by John Romita, this obese crime lord became a major Marvel villain.

Spider-Man's troublesome boss, newspaper editor J. Jonah Jameson. Cover: John Romita.

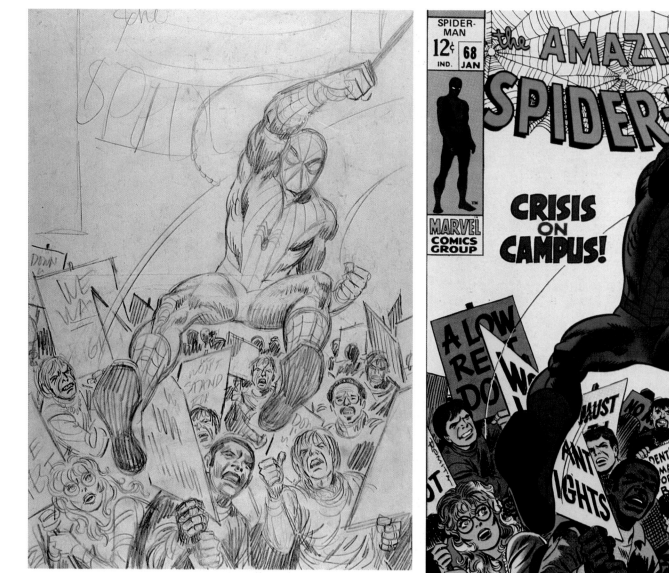

▲ **John Romita's rough sketch and the finished product; another classic cover for** *Amazing Spider-Man* **(January 1969).**

Self-portrait of Gene Colan at his drawing board.

and say, 'How you feeling, Dad?' He had all this sympathy for me, and he saw the worst, and it never deterred him."

Like most freelancers, Romita worked long, hard hours to meet unforgiving deadlines, and his work on the printed page and behind the scenes continues to make him a key figure in the history of Marvel.

The Dean of Light and Dark

Gene Colan had sat out the 1950s slump in comics by working in advertising. "I settled into a job where I punched a time clock, and I really didn't like it," he says. "When the comics industry started to gradually come back, I would call Stan from time to time to ask if there was anything, and finally he said, 'Things are beginning to pick up, come on.' It didn't pay that well when I first came back. All I cared about was to be doing my craft."

Stan Lee, who livened up each story's credits by giving everyone nicknames, called him Gene "The

Dean" Colan. Developing a bold and unusual style, Colan emphasized areas of light and darkness rather than simple outlines. "I think in terms of shadows and weight," he says. "And I'm highly influenced by film. You have to be, because you're dealing with continuity, with drawings that tell stories. You can see composition on the screen." Colan never deliberately planned to develop a unique technique, but believes that "when you like your work, you'll do something with it that nobody else will do."

Upon his return in 1965, Colan took to The Marvel Method at once. "It was great for me," he says. "I could put in almost anything I wanted." He worked with writer Roy Thomas on Sub-Mariner and Dr. Strange, then joined forces with Lee for the definitive version of *Daredevil*, which Colan continued for years. "I had a lot of fun," he says, "Stan gave the artist a lot of latitude." Colan recalls that he once devoted "five or six pages" to a car chase that annoyed Lee because of its length—but only until he saw the fan mail the sequence inspired.

◄ Daredevil beats traffic in Gene Colan's carefree page showing life in New York. From *Daredevil #26* (March 1967). Script: Stan Lee.

▲ The Vision, a new character with an old name, became an important addition to The Avengers. Cover: John Buscema.

Marvel a technique that employed dramatic angles and a remarkable attention to anatomical accuracy. "He draws like a classical artist," says Stan Lee, "like Michelangelo. Buscema is one of the all-time greats." He also possesses the ability to tell a story so vividly in pictures that words sometimes seem almost superfluous. "Stan wanted that kind of thing," Buscema says.

Gene Colan's pencil work demonstrates his unusual use of light and shadow.

In 1967, about a year after his return, Buscema teamed up with writer Roy Thomas to work on *The Avengers*, the super group with the shifting membership. "We turned out some nice stuff," admits Buscema. His elegant groupings of figures brought dignity and a sense of purpose to the various characters, while Thomas juggled relationships, intensified emotions and even quoted poetry to give life to the stories.

Thomas liked the idea of an all-star group and wanted popular characters like Thor and Iron Man to rejoin The Avengers on a permanent basis. "Stan always let me bring them back for an issue or two and then I'd have to take them out again," Thomas says. "Eventually, I just put them in without asking and it worked out very well." In the meantime, Thomas created an important new Avenger called The Vision.

Always conscious of the company's history, Thomas had intended to revive the supernatural character called The Vision that Simon and Kirby had originated in the 1940s, but "Stan insisted on an android," says Thomas. The new Vision, tormented by his status as an artificial being, became a memorable addition to The Marvel Universe, especially when he discovered human feelings in a story Thomas called "Even an Android Can Cry."

Self-portrait of John Buscema, who returned to Marvel in 1966.

The Reluctant Draftsman

"I didn't want to hear about comics," says John Buscema. "I had had a bad experience in the '50s." On the other hand, his advertising job forced him to spend roughly six hours a day commuting to and from Manhattan. "It was brutal," he says. "I never saw my wife." Selling the family home and moving loomed as a real alternative when Buscema received a call from Marvel. "When I realized there was plenty of work, I dropped the advertising and went back into comics because I was able to work at home."

Buscema had honed his skills, and he brought to

The Expanding Universe

The peak of activity during The Marvel Age occurred in 1968. Sales were reported at

◄ Gene Colan's technique
creates a mood of menace
as Captain America's
features dissolve into those
of The Red Skull.
Inks: Joe Sinnott.
Script: Stan Lee. From
Captain America #119
(November 1969).

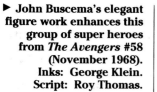

▶ John Buscema's elegant figure work enhances this group of super heroes from *The Avengers* #58 (November 1968). Inks: George Klein. Script: Roy Thomas.

◄ On this extraordinary page, writer Roy Thomas quotes poet Percy Bysshe Shelley while penciler John Buscema finds irony in a city dump. Inks: George Klein. From *The Avengers* #57 (October 1968).

◄ Fawcett Captain Marvel by C. C. Beck.

◄ Second Marvel Captain Marvel by Jim Starlin.

► Third Marvel Captain Marvel by John Romita, Jr.

◄ First Marvel Captain Marvel by Gene Colan.

THE CASE OF CAPTAIN MARVEL

In 1940, a few months after the first issue of *Marvel Comics* appeared, a character called Captain Marvel was introduced by rival Fawcett Publications. This super hero was totally unrelated to the Timely-Atlas-Marvel line of comic books, although Jack Kirby drew one of his first adventures. Nevertheless, Fawcett's *Captain Marvel Adventures* became the most popular super hero series then being published; it sold a million and a half copies twice a month.

Summoned by the magic word "Shazam," Captain Marvel was a crimson-clad character whose sense of humor pleased almost everyone except the publisher of *Superman,* DC Comics. DC accused Fawcett of having committed copyright infringement by making Captain Marvel too similar to Superman. In 1953, Fawcett and DC finally settled out of court, and Captain Marvel vanished.

In 1966, M.F. Enterprises, a minor comics publisher, came up with a dreadful new character named Captain Marvel

whose powers enabled him to dismember and reassemble himself. He lasted only four issues, but Stan Lee realized that the name was up for grabs. "I thought it would be terrible," he says, "if somebody else had the name when we were called Marvel Comics. After extended legal and business negotiations, we got ourselves the rights to the name, but DC ended up with the rights to the old character. I thought we'd better do a book, so I wrote one about an alien from another planet."

The Marvel version of Captain Marvel, drawn by Gene Colan, was a member of the Kree race named Mar-Vell. After several years of different writers, artists and costumes, Marvel's Captain Marvel was finally killed off. Meanwhile, DC published the original Fawcett hero under the title *Shazam.*

Just to confuse matters completely, yet another Captain Marvel was introduced by Marvel in 1982 and later joined The Avengers. This one is a black woman.

Marvel began making fun of itself. Cover above: *Not Brand Echh* #1 (August 1967) by Jack Kirby. **Cover below by Marie Severin (June 1968).**

50,000,000 copies annually, and the company now had the clout to rearrange its distribution deal with DC and publish as many books as the market would bear. As a result, the characters who had been allotted only half a comic book were launched in their own titles: *The Incredible Hulk*, *The Invincible Iron Man*, *Dr. Strange*, *The Sub-Mariner*, *Captain America* and *Nick Fury, Agent of S.H.I.E.L.D.*

In fact, Marvel was so confident that a year earlier, in 1967, it had launched *Not Brand Echh*, a monthly comic book devoted to spoofs of the company's own heroes. These parodies were frequently written and drawn by the original creators of the characters, but one of the mainstays of the series was Marie Severin, a gifted caricaturist who had worked for years on Marvel's production staff. One of the first women to gain prominence as a comic book artist, she also depicted the adventures of super heroes like The Hulk and Dr. Strange.

Stan Lee tried a couple of experiments while things were hot: for example, he put a high twenty-five-cent cover price on the unusually long first issue of *The Silver Surfer* (August 1968). Beautifully drawn by John Buscema, this comic book represented an attempt to upgrade the medium with a serious character of whom Lee had grown very fond. "It's the most wonderful series I know," says Lee. A month earlier, Lee had put Marvel's most popular hero into a magazine-size, black-and-white format: *The Spectacular Spider-Man*. Unfortunately, its failure after only two issues was an omen of things to come.

The Swing of the Pendulum

In the fall of 1968, with Marvel apparently at its peak, Martin Goodman sold the companies he had started in 1932. The buyer was Perfect Film and Chemical Corporation, which soon changed its name to Cadence Industries. Within the Cadence structure, all of Goodman's publishing enterprises were grouped together under one company name, Magazine Management, and Goodman continued as president and publisher. Superficially, nothing had changed.

By 1969 it was evident that Goodman had picked his time wisely, however, for the entire comic book industry was experiencing a slump. This was not an out-and-out disaster, but sales were down everywhere. One obvious reason was an increase in the price of an average issue from twelve to fifteen cents. While those three pennies may sound like nothing today, in 1969 they represented enough of a jump to discourage many young customers. The slump also represented a natural swing of the pendulum. Business had been on the rise at Marvel for almost a decade, and DC had been on a recent roll thanks in part to the fad inspired by the campy television series *Batman* (1966–1968). Now the boom was over, and some

insiders blamed the comic book companies for expanding too fast and spreading themselves too thin.

For the first time in years, Marvel was dropping titles instead of adding them. *Not Brand Echh* and *Dr. Strange* were among the first cancellations; perhaps the biggest disappointment for Stan Lee was having to drop *The Silver Surfer*, the philosophical super hero. "The publisher said if we gave him more action and treated him more like a normal super hero, the sales would pick up," says Lee. "I didn't want to change him, so I said let's just drop the book."

▲ Flashy graphics by artist Jim Steranko enliven the cover of *Nick Fury, Agent of S.H.I.E.L.D.* #1 (June 1968).

▶ Marvel's expansion in 1968 promoted several heroes into their own comic books. *Captain America* #100 (April 1968) by Jack Kirby and Syd Shores. *Iron Man* #1 (May 1968) by Gene Colan and Bill Everett.

▶ *The Incredible Hulk* #102 (April 1968) by Marie Severin. *The Silver Surfer* #1 (August 1968) by John Buscema. The Surfer's book was twice the average length and twice the price.

Hanging Tough

Anticipating better days ahead, Marvel guaranteed itself better access to the marketplace by ending the distribution arrangement with DC that had been in force for more than a decade. A new deal with a large general magazine distributor, the Curtis Circulation Company, allowed for new strategies and a greater opportunity for independence. Marvel was determined to bounce back.

One title, *The X-Men*, hung on by its fingernails. Working with writer Roy Thomas, a young artist named Neal Adams infused the group with new life. "We had some good times," recalls Thomas, who usually maintained strong control over his plots but gave a lot of leeway to this particular artist. "Neal Adams wanted to make his mark doing comics," Thomas says, and Adams succeeded using a startling technique that combined vigorous figures and unusual arrangements of panels that took their shape from the action instead of merely confining it. Even this superior series of stories did not exactly save *The X-Men*, but instead of being canceled, the title was continued after March 1970 with reprints of old issues. Someone at Marvel must have looked into a crystal ball and seen that *The X-Men* was destined to one day become the most popular comic book series published in the United States.

The sinister but enticing Queen of the Mutants holds the awestruck heroes at bay on this cover by Jim Steranko for *X-Men* #50 (November 1968).

MARVEL GETS ANIMATED

In 1966 television was ready for Marvel: a half-hour animated cartoon series called "The Marvel Super Heroes" was syndicated to stations around the country. The stars were The Hulk, Iron Man, The Sub-Mariner, Thor and Captain America. Produced by the Grant-Ray-Lawrence Company, the shows featured extremely limited animation, but, Stan Lee says, "they used real Marvel stories and in some crazy way their shows captured the spirit of Marvel. The theme songs were wonderful—twenty-five years later people still remember them."

By 1967, Marvel cartoons were ready for Saturday morning on the national ABC network. Half-hour programs featuring The Fantastic Four and Spider-Man appeared back-to-back until 1970, and then went into syndication. Grant-Ray-Lawrence did Spider-Man, while The Fantastic Four were animated by Hanna-Barbera Productions.

These were only the first of several Marvel television programs that eventually included not only more cartoons, but a live-action series and dramatic features as well.

The Marvel Theme Song

Meet the bulky, kinda sulky, kinda Hulky super hero, Altruistic and electrically transistored super hero, An exotically neurotic and aquatic super hero, The Marvel Super Heroes have arrived.

Super powered from their foreheads to their toes, Watch them change their very shape before your nose.

See our cane-striking super heroes change to Viking super heroes, Our zingin', real swingin', shield flingin' super heroes. They're the latest, they're the greatest, ultimatest super heroes, The Marvel Super Heroes have arrived.

► Havok, the brother of
Cyclops, joins The X-Men.
The innovative cover
design was the work of
Neal Adams. *X-Men* #58
(July 1969).

◄ Neal Adams shattered comic book layout conventions with pages like this one from *X-Men* #57 (June 1969).

ESCAPE ARTIST: JIM STERANKO

Perhaps the most innovative new talent to emerge at Marvel during the late 1960s was Jim Steranko, whose bold innovations in graphics, layout and design startled the readers of *Captain America, The X-Men* and *Nick Fury, Agent of S.H.I.E.L.D.* Working in every genre from romance to the supernatural, Steranko transformed the look of the comic book page. He played tricks with space and time using unusual arrangements of panels, and utilized the techniques of print advertisements and posters in his quest for the ultimate impact. He even supervised the coloring of his pages and covers, which sometimes created optical illusions. "You couldn't take your eyes away from his work," says Stan Lee. "His style was explosive. He drew the way they're trying to draw today."

A writer as well as an artist, Steranko had worked as everything from a musician to a magician. He executed an escape act as surprising as anything he had performed on the stage when he dropped out of comics as the 1960s came to a close. Reportedly too much of a perfectionist to be tied down by deadlines, Steranko had other ambitions and interests. He wrote a two-volume history of Golden Age comic books, and later published his own film magazine. One of the first of a new breed of artists who viewed comics more as a means of self-expression than as a business, Steranko created a sensation and then decided to disappear.

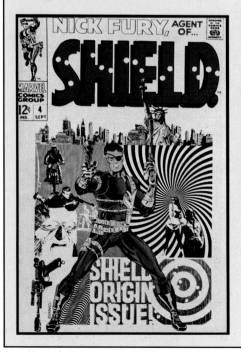

◀ For this cover (September 1968), Steranko dropped the color from the background, employed disorienting op art effects, and used high-contrast photographs in a collage to convey the impression of a nation threatened by violence. The title is even full of bullet holes.

▲ For the first issue of the short-lived *Tower of Shadows* (September 1969), Jim Steranko wrote, penciled, inked and colored a horror story called "At the Stroke of Midnight." His bold approach to color, and the technique of breaking the narrative into tiny panels, created a startling impression. The central row of panels, which divide a large scene into smaller sections, achieve an effect similar to a motion picture camera panning across an elaborate set.

Farewell to The King

An era ended in 1970 when Jack Kirby left Marvel to work for rival DC Comics. "I remember going to the office and seeing a cigar stuck to the wall, and a little note under it saying, 'I quit,'" recalls artist Don Heck. "Jack was living out in California by then, so somebody else must have done it, but that's how I knew he'd left."

Over the years since 1970, Jack Kirby has occasionally displayed some acrimony toward Stan Lee, usually in the pages of fan magazines. Clearly, Kirby feels that he has not received all the credit due him for his contribution to Marvel. Interviewed for this book, Kirby chose to discuss his departure from Marvel only in general, polite terms, as part of a pattern that marks the lives of many freelancers. "Either I got more money from DC," he says, "or I got into an argument with the editor or some official at Marvel. That kind of thing went on."

"I used to wonder why he left," says Stan Lee. "When he went to DC, he insisted that he be the writer and the editor and the artist. And I said to myself that he was just sick of the credits always saying, 'By Stan Lee and Jack Kirby,' with me as the editor. I think he wanted to prove how good he was without me, but I have no way of knowing if that's right."

In the course of attracting the attention that helped Marvel to thrive, Stan Lee inevitably received a good deal of publicity himself. In some quarters the perception arose that Lee had built up

the company's roster of heroes almost single-handedly. More recently, admirers of Jack Kirby have concluded that Kirby was the company's true creative force; these Kirby aficionados cite as proof of their argument The Marvel Method, which placed such major responsibility on the artist's shoulders. The fact seems to be that Lee and Kirby worked as a team. Each of them has done splendid work without the other, yet the bulk of the achievements for which each will be remembered occurred during their collaboration.

The roll call of the comic book characters they created together during The Marvel Age is nothing short of incredible, especially since all continue to be viable commercial properties after a quarter of a century or more: The Fantastic Four, The Hulk, Thor, Iron Man, Sgt. Fury and His Howling Commandos, The Avengers, The X-Men, The Silver Surfer and Nick Fury, Agent of S.H.I.E.L.D. Lee and Kirby also successfully revived Captain America, The Human Torch and The Sub-Mariner. Lee, of course, also worked separately on heroes like Spider-Man, Dr. Strange and Daredevil. This record of accomplishment by a pair of collaborators has no parallel in the history of comic books. It is without question a remarkable body of creative work.

When he handed out nicknames to the Marvel artists, Stan Lee dubbed Jack Kirby "King." Endlessly inventive, and capable of imbuing every line he draws with a feeling of latent power, Kirby is one of a small handful of comic book artists universally regarded as touched with greatness. In the field of the super hero, Kirby is generally considered to have no peer.

Stan Lee's emotional intensity, tempered with a sense of irony, has made him one of the most forceful and original writers in the medium. As an editor, his story sense, organizational skill and flair for promotion are unsurpassed. Like producer Walt Disney, he seems to possess a special gift for bringing out the best in the talented people working around him. He, more than anyone, is responsible for the continuity of the Marvel image.

Their colleague John Buscema puts it as well as anyone can: "I think they're the greatest team in comics ever. And they worked so well together, Stan and Jack. It was unbelievable."

▲ Jack Kirby's cover (July 1970) celebrates one hundred issues in collaboration with Stan Lee on the flagship title of Marvel's renaissance, but after two more issues, Kirby left Marvel.

◄ Jim Steranko slyly circumvents The Comics Code in a virtually wordless page that is nonetheless rife with innuendo. From *Nick Fury, Agent of S.H.I.E.L.D.* #2 (July 1968).

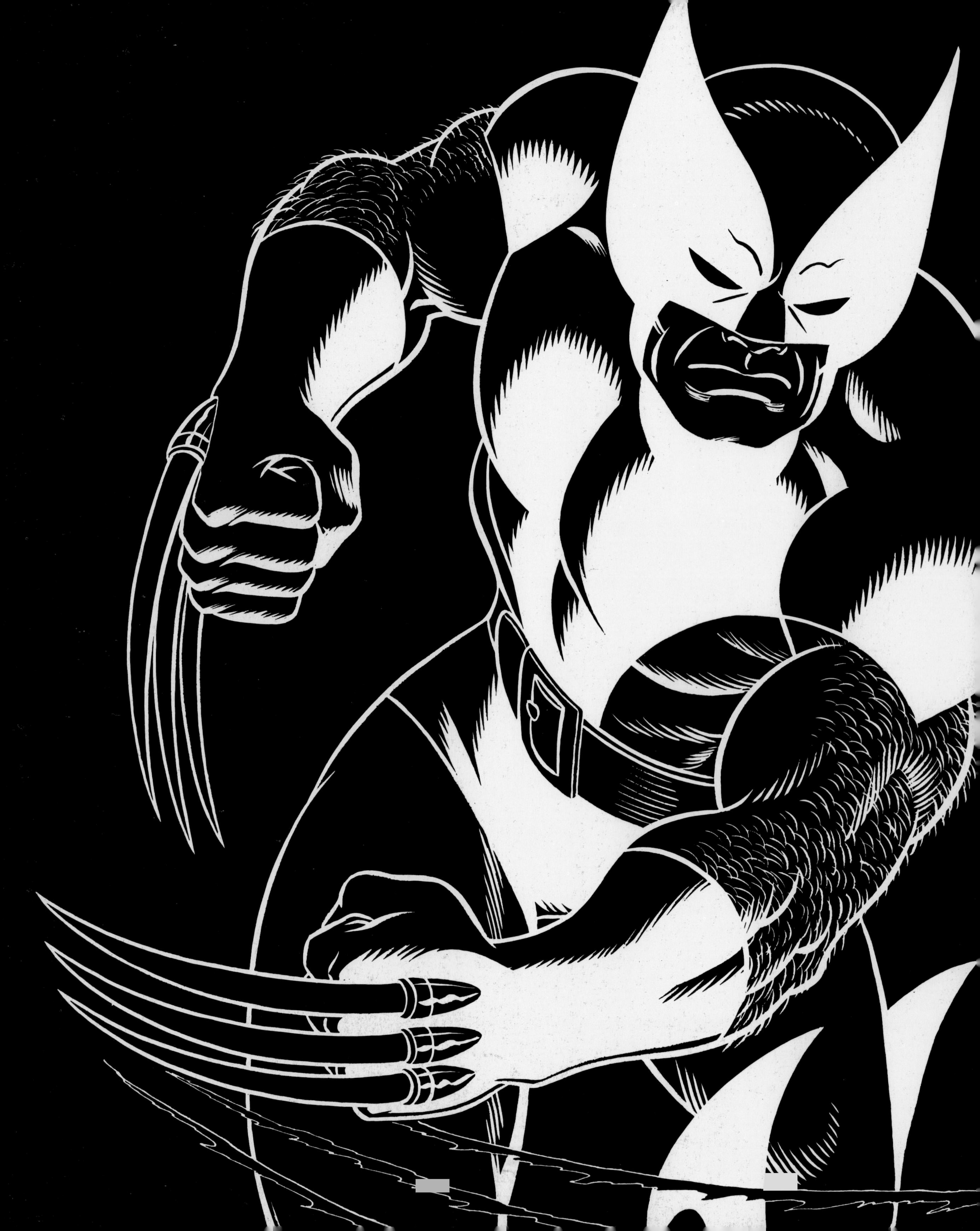

CHAPTER FIVE

Research and Development (1970 – 1978)

Now the industry leader, Marvel unleashes a young generation of creators, and the result is a period of wild artistic exploration. Innovative characters range from a savage barbarian to an international brotherhood of mutants, but the expansion creates some growing pains.

The era following The Marvel Age was marked by dramatic and incessant change. New concepts, new characters and new comic book series were introduced with wild abandon. A new generation of creative talent began to flex its muscles, bringing youthful enthusiasm to a series of experiments that sometimes ended in failure, but often led to a surprising level of success.

This energetic if sometimes undisciplined expansion, which Stan Lee dubbed "Phase Two" of the new Marvel, produced its share of growing pains. After Lee's reign of more than a quarter century as editor-in-chief came to an end in 1972, the head editorial post was occupied by five men in less than five years. Meanwhile, company presi-

dents came and went frequently until finally, in 1975, one arrived with the acumen to bring about long-term financial stability in a changing market. If chaos occasionally seemed to reign, however, the eventual result of this upheaval was Marvel's transformation into the unquestioned leader of the comic book industry.

An important influence on Marvel's new direction was provided by writer Roy Thomas, whose work had brought him some influence within the company, and who continued to embody the aspirations of younger writers and artists. Partly because he retained a fan's enthusiastic interest in the characters and the workings of the company, Thomas was functioning, he explains, as an unofficial "assistant editor, although I was hired officially as staff writer." He helped to coordinate crossovers, recruit new talent and initiate innovative projects.

A Prehistoric Premiere

Marvel's first major success of the decade, *Conan the Barbarian*, made its debut in October 1970. Conan was an adaptation rather than a Marvel creation, but the comic book version helped to make the barbarian famous. "It wasn't totally my idea," says Roy Thomas, "but I was the one who shepherded it, which is why I ended up writing it."

In fact, letters from fans suggesting the series had first set Thomas on the trail of Conan, a hero who had been created in 1932 by writer Robert E. Howard for the old pulp magazine *Weird Tales*. A soldier of fortune wandering through imaginary prehistoric realms populated by wizards and demons, Conan was the most famous character in the literary genre known as sword and sorcery. Howard's stories had been enjoying some success in paperback reprints, and Thomas quickly realized that they were suitable for comic book treatment. "I thought it was a good direction to go in," he says, "and to some extent it was a move away from typical comic book material. I wanted to widen the horizon."

Conan the Barbarian was something of a gamble for Marvel. The series contained the usual elements of action and fantasy, to be sure, but it was set in a past that had no relation to The Marvel Universe, and it featured a hero who possessed no magical powers, little humor and comparatively few moral principles. Furthermore, Marvel generally shied away from adaptations of "outside" material because a fee was required for permissions. "I managed to sell Martin Goodman on the idea of actually paying a little money for it," says Thomas, "which was my major accomplishment." The gamble paid off, and *Conan the Barbarian* is still going strong after more than twenty years. As a result, Marvel was encouraged to publish more and more comic books with stories based on characters from other media.

▼ A new kind of hero for Marvel, where young blood stirred with the decade's dawn: *Conan the Barbarian* #1 (October 1970). Cover: Barry Windsor-Smith.

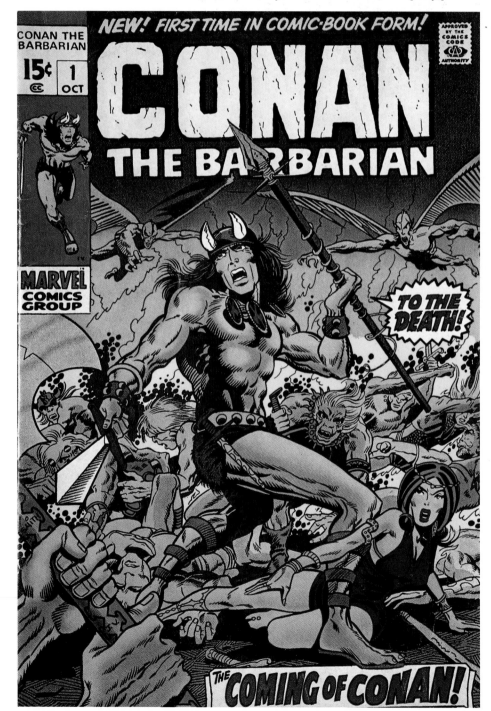

◄ With each new issue of *Conan the Barbarian,* Barry Windsor-Smith's style became more elaborate, ornate and exotic.

◄ In the wake of Conan's success came other barbarians based on the fiction of Robert E. Howard. Marie Severin did the honors for *Kull the Conqueror* #1 (June 1971). Six years later, Frank Thorne did the cover for *Red Sonja* #1 (January 1977).

Problems for Captain Marvel inaugurated the nine-month epic Kree-Skrull War. Cover: Sal Buscema.

For the saga's climax Roy Thomas revived Golden Age heroes. Pencils: Gil Kane. Inks: Bill Everett.

The Style for Sorcery

The artist chosen to depict Conan's adventures proved to be an inspired selection. Born in London, Barry Windsor-Smith was only twenty-one when he began to work on the first issue of Conan. His initial efforts were slightly sketchy, but his technique progressed by leaps and bounds. Within a few months he had achieved a style never seen in comics before. "He just burst out in a different way than I would have imagined," says Thomas, "because I had no idea he was going to work into that art nouveau kind of style." "Art nouveau," "art deco" and "Pre-Raphaelite" are terms frequently used to describe the fine-art influence in Windsor-Smith's ornate, intricately detailed work. His Conan was less a lusty brawler than a lean, catlike figure moving through vistas of dreamlike decadence.

Windsor-Smith's drawing was complemented by the scripts Thomas provided, which were often based on his own ideas rather than material derived from Howard. One especially felicitous extrapolation was Red Sonja, a minor Howard character transformed by Thomas into a companion for Conan. The beautiful swordswoman was popular enough to earn her own comic book and even a 1985 motion picture. In fact, the success of Conan led to a rash of sword and sorcery comic book series from various publishers, but only the original proved to have staying power.

War in Space

More typical of Thomas, and of Marvel, was an elaborate story sequence known as "The Kree-Skrull War," which ran for nearly a year in *The Avengers* (June 1971 to March 1972). The Avengers were already an all-star group of heroes gathered from a number of different Marvel comic books, but this plot involved concepts and characters from several more Marvel stories, past and present. Captain Marvel, originally an officer of the interstellar Kree space fleet, was called into battle with an alien race of old *Fantastic Four* villains, the Skrull, and before the dust settled The Avengers were confronting a number of almost forgotten Golden Age characters, including The Angel and The Fin. This wild tale, almost impossible to summarize, attempted to tie together more than thirty years of the company's stories, while at the same time it demonstrated that plot lines could be extended almost indefinitely. More than any previous work, "The Kree-Skrull War" solidified the idea that every comic book Marvel had ever published was part of an endless, ongoing saga. This was The Marvel Universe with a vengeance. The

◄ Ant-Man's finest hour, as he dismisses his insect companions and ventures alone into unknown territory: the interior of the stricken body of The Vision, a man-made android. Neal Adams' pencils (top) appear below in the printed version, inked by Tom Palmer. From *The Avengers* #93 (November 1971).

first issue of this epic was drawn by Sal Buscema, and the last by his brother, John Buscema, but most of the artwork was provided by the innovative Neal Adams, who also created some of the more bizarre twists in the tale. For one especially memorable sequence, Adams conceived the idea of shrinking Ant-Man down to microscopic size so that he could enter and repair the broken body of the android called The Vision. In this weird environment of wires, tubes, chemicals and crystals, the ordinarily lackluster Ant-Man enjoyed his finest hour.

Spidey Fights Drugs

Stan Lee, still editor-in-chief, continued to write some of Marvel's most popular comic books. He worked with artist John Buscema on *The Fantastic Four* and *The Mighty Thor*, but nothing Lee did in this period was as important as the three-part story he wrote for *The Amazing Spider-Man* #96–98 (May–July 1971). This was a narrative of considerable social significance, and one that changed the face of comic books forever.

"I got a letter from the Department of Health, Education and Welfare," recalls Lee, "which said, in essence, that they recognized the great influence that Marvel Comics and Spider-Man have on young people. And they thought it would really be very beneficial if we created a story warning kids about the dangerous effects of drug addiction. We were happy to help out. I wove the theme into the plot without preaching, because if kids think you're lecturing them, they won't listen. You have to entertain them while you're teaching."

Drawn by veterans John Romita and Gil Kane,

the three issues were largely devoted to Spider-Man's battle against his old foe, The Green Goblin. Along the way our hero discovers that his college roommate has been taking pills that eventually cause his collapse and hospitalization. Spidey has to fend off the villain while rescuing his friend, who turns out to be The Green Goblin's own son.

"It was a good story," says Lee, "and everybody involved was very happy with it. As usual, we sent the book to the Comics Code office, and, amazingly and ironically, they said they had to reject it." The Comics Code, all-powerful in the industry for sixteen years, prohibited absolutely any mention of drugs for any purpose.

"I told them this was a story showing the evils of drug addiction," says Lee, "and they said, 'Sorry, you can't do it.' I said that I didn't do it on a whim, but at the request of the United States Government, and they said, 'Sorry, you can't do it.' Well, at that point I figured the Code office was wrong."

Cracking the Code

Marvel decided to publish the three antidrug issues of *The Amazing Spider-Man* without the Comics Code's seal of approval. It was a risky move, but Lee decided that "we would do more harm to the country by not running the story than by running it. And I must say that we got a favorable reaction from the press all over the country, and from parents and educators too. Everybody loved what we had done. And because of that, the Code was changed."

As a result of Marvel's successful stand, the Comics Code had begun to look just a little foolish. Some of its more ridiculous restrictions

▼ **Stan Lee's antidrug story in three 1971 issues of** *The Amazing Spider-Man* **challenged the strictures of the Comics Code and appeared without its seal. Covers by Gil Kane (left and right) and John Romita (center).**

◄ Peter Parker's college roommate falls victim to drugs in a story that revolutionized the comic book industry. From *The Amazing Spider-Man* #97 (June 1971).
Script: Stan Lee.
Pencils: Gil Kane.
Inks: Frank Giacoia.

Marvel's first black-and-white comics magazine (May 1971), with a painted color cover by John Buscema.

were abandoned because of Lee's decision, ultimately affording the comics industry some measure of the freedom available to other media.

While Spider-Man's antidrug series was running, Stan Lee launched a new publication that was intended to run without any Comics Code approval, revised restrictions notwithstanding. This was *Savage Tales* (May 1971), an oversize comics magazine printed in black-and-white rather than color. "We were trying to see if maybe we could get an older audience," explains Lee, who put a price tag of fifty cents on the first issue at a time when a color comic book cost fifteen cents. "It was really an experiment to start another little line of books that wouldn't have a high overhead." The lack of color made the magazine look more serious and adult than an ordinary comic book, it kept printing costs down, and it also enabled Lee to provide more work for his growing stable of artists.

The highlight of *Savage Tales* #1 was a finely crafted Conan adventure by Roy Thomas and Barry Windsor-Smith. The first issue also introduced a horror character called Man-Thing, who coincidentally appeared just a few weeks before a similar DC Comics monster called Swamp Thing. Marvel's creature from the bogs had a script by Gerry Conway, while DC's was the creation of writer Len Wein; each of these two writers later created some of Marvel's most sensationally successful heroes.

Savage Tales got off to a rocky start; in fact, two years elapsed before a second issue was published. Yet Lee persevered, and in the next few years Marvel established a number of black-and-white magazines, gaining a substantial share of the market originally created by maverick publisher James Warren with his horror comic *Creepy*.

Marvel Pulls Ahead

As 1971 drew to a close, publisher Martin Goodman initiated an ingenious sales strategy, a complicated series of changes in the size and price of the standard color comic book, that gave Marvel a commanding lead in overall circulation. Marvel had been growing steadily for a decade, but Goodman's new maneuvers finally put it over the top.

The covers of the October 1971 comic books proclaimed that the price was "still fifteen cents"—for thirty-six pages (including covers), but inflation had made a price increase inevitable. When the increase came, however, it was more than a matter of the traditional two or three pennies. In November 1971 the standard comic book price jumped to twenty-five cents, but the number of pages was raised to fifty-two. Rival DC Comics made the same change simultaneously—the two industry leaders could rarely keep secrets from each other, especially since many free-lance writers and artists worked for both companies.

▶ Thumbnail sketches by John Romita for a story that appeared in *Savage Tales* #1. In these compact drawings, the artist laid out the design for eight comic book pages on a single sheet of paper.

After only one month of the new prices, in December 1971 Marvel dropped back to thirty-six pages at the price of twenty cents. Marvel books were now considerably less expensive for young readers who had to count their nickels and dimes. Moreover, since Goodman had in effect created the appearance of a bargain while raising the price by one third, he had increased profits sufficiently to offer a larger percentage of the retail price to his wholesale distributors. As a result of this advantageous arrangement, circulation increased, and the twenty-cent Marvel comic books were more widely distributed than ever before.

Frank Brunner's January 1974 cover.

Writers and artists were frustrated at having to switch from one length to another and then back again, but when the smoke cleared, Marvel had the biggest sales in the business. "It really worked," says Roy Thomas. "DC hung on to those large books for about another year, and they took a bath."

Horrible Heroes

Seizing the advantage the new price policy had provided, Marvel embarked on a period of rapid expansion. As a result of salutary changes in the Comics Code, the use of traditional horror characters, like vampires and werewolves, was now possible. The horror genre was popular in films and on television, and Marvel had been daintily trying it, under the old Code restrictions, in anthology titles like *Chamber of Darkness* and *Tower of Shadows*. Despite some superior work, however, nothing had really clicked. A new approach was needed.

Ultimately, Marvel hit upon the idea of combining horror with heroics, making a monster (often sympathetic) the protagonist of his own comic book series. Man-Thing had already been introduced, and after a few more anthology appearances he was rewarded with his own book, *Man-Thing* #1 (January 1974). *Ghost Rider* (September 1973) and *Werewolf by Night* (September 1972) evolved via a similar route. The already familiar title characters in *Tomb of Dracula* (April 1972) and *The Monster of Frankenstein* (January 1973) rose from the grave and won their own books without any previous testing in anthologies.

The horror heroes achieved varying degrees of popularity. Ghost Rider, a supernatural motorcyclist whose head periodically changed into a flaming skull, proved a solid success. He lasted ten years, and Dracula did almost as well, but their compatriots soon fell by the wayside. Marvel's new policy of expansion involved blanket coverage of a genre, and permitted the marketplace to decide which characters would stand the test of time. This scattershot approach, combined with a reliance on many characters and concepts from the past, created the paradoxical impression that Marvel was moving forward by looking backward.

Expansion also meant a new division of labor. Writer Roy Thomas, working in the established Marvel Method under Stan Lee's supervision, created story lines for the horror heroes and then turned them over to various artists. Thomas received no credit, however, because the actual scripts were written by someone else. The dialogue for the debuts of most of the new Marvel monsters was provided by young Gerry Conway, who had been only seventeen when Thomas originally recruited him in 1970. "At that time," says Conway, "Roy came up with the ideas and the initial plots, then let other people execute the stories." The experience Thomas gained in creating concepts for new books and finding new writers would soon be put to the test.

The Changing of the Guard

In September 1972, Stan Lee dropped a bombshell: his column, "Stan's Soapbox," published in all Marvel comic books, announced that Lee had assumed a new corporate position and that Roy Thomas had become the company's new editor-in-chief. "Roy was great," says Lee today. "He saved my life when I stopped editing, because I had to find somebody who could follow my style fairly well. Roy fit the bill beautifully."

"The main thing, really," says Thomas, "was that Stan became publisher—and I was the next person in line to become editor." As publisher, with responsibility for supervising Marvel's continued expansion, Stan Lee was obliged to relinquish his role as Marvel's most important writer. He publicly acknowledged that a new generation of writers

Werewolf by Night makes his debut in *Marvel Spotlight* #2 (February 1972). Cover: Neal Adams.

Bram Stoker's classic character emerges from *The Tomb of Dracula* #1 (April 1972). Cover: Neal Adams.

Mary Shelley's 1818 creation in *The Monster of Frankenstein* #1 (January 1973). Cover: Mike Ploog.

"Give me a good horror story, and I'll do that to a fare-thee-well," says artist Gene Colan, who got his chance when writer Marv Wolfman adapted the character introduced in Bram Stoker's 1897 novel. This bad guy enjoyed a good long run.

THE VILLAIN TO BEAT: DRACULA

With an unbroken run of seventy issues over the course of more than seven years, Marvel's *The Tomb of Dracula* was the most successful comic book series to feature a villain as its title character. Gene Colan, who did the penciling for every issue from the first in 1972 to the last in 1979, modestly attributes the long run to the inherent popularity of novelist Bram Stoker's creepy creation. He might well have added that he drew the character and his dark domain with considerable flair.

"I heard they were going to do Dracula and I wanted to draw it very much," says Colan, who drew samples on his own time to convince Stan Lee he was the man for the job. "I wanted an opportunity to draw atmosphere—the darkness, the bleakness, the mist." Colan's shadowy style, deftly inked by Tom Pal-

mer, was perfectly suited to the subject.

Colan modeled his version of the vampire on actor Jack Palance, who, by an almost eerie coincidence, was to play the role on television in 1973, a year after the comic book series began.

"Gene Colan's stuff was brilliant," says Marv Wolfman, who started writing the series with the seventh issue and stayed with it until the end. Wolfman had never been much of a horror fan, which, he says, "kept me from doing anything standard, because I had no idea what standard was. We did people-oriented stories." Wolfman invented a constellation of fresh new characters to interact with the brooding, driven villain, and the mix of strong writing and imaginative art was a powerful brew that kept Dracula alive in his own comic longer than any other bad guy.

would now begin to carry the load. "It's time for Phase Two to begin," wrote Lee. "Marvel's still much too young, too zingy, too bright-eyed and bushy-tailed to settle back and bask in the sun of yesterday's success."

In his new role as publisher, Lee explains, "I was deciding what books we would publish and what to concentrate on, and I worked with the editor and oversaw most of what we did. But, I must say, I concentrated a great deal on publicizing and promoting the company. I was always somewhere making goodwill appearances and doing interviews about Marvel. And I did a tremendous amount of college lecturing, just to spread the word and try to get people interested in Marvel and in comics. And I really think it had some effect; a ground swell just kept growing and growing."

Stan Lee lectures on Marvel at Carnegie Hall, January 5, 1972.

Lee, who has retained the title of publisher to the present day, was also appointed Marvel's president in 1972, but gave up that position "after a year or two. I was spending most of my time going to meetings and looking over balance sheets and annual reports, and I didn't have time to do the thing I thought I did best, which is the creative part of comic books."

Amidst all these changes, Martin Goodman

The Carnegie Hall poster includes pieces of Captain America, Daredevil, Spider-Man, Thor, The Hulk, Iron Man, The Thing and The Silver Surfer.

◄ Ghost Rider, a motor-cyclist under a curse, made his debut in *Marvel Spotlight* #5 (August 1972). Script: Gary Friedrich. Art: Mike Ploog.

▶ Luke Cage later became Power Man and enjoyed a run of fourteen years. Cover: George Tuska.

▼ An atmospheric page from *Jungle Action* #10 (July 1974) features Marvel's Afro-American super hero The Black Panther. Script: Don McGregor. Pencils: Billy Graham. Inks: Klaus Janson.

ended his association with Marvel—the company he had started forty years earlier with a minor pulp magazine called *Complete Western*. Although Goodman had sold Marvel to Cadence Industries in 1968, he had stayed on staff for four years. But disagreements arose between him and Stan Lee over the direction the company should take. Ultimately, Cadence executives decided to back Lee's strengths in creativity and publicity instead of favoring Goodman's undeniable business expertise. Economic and managerial skills seemed easily replaceable, but in fact it took several years to find an executive capable of reestablishing Marvel's firm financial footing.

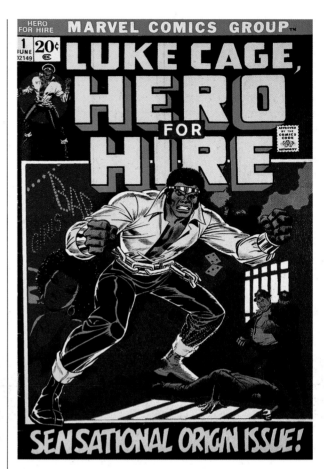

Affirmative Action

Meanwhile, Marvel continued to expand at a tremendous pace. "If we even talked about an idea for a book," recalls Roy Thomas, "it immediately had to go onto a schedule and be out a few months later. Stan kept coming into my office with yet another title. In the long run, most of them didn't really work, but they made some money, and we explored some new areas."

A conscious effort was made to include women and minority groups in the ranks of Marvel's heroes. "Stan really wanted to do both of those things," says Thomas. In fact, Lee and Jack Kirby had introduced a black super hero, The Black Panther, in an issue of *The Fantastic Four* as early as 1966. In his secret identity he was T'Challa, the king of an imaginary African nation. After spending several years as a member of The Avengers, The Black Panther received his own series in 1973 in the pages of *Jungle Action* #5. The scripts by Don McGregor emphasized the character's innate dignity, and many of the stories were illustrated by a young black artist named Billy Graham. *The Black Panther* #1 finally appeared in 1977.

When Stan Lee created *Luke Cage, Hero for Hire* in 1972, it was the first Marvel comic to take its title from a black character. Billy Graham inked veteran George Tuska's penciling, and the first writer on the series was the talented Archie Goodwin. Roy Thomas and artist John Romita also had a hand in the creation of Luke Cage, who was at the opposite end of the spectrum from T'Challa. A streetwise, tough former urban gang member, Cage is framed for a crime he did not commit. In prison he volunteers for a medical experiment that gives him extraordinary strength; he then escapes and becomes a mercenary "hero for hire." With issue #17, *Luke Cage* became *Power Man*, a comic book series that continued until 1986. Under one name or another, he was Marvel's most successful minority super hero.

In *Master of Kung Fu* (April 1974), Marvel presented an Oriental hero, an idea that was perhaps overdue after so many Asian villains had been seen in Marvel's pages during previous decades. To acknowledge the guilty past, writer Steve Englehart and artist Jim Starlin declared that their protagonist was the good-guy son of the famous bad guy Dr. Fu Manchu. This sort of stunt, combined with the fact that the series was evidently intended to capitalize on the fad for martial arts in the movies, might have condemned the nimble Shang-Chi to a short career, and in fact the original creators soon abandoned the character. But ingenious writing by Doug Moench and energetic art by Paul Gulacy brought *Master of Kung Fu* new life, and the series survived until 1983.

Marvel even tried an American Indian hero who was featured in *Red Wolf* (May 1972). The western setting was out of vogue, however, and this experiment lasted for only nine issues.

Fabulous Females

Women had long been an integral part of Marvel's super hero teams, but the rise of the feminist movement encouraged the company to invent some new women intended to stand on their own. Providing female characters with successful solo careers continued to be an uphill fight, however, as three 1972 experiments demonstrated. The most interesting attempt came in the pages of *The Cat* (November 1972), which introduced a policeman's widow named Greer Nelson. She returns to college and meets a female professor who has designed a device to "make it possible for any

▲ Mood and menace in a powerful page from *Master of Kung Fu* #38 (March 1976). Script: Doug Moench. Pencils: Paul Gulacy. Inks: Dan Adkins.

◄ Marvel gave female crime-fighters a try with *The Cat* (November 1972). Pencils: Marie Severin. Inks: Wally Wood.

A color hero went black-and-white in *The Rampaging Hulk* #1 (January 1977). Cover: Ken Barr.

Vampires were more villainous in the black-and-white *Dracula Lives!* Cover: Luis Dominguez.

Marvel's most successful black-and-white comic, *Savage Sword of Conan*, began in 1974 and continues today. Cover: Steve Hickman.

The first of Marvel's oversize black-and-white comic books returned for its second issue in October 1973, but regular publication did not begin until March 1974. Cover: John Buscema.

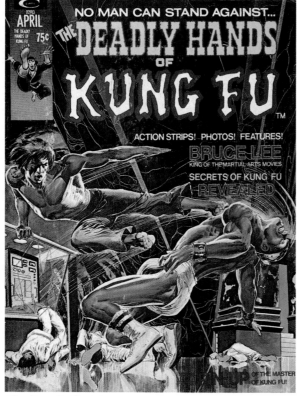

The Deadly Hands of Kung Fu combined comics with articles and photographs documenting the martial arts craze inspired by movie stars like Bruce Lee. Cover: Neal Adams.

Horror was a mainstay of the black-and-white books, and the zombie introduced twenty years earlier received his own title with *Tales of the Zombie* #1 in 1973. Cover: Boris Vallejo.

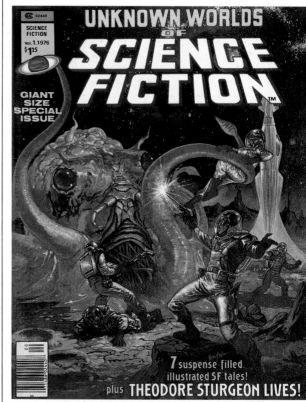

By the time *Unknown Worlds of Science Fiction* made its debut in 1976, the black-and-white comic book phenomenon was slowly winding down. Cover: Don Newton.

woman to totally fulfill her physical and mental potential—despite the handicaps that society places upon her." No mental potential is required to guess that Greer receives the traditional comic book treatment and ends up fighting crime in a set of tights. With a script by Linda Fite and penciling by Marie Severin, *The Cat* had perhaps too much feminist doctrine for the average reader—it folded after four issues. Yet Greer Nelson continued to pop up in various Marvel comics, and eventually another machine transformed her into a furry, feline female called Tigra, who seemed to be more interested in cuddling than combat. Like count-less colleagues, she ended up joining The Avengers group.

Night Nurse, about a dedicated young woman in white, started and stopped simultaneously with *The Cat. Shanna the She-Devil*, a series featuring a beautiful "veterinarian and ecologist" who moves to the jungle and dons a leopard skin, began in December 1972 and ended five issues later. "It's kind of a shame," says Roy Thomas. "You could get blacks to buy comics about whites, but it was hard to get whites to buy comics in which the main character was black. And it was even harder to get boys to buy comics about women."

Marvel in Monochrome

"Stan really wanted to go with the black-and-white magazines," says Roy Thomas. "One day there was one book, and the next day we had two, and the next day we had four." *Dracula Lives*, *Vampire Tales* and *Tales of the Zombie* were all launched in 1973; the latter revived the zombie character originally created by Bill Everett and Stan Lee back in 1953.

In short order, the black-and-whites became a separate division with their own editor. Marv Wolfman, who had developed a reputation for handling horror characters like Dracula, was the man for the job. "Roy asked me to head up the magazine line," says Wolfman. "I had written sev-eral stories for the first issues, so I was involved from day one."

Upon assuming the editorship, Wolfman was immediately called upon to create a black-and-white humor magazine. "I was asked to edit *Crazy*, and essentially given about six weeks to assemble an entire staff, establish a look and get all the material. And I wasn't allowed to use the regular Marvel staff. The trick I discovered was to use artists who were newspaper editorial cartoon-ists; they are phenomenally good artists and accustomed to working incredibly fast." Off to a good start, *Crazy* held on for ten years, and is re-membered fondly by humor magazine aficionados.

More black-and-white titles appeared in 1974: a revival of *Savage Tales*, *The Deadly Hands of Kung Fu*, *The Savage Sword of Conan* and, adapted from the movie, *Planet of the Apes*. The next year brought *Marvel Preview* and *Unknown Worlds of*

Science Fiction.

Yet for all the effort expended on them, the magazines never really took off, and only *Savage Sword of Conan* has continued to the present day. "The readers liked color," says Stan Lee. Not enough readers appreciated the chance to see clean, crisp, large reproductions of unadorned pencils and inks; and these publications never really fulfilled Marvel's original intention, which was to move beyond the Comics Code restrictions on sex and violence.

Art Expert

In July 1973, Stan Lee announced that John Romita had been officially appointed Marvel's art director. This was a post that Lee himself had held

▲ Justification for the black-and-white comics is found in beautifully rendered pages like this one by Barry Windsor-Smith from *Savage Tales* #2. Script: Roy Thomas.

SPACED OUT: JIM STARLIN

With his vision of troubled characters playing out their psychodramas against a vast background of interstellar chaos, Jim Starlin rapidly succeeded in establishing himself as one of the most unusual comic book artists of his generation. In a brief stint with Marvel, which included work on two characters that had previously never quite made their mark, Starlin managed to build a considerable cult following.

Assigned to do the art on *Captain Marvel* in 1973, Starlin quickly assumed the writing chores as well, taking strong control of the character. Billed as "The Most Cosmic Super Hero of All," Captain Marvel was transformed from a soldier of the spaceways into a dreamer who wandered throughout the universe on a philosophical quest for truth. And Thanos, the villain who opposed him, was

revealed as a mystic, motivated by his love for the female figure of Death.

This was heady stuff for a comic book, and after ten issues on *Captain Marvel*, Starlin brought the same approach to *Warlock*, another science fiction title in need of renovation. In short order, Adam Warlock became a split personality battling his darker half for control of his soul; in the process he ultimately sacrificed his life.

With his ambitious themes and powerful drawing style, Starlin brought a new dimension to comics and also demonstrated the opportunities available to a combination writer-artist. The prospect of providing prose as well as pictures proved to be increasingly attractive to successful pencilers in the years to come.

Captain Marvel endures intense interstellar mind games (below, left) while Warlock (below, right) contemplates his place in the universe. Script and pencils: Jim Starlin.

during his tenure as editor, but an increasing number of publications meant that no one person could realistically manage both jobs at once. Editor Roy Thomas welcomed the change. "It made a lot more sense," Thomas says. "Romita was so valuable in so many ways. He's been there ever since."

Unofficially, Romita had been moving into the position for some time, and might have become art director sooner if not for his important work drawing and plotting the best-selling adventures of Spider-Man. "I had already taken on the chore of talking to artists and transmitting Stan's thoughts," says Romita. "I was like an assistant art director. I was doing sketches and supervising the penciling, and I was generally in charge of the covers as far as quality and scheduling were concerned. And that's still my primary assignment."

Perhaps the most satisfying part of Romita's job as art director was designing the new characters dreamed up by various writers and editors. "They would come to me, and we would try to tie themes and elements together to create the look of the character. Sometimes they would just throw a name at me, and I would come up with the visual image and they would build on it. I take a certain amount of pride in that." To this day, Romita does uncredited design work on a number of Marvel's most popular heroes and villains.

At the same time that Romita became art director, Marie Severin took on the job of overseeing the color on all of the company's comics. The Marvel staff was growing, but some freelancers were growing restless.

Leaving the Nest

It was a sign of the times when artist Barry Windsor-Smith decided to leave Marvel in early 1973. After twenty-four issues of *Conan the Barbarian* he was ready to move on. In fact, Windsor-Smith was preparing to say good-bye to comics entirely. Meanwhile, Neal Adams, who had made his mark with *The X-Men* and *The Avengers*, had adopted a similar attitude; he even began to organize artists who were dissatisfied with conditions in the industry, and made a special effort at DC to gain recognition and recompense for the forgotten creators of Superman.

The defection of such talented young artists symbolized the problems in the comic book

industry—comics were at once a business and an art form. Idealistic talent often bridled at editorial restrictions and the exigencies of deadlines and schedules. Faced with the choice of rushing a job or missing a deadline, many artists opted for the latter, even if it meant late publication or filling in with a reprint.

Windsor-Smith particularly resented the fact that his increasingly intricate work did not earn him a higher page rate than he would have earned for a mediocre effort, and he found it frustrating that superior technique resulted in a loss of output and thus a loss of income. "It's a hell of a fight," he said at the time, "and I'm tired of fighting."

Roy Thomas, a contemporary of the rebellious artists, seems to have understood their position. "They were actually trying to make a mark of some sort," he says, "and they took what they did very seriously. They weren't just in it for the money."

As art director, John Romita was disappointed. "There was a whole generation of artists in the 1970s," he says, "who were very thoughtful young people, but they were not team players. Guys who we thought would follow through in the way that other artists traditionally had, left to create their own businesses and to do their own artistic experiments." Yet Romita acknowledges that these independent spirits eventually helped to improve the position of talent in the industry. "I think their instinct was right," he says today. "I would never have thought to hold back my services or to walk. They deserve some of the credit for everybody getting a better shake these days."

The Big Gun

While many of Marvel's attempts to invent new heroes didn't really work out, a character came in through the back door who was destined to emerge as one of the hottest heroes of the 1980s. His name was The Punisher.

Gerry Conway, who had taken over from Stan Lee as Spider-Man's writer, says, "I wanted to do a dark, street-tough kind of opponent for Spider-Man. I came up with the character, took it to Roy, and we decided to do it. John Romita developed the costume. My original sketch was of a guy in a black jumpsuit with a little white skull on his chest, and John did a wonderful thing

Publisher Stan Lee and art director John Romita contemplate a Spider-Man cover in 1976.

◄ John Romita's design sketch for a menacing antihero: The Punisher.

▲ The Punisher makes his debut by kicking the stuffing out of a well-meaning Spider-Man. From *The Amazing Spider-Man* #129 (February 1974). Script: Gerry Conway. Pencils: Ross Andru. Inks: Frank Giacoia.

The Punisher was presented in 1974 as a hit man for hire. A year later, in *Marvel Preview* #2 (below), creator Gerry Conway revealed the hero's origin as a soldier seeking vengeance. Art: Tony DeZuniga.

where he took the skull, made it huge, and made the teeth of the skull form a cartridge belt. It looked terrific."

When The Punisher first appeared in *The Amazing Spider-Man* #129 (February 1974), Ross Andru drew the character's craggy, scowling features and sent him out with a concussion rifle to kill Spidey. Acting under the misapprehension that Spider-Man is a criminal, The Punisher relents upon realizing the truth, but vows to continue his vigilante mission of eradicating felons. "Something tells me," says Spidey, "that man's got problems that make mine look like a birthday party."

The Punisher began making further guest

THE PUNISHER

The Punisher is Marvel's most dangerous hero. Although he possesses no special abilities beyond those of a highly trained and motivated soldier, his ruthless commitment to a war on crime has turned his life into an endless, bloody battle. While other Marvel heroes generally kill with the utmost reluctance, The Punisher positively relishes his role as an executioner. The gigantic skull emblazoned on the front of his black costume sums up his public persona.

Writer Gerry Conway and art director John Romita first conceived The Punisher as a grim gunman, and when he first appeared in 1974 the character was an assassin for hire, albeit one who would only eliminate criminals. The idea of killing for cash was dropped almost immediately, however, and The Punisher was transformed into a crusader motivated by revenge, although he was not above pocketing the ill-gotten gains of his victims. His wife and children had been murdered after accidentally witnessing a gangland execution, so he wreaked vengeance on the brutal perpetrators and has subsequently stalked all lawbreakers. Outwardly he is stoic, but beneath the surface he is tortured by the guilt of a survivor. Yet there are also hints that his loss may have been a blessing in disguise, that he was born for his job and could not be happy without it.

The death's-head symbolizes The Punisher's tough tactics.

Despite his obsession, The Punisher is in some ways a very practical man, and much of his appeal is based on his use of authentic weapons and technology. This disturbing hero is one of the most convincing in comic books, and hardware is part of his charm. His no-nonsense attitude challenges psychological and sociological excuses for evil: he just finds bad guys and shoots them. Although in some respects The Punisher is a throwback to the pitiless heroes of the old pulp magazines, he is also a symptom of our times, or perhaps a commentary on how we see ourselves today. Captain America came wrapped in Old Glory, but The Punisher's costume appears to be made out of a pirate's flag.

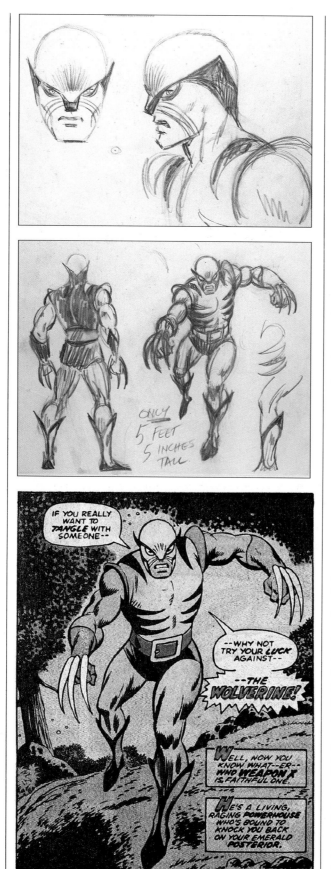

Original design sketches by John Romita emphasized Wolverine's small stature. This helped dramatize his fearless nature when he challenged The Hulk in the last panel of *The Incredible Hulk* #180. Pencils: Herb Trimpe. Inks: Jack Abel. Script: Len Wein.

appearances almost immediately. He acquired a name and an origin: he was Frank Castle, an ex-Marine who transformed himself into a one-man army after his family was slaughtered by thugs. He was grim and brutal, and the fans loved him.

"From the moment that I wrote him," Conway says, "I thought he would become a star character. Every time he appeared in a Spider-Man book, it sold well. But he had no super powers, and at that time there was a strong feeling that a character without super powers couldn't carry his own book. The other feeling was that The Punisher was so violent that we couldn't really give him a regular color comic book." It would take a new decade, with a new attitude toward crime, to elevate the vengeful Punisher to his full commercial potential. "I was years ahead of my time," says Conway with a laugh.

Someone Sharp

Later in 1974, Marvel planted another time bomb with the introduction of a second wild and dangerous character who would gradually develop into a 'sensational success. One of the most enigmatic figures in comic books, with a background and a psychology that remain shrouded in mystery, he is known as Wolverine.

"I took Len Wein to lunch one day," says Roy Thomas, "and we talked about how to create a Canadian character for the comics, because we had a fair amount of sales there. I thought Wolverine was a good name, and I said I wanted him to be a little, scrappy guy. Then I left it to Len."

Wein, a friend of Gerry Conway's, had freelanced for various publishers, but gradually turned his attention exclusively to Marvel; by 1974 he was writing the adventures of several heroes, including The Hulk. So it was on the last page of *The Incredible Hulk* #180 (October 1974) that readers first encountered Wolverine, an apparently unstable agent of the Canadian government, known as "Weapon X." In the next issue, protagonist and antagonist faced off, with Wolverine demonstrating his agility, his resiliency and also a set of razor-sharp claws forged from a mythical Marvel metal known as adamantium.

The deadly claws were the key to Wolverine, a character with a pronounced mean streak. "When you're given the name Wolverine," says Wein, "you do research on what the animal is. And the wolverine is a very small, very nasty little animal with claws. What made Wolverine a hero was that his natural inclination was to disembowel an antagonist without a second thought, but he would restrain himself." Actually, the claws were employed quite liberally in the character's first appearance, although admittedly against the invulnerable Hulk. Over the years, various writers have portrayed Wolverine as both a raging killer and a model of admirable self-control. And the claws, which initially seemed to be attached to gloves,

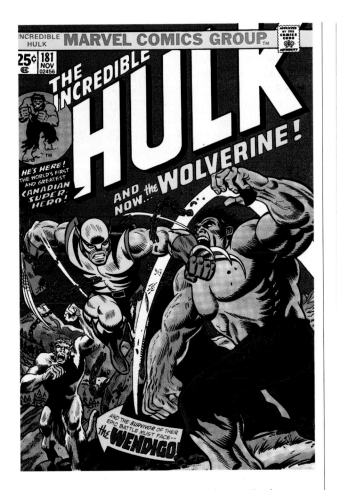

"The World's First and Greatest Canadian Super Hero" got full star treatment when he battled the title character in *The Incredible Hulk* #181 (November 1974).

Known today simply as *The Spectacular Spider-Man*, this book started in December 1976. Cover: Sal Buscema.

With simplified scripts for younger fans, this book ran from 1974 to 1982. Cover: John Romita.

were later revealed to be retractable surgical implants. Their origin remains a secret.

This frightening but fascinating figure, who, like The Punisher, seemed as much villain as hero, sported a costume designed by art director John Romita, and was drawn by The Hulk's regular artist at the time, Herb Trimpe. Wolverine was a mutant, and had the power to heal any wound he received. This last attribute was added almost as an afterthought by Len Wein, because he and Roy Thomas had been thinking of reviving Marvel's old mutant group, The X-Men. By the time that project came to fruition, however, Thomas had resigned and Wein had replaced him as editor-in-chief.

Room at the Top

Although he had demonstrated considerable skill in hiring promising people and overseeing the introduction of fresh ideas, Roy Thomas was not comfortable with the idea of being an executive. "Basically," says Thomas, "I'm not a person who's very interested in business or, God forbid, working my way up the corporate ladder." His natural inclination was to identify himself with writers and artists, rather than management, and he recalls that "things were becoming a little bit strained. I just wasn't enjoying the job. I felt that I was wasting too much time on things that I really hated spending time on."

Thomas left the job at the end of 1974, the first in

a succession of talented writers who discovered that the job of editor-in-chief was something of a burden. But he was far too valuable for Marvel to lose him entirely. Instead, he was designated "editor emeritus," a title soon abandoned, but intended, in essence, to convey that Thomas would continue as a writer and would also edit the comic books he wrote. He would thus retain a measure of control while simultaneously lightening the load of his successor. It seemed a good idea at the time, but the concept eventually led to controversy. For the time being, however, Thomas was happy. "I only wish I'd stayed just a little longer. Then I would at least have had my name as editor on *Giant-Size X-Men*, which became such a classic."

Mutants on the Move

Giant-Size X-Men (May 1975) has become a landmark in the history of comics. It introduced the most successful team in the history of the medium, and the most popular comic book series of recent times. Furthermore, the series it launched made the term "mutant," once considered too esoteric for comic books, a household word. The story of the comic's creation, a patchwork of the old and the new, of inspiration and confusion, is almost as fantastic as the book itself.

Roy Thomas was still editor-in-chief when the idea first came up at a meeting he attended with

The Sentinels were giant robots designed to eradicate mutants. Cover: Dave Cockrum.

Jean Grey, formerly Marvel Girl, becomes the infinitely more powerful Phoenix. Cover: Dave Cockrum.

▶ **A new group of mutants burst on the scene in *Giant-Size X-Men* #1 (May 1975). They became established as the regular team in the following issue, *X-Men* #94 (August 1975). Covers: Gil Kane and Dave Cockrum.**

publisher Stan Lee and Marvel's president Al Landau. Appointed by Cadence Industries, Marvel's parent company, Landau had no direct publishing experience, but he headed Trans World Features Syndicate, an organization that licensed American publications like Marvel's for reprinting around the world. As Thomas remembers the meeting, "Al Landau said that if we could come up with a group book that had characters from several different countries—and of course we would target particular countries—we could sell the book abroad." Thomas immediately thought of The X-Men, the Stan Lee–Jack Kirby creations that he had scripted before they were discontinued in 1970.

Thomas turned the idea over to Len Wein and artist Dave Cockrum, suggesting that one or two of the old characters be retained at first to travel around the world recruiting new members for the group. By the time *Giant-Size X-Men* was published, Wein was its editor as well as its writer. Ironically, the concept of using characters from countries where sales might be improved, which was originally the whole point of the publication, somehow never trickled down to Wein and Cockrum. "The marketing aspect was not on my mind at all," says Wein. "Dave Cockrum and I just looked for an interesting combination—someone from here, someone from there." With countries of origin like Russia and Kenya, where big sales were highly unlikely, the new *X-Men* might well have been considered an automatic failure had anybody cared about the original marketing motive.

The Second Time Around

Giant-Size X-Men (the title describes the length of the book, not the stature of its heroes) had room for all the original X-Men as well as the new ones created for a special mission. After the first few issues the roster included only two old-timers: Cyclops, whose gaze had the power of a laser beam, and Dr. X, the wheelchair-bound mentor of the mutants. The new characters were the wild Canadian Wolverine, as Wein had planned; Storm, a beautiful black woman with the power to control the weather; Colossus, a hefty Russian peasant with skin that could change to steel; and Nightcrawler, a furry German circus freak with the gift of teleportation.

"Dave Cockrum had a book full of dozens and dozens of characters he had designed that he hoped to make use of someday. Dave and I sat down and went through the book," says Wein. "We combined costumes and characters and powers, mixing and matching everything until we got a group that worked." Cockrum's energetic drawing and strong sense of design had a major impact on the series, which, in Wein's words, was "a solid hit from day one. Later it really went through the roof."

Yet Wein abandoned the new X-Men while they

were still getting off the ground. "When I was editor-in-chief," he explains, "I couldn't write as much as I wanted to because of time constraints. I was down to writing just *X-Men* and *The Incredible Hulk*, and one of them had to go. And The Hulk had always been my favorite Marvel character. Who knew?" Wein's assistant, Chris Claremont, was contributing to the writing by the second issue, and had taken over completely by the fourth.

Mr. X

Chris Claremont has been writing the adventures of The X-Men for more than fifteen years, an extraordinary record in a business where rapid turnover is the norm. His record is even more extraordinary because he never intended to enter the comic book business at all. Born in 1950, Claremont had not read the old *X-Men* as a boy, but he had read Stan Lee's and Jack Kirby's *The Fantastic Four*; he especially savored the classic issues that introduced Galactus and The Silver Surfer. The idea of portraying heroes in conflict against a background of cosmic proportions evidently was not lost on him.

At the suggestion of a family friend, Claremont came to Marvel casually for a two-month college internship in 1969. Claremont's real interest was acting, but when he returned to Bard College he submitted some plot ideas to Marvel, and after graduating in 1972 he began to sell some stories. "I viewed it as a convenient way to pay the bills while I was trying to get acting gigs," he says. "And then in the spring of 1974, Marv Wolfman offered me a position as his assistant editor on the black-and-whites. And I said I'd work for six months to build up some money, and then do summer stock. Instead, Roy quit as editor-in-chief and Len took over and gave me *The X-Men*. The rest, as they say, is history."

If Claremont abandoned the theater, he found plenty of room for drama in the pages of *The X-Men*. "For the first couple of years, Dave Cockrum and I were making it up as we went along," says Claremont. "And our interests meshed." Len Wein's original ideas were modified in the process. Wolverine, who, Claremont says, had been conceived as a "smart-mouthed teenager," became older and more experienced. Wein's Nightcrawler was going to be "bitter, twisted and tormented," according to Claremont, "but we took the approach that Nightcrawler thought it was incredibly cool to be blue and furry. The book took a totally new direction."

The fluid nature of the new *X-Men*, with members coming and going and no personalities etched in stone, was an innovation that worked. Marvel's new readers seemed to relish the excitement of change more than they craved the comfort of stability. "The trick with *X-Men*," says Claremont, "was that you couldn't read just one issue.

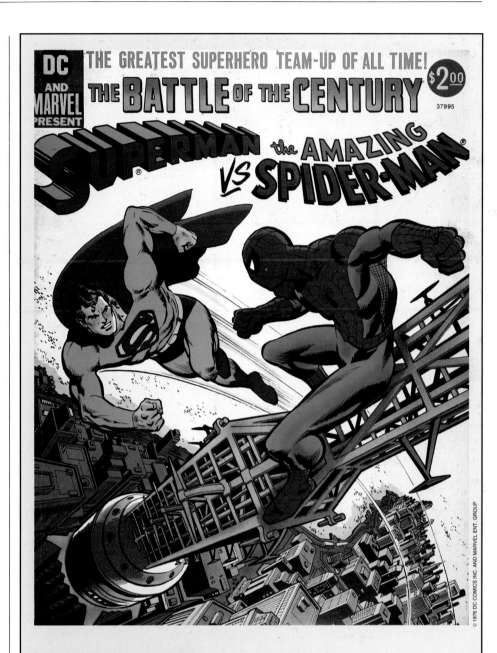

SPARRING PARTNERS

Marvel Comics and DC Comics have always been competitors, and by extension, their corporate symbols Spider-Man and Superman have been rivals as well. Before the two heroes could come to blows, however, their respective companies had to come to terms. Fortunately, Marvel publisher Stan Lee and his DC counterpart Carmine Infantino had worked together in Marvel's early days, and because of their long-standing relationship they were able to reach an agreement that created a special moment in comics history. The result, *Superman vs. The Amazing Spider-Man* (1976), was a huge, tabloid-size ninety-two-page comic book that brought the two red-and-blue-clad adventurers together to trade punches and then, naturally, save the world.

Of course, the vaunted battle between two good guys had to be explained away as a mistake engineered by the story's villains, and along the way, Spider-Man good-naturedly nursed his bruised knuckles while admitting that he couldn't match The Man of Steel's raw power. Still, Spidey's vulnerability has always been part of his charm, and he managed to hold his own when it really mattered, using his knowledge of psychology to divide and conquer the forces of evil. The script for this epic was written by Gerry Conway, with pencils by Ross Andru and inks by Dick Giordano. "We were told it couldn't be done," Stan Lee wrote at the time. But Marvel and DC did manage to lay down their arms long enough to fulfill fan fantasies and make a tidy profit into the bargain.

▶ All of the original X-Men except Cyclops resign, and Wolverine makes his presence felt, in a key scene from *X-Men* #94 (August 1975).
Plot: Len Wein.
Script: Chris Claremont.
Pencils: Dave Cockrum.
Inks: Bob McLeod.

X-MEN

"All-New All-Different"

make a point of following the developments in each issue have turned The X-Men into the most popular comic book heroes of modern times. These mutants are adults, unlike their predecessors, and their autonomy was affirmed when Professor X, who treated the team as his pupils, was whisked away to enjoy a romance on a distant planet. On their own, The X-Men are careerists like the baby boom generation they represent: single people who make the workplace the center of their lives and struggle to form lasting bonds in a mobile and unstable society. Any super hero can make enemies; what sets The X-Men apart is their friendship.

The ever-changing roster of X-Men has included such mutants as (clockwise from top center): Colossus, Thunderbird (quickly killed in the line of duty), Cyclops, Wolverine, Nightcrawler, Marvel Girl and reserve member Polaris.

The revised and revamped X-Men, complete with new concepts and new characters, took comic book readers by storm. When writer Len Wein and artist Dave Cockrum resurrected the moribund series in 1975, their strategy was to pack the book with mutants, including seven new ones who had been recruited by their mentor Professor X to lend a hand to the original group. Within a few issues most of the old members had quit. Not even their successors were secure, however: by the end of their third appearance one of them was dead. Such startling switches defined the new X-Men, who had to accept instability as a way of life. They are the apotheosis of Marvel's long-standing policy of letting its characters develop over time; in fact, introducing new personalties and exploring altered relationships have become crucial elements in the success of the comic books.

The intricacy characteristic of X-Men plots demands intense involvement from readers, and perhaps as a result The X-Men have not received as much recognition from the general public as personalities like The Hulk or Spider-Man. "As the characters grew more complex, it became harder to define them," says Chris Claremont, the writer who has worked continuously on the new X-Men since their second appearance. Nonetheless, committed fans who

Alex Schomburg returned to Marvel in 1977 to do the cover for *The Invaders Annual* #1.

An oddball group rendered handsomely by Gil Kane and Dan Adkins.

Marvel's major misfits became *The Defenders* in August 1972. Cover: Sal Buscema.

Character sketch by John Romita for Ms. Marvel, whose comic book started in January 1977.

Something about it would be so interesting that you'd want to come back for the next one."

The new X-Men were off to a strong start. A colorful cast had been assembled, and the theme of noble mutants fighting to protect the human race that feared them had innate appeal. Yet Claremont admits that "we had no idea where we were going or what we were doing." The team was still a few years away from becoming the most phenomenal success in contemporary comic books.

New Clubs with Old Members

While The X-Men were the most important super hero group created in the 1970s, they were hardly alone. In fact, Roy Thomas unleashed another group almost simultaneously with the first issue of *The Invaders* (August 1975). "I was always interested in the old comic book characters from the 1940s," says Thomas, and he particularly remembered Golden Age artist Alex Schomburg's covers featuring Captain America, The Sub-Mariner and the original Human Torch fighting side by side against the Nazis. No related stories had appeared inside the comic books, however, and Thomas decided to rectify the matter. Schomburg was

brought back to do a cover, but the series was regularly illustrated by Frank Robbins. Despite the historical slant, perhaps a trifle esoteric for young readers, *The Invaders* ran a respectable four years.

Another new club with old members was *The Champions* (October 1975), an unlikely combination of retired X-Men like The Angel and Iceman working with the spectral Ghost Rider and the Greek god Hercules. This unfocused team only lasted for seventeen issues. In another experiment even Marvel's most notorious loners were asked to work as team players: *The Defenders* (August 1972) brought together The Hulk, The Sub-Mariner and Dr. Strange. Conceived by Roy Thomas, and drawn for a long stint by Sal Buscema, The Defenders endured many membership changes and managed to survive until 1986.

The Revolving Door

Len Wein, who had made a significant and lasting contribution to Marvel with the creation of Wolverine and the new X-Men, resigned as editor-in-chief in the summer of 1975. "It was a very interesting time," he says, "but I was the sole editor of fifty-four titles a month. It was just outrageous. . . I had one assistant. I was spending half my time upstairs fighting the usual business battles, and it just wasn't any fun. After eight or nine months, it was killing me. And so I arranged the same kind of deal for myself that Roy Thomas got when he stepped down from the job, which was to become a writer-editor. Within a couple of months I found myself writing Spider-Man, Thor, The Hulk and The Fantastic Four." Wein stayed on for a couple of years and then moved over to DC, following the increasingly common back-and-forth personnel migration pattern between the two companies.

Wein's replacement was Marv Wolfman, who had been editing Marvel's line of black-and-white comics magazines. Archie Goodwin, who took Wolfman's old job and who would become editor-in-chief himself within a year, says, "it was pretty much of a revolving door."

Wolfman describes his trip through the revolving door as "pretty fast." He was happy editing, "even though we were publishing an ungodly amount of stories," but he had the usual complaint: "I didn't like the fact that I was dealing with business and not editorial." Like his predecessors, Wolfman promoted new projects. "We did a lot of experimenting with different things. Some of them worked and some of them didn't. Howard the Duck was one of my favorites; there was a lot of negative feeling about Howard amongst the staff, because nobody had done anything that ludicrous before."

By 1975, Marvel was drifting into deep water. Its sales were the highest in the industry, but profits had somehow dwindled dangerously. The number of available retail outlets was shrinking as independent newsdealers were replaced by chain stores, whose accountants often found the few pennies of profit on a comic book not worth bothering about. "I knew there were financial problems," says Wolfman, "because every so often, new, tighter budget rules would come down. The newsstand market was dying, and DC was having the same problems. At the same time, paper prices zoomed. Marvel needed to turn things around. That's when Jim Galton came in."

Taking Care of Business

James Galton became Marvel's new president in 1975, and he held the position until 1990. Previously a publisher of paperback books at Popular Library, Galton was recruited by Cadence Industries to exert some control over Marvel's foundering finances. "The independent wholesaler distribution system for comic books was pretty much the same kind of system that the paperback book industry had been using," Galton says. "So from a marketing standpoint, I was familiar with the system and there were great similarities between the two industries."

Someone with solid experience was what Marvel needed. "I think that by June 30th of the year I arrived, Marvel had lost two million dollars," Galton says. "The previous management didn't have a clue as to how to run the company." With the cooperation of publisher Stan Lee, Galton proceeded to make some changes. "Stan and I worked very well together," Galton says. "He handled the creative side and I handled the business side, and we respected each other's expertise."

"Jim was just wonderful," says Stan Lee. "I've never enjoyed working with anybody more. He was one of the most capable, intelligent, honorable people I've ever known, and we became very good friends."

"The first thing I had to do was pare production," Galton says. "The number of titles had proliferated geometrically. The editorial department was putting out new series without considering whether or not the books were marketable. In addition, the delivery of books was off schedule and chaotic. This damaged credibility with the distributors and, more importantly, affected ultimate sales: the reader could not rely on getting the next issue of a book at the appropriate time. I also made substantial changes in the sales and circulation areas."

It fell to editor-in-chief Marv Wolfman to see that art and scripts were delivered in time to meet publication schedules. Late work meant that the comic books would not ship regularly, and sometimes an old book would have to be reprinted to fill in the gap. Neither alternative was good for sales, but screaming at the artists and writers seemed to have no effect. "So we created a phony comic book called *Marvel Fill-In Comics*," says Wolfman, "and we put it on the publication schedule." Writer Bill Mantlo, usually working with artist Sal

▲ *What If?*, conceived by Roy Thomas, began in January 1977. Cover: George Perez and Joe Sinnott.

▼ Marie Severin's 1977 map of the Marvel offices shows a lot of people on the premises who really only dropped in from time to time.

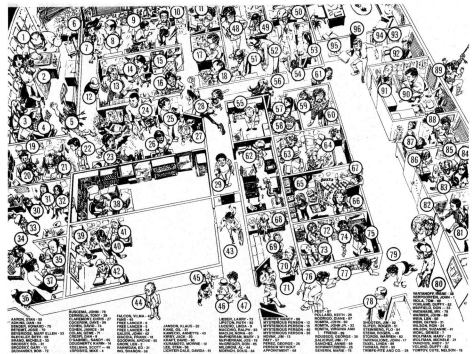

AARON, STAN - 55
ADKINS, DAN - 64
BENDER, HOWARD - 75
BETEMER, JOSIE - 70
BEVERIDGE, MARY ELLEN - 53
BLECKLEY, BETH - 59
BRAND, MICHELE - 32
BRODSKY, SOL - 81
BRODSKY, GARY - 11
BUDIANSKY, BOB - 72

BUSCEMA, JOHN - 76
CERNIGLIA, TONY - 39
CLAREMONT, CHRIS - 27
COCKRUM, DAVE - 58
COHEN, DAVID - 74
COHEN, JANICE - 34
COLAN, GENE - 71
CRESPI, DAN - 71
D'GABRIEL, SANDY - 65
DOUGHERTY, KARIN - 14
EDELMAN, SCOTT - 46
ESPOSITO, MIKE - 4

FALCON, VILMA - 4
FANS - 45
FREE LANCER - 8
FREE LANCER - 54
FREE LANCER - 54
GALVIN, JOHN - 42
GIACOIA, FRANK - 18
GOODWIN, ARCHIE - 50
GROW, LEN - 2
HANNIGAN, ED - 21
ING, SHARON - 56

JANSON, KLAUS - 20
KANE, GIL - 91
KAWECKI, ANNETTE - 43
KIRBY, JACK - 93
KRAFT, DAVID - 80
KURAMOTO, MORRIE - 10
LEE, STAN - 96
LICHTER-DALE, DAVIDA - 61

LIEBER, LARRY - 73
LIPSTON, RUTH - 92
LUCERO, LINDA - 9
MACCHIO, RALPH - 83
MACLIN, NORA - 65
McPHERRAN, MARY - 33
McPHERRAN, JOE - 15
McGREGOR, DON - 85
MR.GROW, AL - 44
MOENCH, DOUG - 84

MURPHY, NANCY - 66
MYSTERIOUS PERSON - 12
MYSTERIOUS PERSON - 15
MYSTERIOUS PERSON - 46
MYSTERIOUS PERSON - 35
NOVAK, JIM - 13
PATY - 57
PEREZ, GEORGE - 26
PERSON WITHOUT APPOINTMENT - 68

PEST - 87
POLLARD, KEITH - 29
RODRIGO, DIANE - 67
ROMITA, JOHN - 90
ROMITA, JOHN JR - 22
ROMITA, VIRGINIA AND FRIEND - 89
ROUSSOS, GEORGE - 36
SALICRUP, JIM - 77
SANCHEZ, ANNIE - 69
SCHWARTZBERG - 25
SEVERIN, MARIE - 79

SHOOTER, JIM - 52
SLIPER, ROGER - 51
STEINBERG, FLO - 94
STERN, ROGER - 49
STOROB, WARREN - 62
TARTAGLIONE, JOHN - 17
TAXEL, LINDA - 88
THOMAS, ROY - 95
TRIMPE-PITE AND CO. - 26

VARTANOFF, IRENE - 78
VERPOORTEN, JOHN - 1
VIOLA, TOM - 46
VORLAND, DUFFY - 82
WARFIELD, DON - 33
WATANABE, IRV - 78
WARNER, JOHN - 86
WEIN, LEN - 60
WEIN, GLYNIS - 31
WILSON, SUZANNE - 41
WOHL, DENISE - 7
WOLFMAN, MARV - 23
WOLFMAN, MICHELE - 31
YANCHUS, ANDY - 37
YOLAND, DUFFY - 82
YOMTOV, CUTE, NELSON - 16

174   RESEARCH AND DEVELOPMENT/MARVEL

MARVEL'S WILDEST WATERFOWL

When he dropped without warning into The Marvel Universe, Howard the Duck created quite a splash. Zapped from another dimension into what he called "a world of hairless talking apes," the cigar-smoking duck (actually a drake, of course) made his debut in a Man-Thing story appearing in the anthology series *Fear* (December 1973). "Howard was created totally as a joke and totally on the spur of the moment," says writer Steve Gerber. In fact, when he took a gander at artist Val Mayerik's first drawing of the duck waddling into what had previously been a horror story, Gerber's immediate reaction was, "I'm in real trouble!"

Actually, Gerber was on to something good, and after a few more guest appearances in various comic books, *Howard the Duck* #1 was launched in January 1976. By then, Howard was so popular that copies of the first issue were hoarded by dealers and distributors as collector's items. "It was just something completely different," says Gerber.

Confronting everything from a vampire cow to a giant gingerbread man, Howard provided a parody of comic book clichés and a dollop of social satire as well. Gerber describes the duck as "a character who is essentially passive and gets dragged into all his adventures," and the slogan on each cover, "Trapped in a World He Never Made!" reflected this. Sympathetic readers responded in droves, and *Howard* was even launched briefly as a newspaper comic strip in June 1977, written by Gerber and drawn by Gene Colan. "Howard was very big," says publisher Stan Lee, who recalls that the duck received thousands of write-in votes when he ran for President of the United States against Gerald Ford and Jimmy Carter in 1976.

Unfortunately, a dispute concerning rights to the character arose between Steve Gerber and Marvel, and without his original writer, the duck went into a tailspin. A settlement was finally reached, but not before *Howard the Duck* ceased regular publication in 1979. A lavish but misguided movie adaptation in 1986 only succeeded in giving Howard a bad name. But if the film laid an egg, Howard himself remains a unique creation who brought a welcome touch of humor into comic books.

▶ **Howard's debut panel is by Val Mayerik; his first cover and fall through space are by Frank Brunner.**

SPIDEY GOES DAILY

Extra proof of Spider-Man's continuing popularity appeared in homes all over the country on January 3, 1977, when the "Amazing Spider-Man" daily newspaper strip made its debut. Written by Stan Lee and drawn by John Romita, the new strip was bucking a trend: the days when adventure strips dominated the newspapers were long past, and simply drawn humor features were now the most popular fare. But Spider-Man, accustomed to adversity, prevailed. The strip's circulation grew, and it continues to be published today. Spider-Man, originally a comic book character, is now one of the few action heroes in the papers, maintaining the comic strip tradition that made comic books possible in the first place.

Both Lee and Romita had come into comic books with the widely shared perception that work on a daily strip would have been a better job opportunity, yet when their chance came, the pair realized at once how much freedom comic books had allowed them.

"The strip format was so restrictive," says Romita, "compared to comic books with full-page shots, panoramic wide-angle shots, tall shots. All of that freedom was gone." Romita dropped the strip after four years to concentrate on his duties as Marvel's art director. Lee has stayed with the strip, and its long run has helped to make Spider-Man one of the few comic book characters who is known even to people who never read comics. Currently, the daily strip is drawn by Larry Lieber, Stan Lee's brother, and the color Sunday episodes are drawn by Flor Dery.

▲ Stan Lee and John Romita dreamed of a daily Spider-Man comic strip years before they were able to convince newspaper publishers that readers would want a super hero. These rare 1970 sample strips, never published, are the first two ever done.

▼ The color Sunday strip, which is seen by many newspaper readers who don't follow the black-and-white daily strip, often concentrates on Peter Parker's private life. This example, however, from July 1, 1990, shows Spider-Man in costume, a super hero temporarily stymied by a super villain.

THE HULK HITS THE TUBE

"Dr. David Banner. Physician. Scientist. Searching for a way to tap ir .o the hidden strengths that all humans have. Then an accidental dose of gamma radiation altered his body chemistry. And now when David Banner grows angry or outraged, a startling metamorphosis occurs...." These words were intoned each Friday night on CBS for more than three years in the late 1970s to introduce *The Incredible Hulk*, one of the few successful efforts to present a super hero on prime time television.

The Incredible Hulk, a two-hour pilot film, aired on November 4, 1977, and was followed up a mere three weeks later by *The Return of The Hulk*. When the regular one-hour series began on March 10, 1978, executive producer Kenneth Johnson, who had directed the original pilot, was credited with developing the show for television. Eighty episodes were produced by Universal, with publisher Stan Lee serving as consultant.

The stars were Bill Bixby and Lou Ferrigno. Bixby, familiar to viewers from his roles in *My Favorite Martian* and *The Courtship of Eddie's Father*, portrayed the scientist David Banner (whose name was pointlessly altered from the original Bruce of the comic book series). Ferrigno, a bodybuilder and former Mr. Universe, took the role of Banner's ominous alter ego. He played the part wearing a wig, contact lenses, a fake nose, false teeth and green body makeup that in one episode was enthusiastically licked off by a trained bear.

Buscema, did a story for each major character, and this fill-in was used when the regular creators fell behind. Oddly enough, this insurance made the regular creators work faster: if the fill-in story was used, they lost income. This stockpile inventory system is still in place.

Brief Chief

Early in 1976, Marv Wolfman went to Stan Lee and resigned as editor-in-chief; he arranged a writer-editor contract and worked on various titles, from *Daredevil* to *Tomb of Dracula*. The problem of retaining an editor-in-chief had become acute. "We used to laugh about it," says Stan Lee. "We used to say, 'Don't paint his name on the door, just tack it up.'"

Gerry Conway, the creator of The Punisher, broke all records for moving in and out of the office. Most estimates place his time on the job at about a month. "I think it was March of 1976," he says. Conway, who believes he might have been editor-in-chief a few months sooner if he hadn't been on vacation when Stan Lee was faced with a previous vacancy, realized he didn't want the job as soon as he got it. "There was never an acknowledgment that no one person could edit fifty books," he says. "Marvel needed to have one person who had an overview capacity, and then needed individuals to have responsibility for the various books. But the person who acknowledged this need would, in effect, be acknowledging a lack of power, or that's how it was perceived."

Of course, the writer-editor idea took some of the pressure off the editor-in-chief, but it led to other problems, as James Galton soon noticed. "It turned out to be a nightmare," he says. "I felt captive to that situation, and I determined that as soon as those contracts ran out, I would not sign another one. Nobody was looking at what the writer was writing—it just got published. We needed more checks and balances."

The Next in Line

Archie Goodwin, who became Marvel's editor-in-chief in the spring of 1976, is widely recognized as one of the best writers in comics. "I was always unhappy that he was an editor because I wanted to get more writing out of him," says Stan Lee. "But he was a very good editor, and he was very good at working with the artists and writers. They got along well with him."

Goodwin first came to prominence as a writer and editor of horror stories for publisher James Warren's *Creepy* and *Eerie*. He worked with top freelancers like Gene Colan and Steve Ditko on these comics, and they got him interested in Marvel. By 1966 he was working on Iron Man with Colan. "My history in comics was always working for a couple of years at one place and moving around," says Goodwin, "so I think I was probably at Marvel a couple of times before I ever began to do editorial work there."

About his promotion to editor-in-chief, Goodwin says he was "next in line" for the job, repeating a phrase most of his predecessors have also used to describe themselves. By the time Goodwin got the job, cutbacks were becoming common, and the company was in a holding pattern rather than in an aggressively ambitious mode. "It was touch and go—we had to find a way to keep books going and keep people working," says Goodwin.

President James Galton's austerity program paid off, however. "Within a year, we were profitable," Galton says. Yet problems remained, and Goodwin was the first to acknowledge them. "The previous administration's policy," says Goodwin, "had been to add more comics when they needed more money. And Marvel hadn't really recovered from that. Plus, everything was structured as if we were still a small operation, the way it was when Stan was in charge. But you stick with the job because your ego gets involved—it was nice thinking you could follow in Stan Lee's footsteps."

Goodwin was also aware of problems with the writer-editor contracts, but could only mark time till they ran their course. "It was a two-edged sword because the writer-editors tended to be a law unto themselves. I was able to get along with most of them, but it was a strange situation."

Help from Hollywood

Marvel got a tremendous boost during this basically quiet period when it acquired the rights to adapt the movie *Star Wars* (1977). Directed by George Lucas, the space fantasy became the biggest money-maker in movie history, and Marvel fans noted that its villain looked very much like Stan Lee's and Jack Kirby's character, Dr. Doom. When the film took off, the six-issue Marvel adaptation followed suit. Second and third printings were called for, and Marvel's *Star Wars* became the first comic book since the Golden Age of the 1940s to sell over a million copies per issue.

"That really worked," says Archie Goodwin, "but I can't take any credit for it. Roy Thomas is the one who brought it to Marvel, and he had to push a little bit to get them to do it. He met with Lucas, and

© LUCASFILM LTD.

◄ The climax of the George Lucas hit film *Star Wars* (1977), adapted for Marvel by writer Roy Thomas and artist Howard Chaykin.

I guess their idea was to put out the comic book prior to the movie's opening to build some interest. Eventually, they made a deal that was incredibly favorable to Marvel, because Lucas really wanted to get the promotion going."

Roy Thomas wrote the six-issue adaptation, and Archie Goodwin took over the regular comic book series that followed: "The film helped create a new interest in comic books, and was very good for the business in general." It was also good for Goodwin, who was hired to do a *Star Wars* newspaper strip as well as the comic book, and was happy to leave his job as Marvel's editor-in-chief behind. "I got into comics because the last thing I ever wanted to be was an administrator," he says.

Archie Goodwin resigned in late 1977. The task of making controversial changes in Marvel's management of talent was left to "the next in line."

Roy Thomas, fourth editor of Marvel Comics.

Len Wein, fifth editor of Marvel Comics.

Marv Wolfman, sixth editor of Marvel Comics.

Gerry Conway, seventh editor of Marvel Comics.

Archie Goodwin, eighth editor of Marvel Comics.

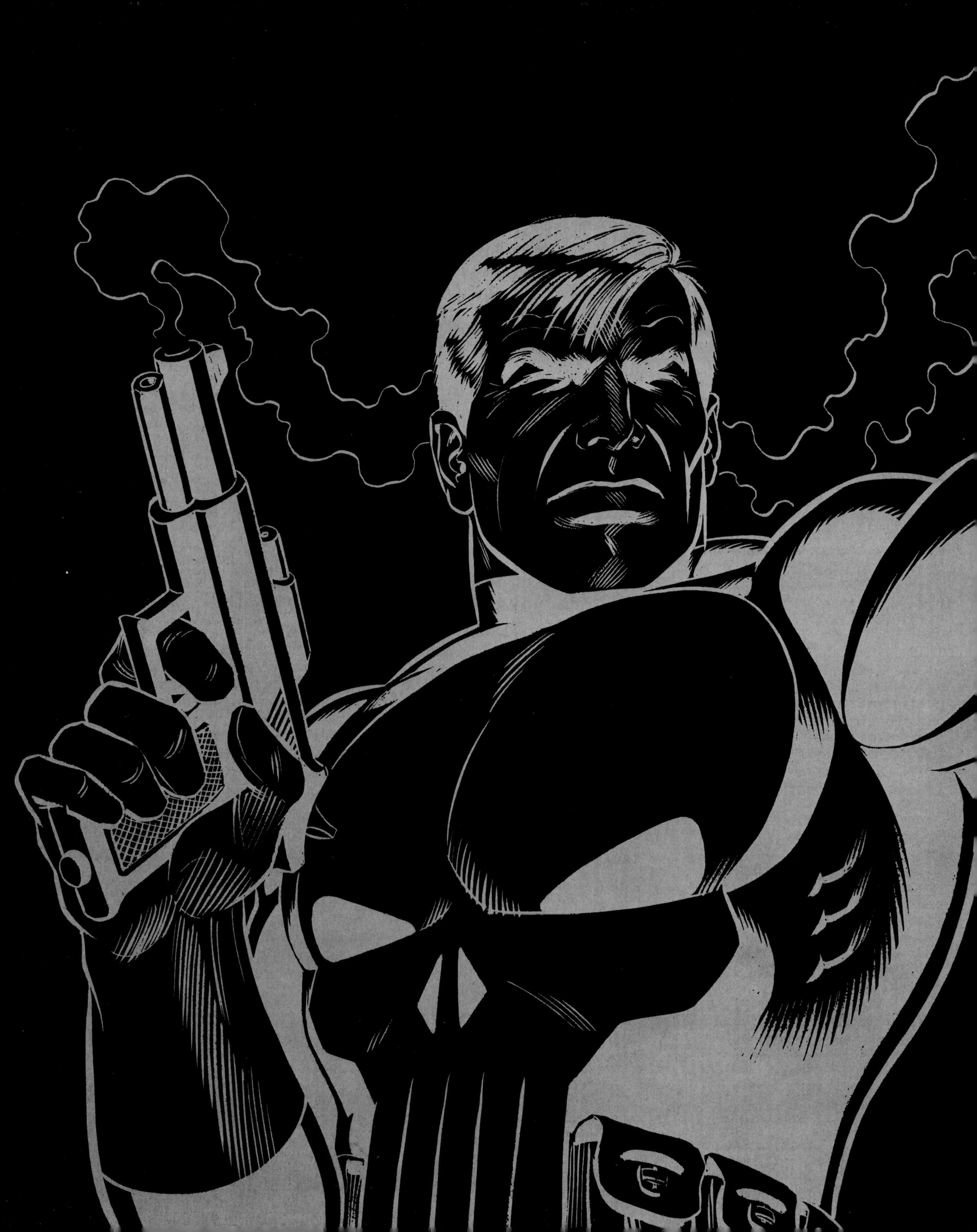

CHAPTER SIX

The Marvel Universe (1978–1990)

Marvel consolidates its gains, introduces
a new editorial system, and finds different publishing
formats and marketing strategies to reach the contemporary
breed of committed comic book collectors. Sensational
success continues as Marvel attracts the artists and writers
who can keep its heroes endlessly appealing.

▲ **Marvel comic books based on popular toys for boys came into vogue at the end of the decade:** *The Micronauts* **(January 1979),** *Shogun Warriors* **(February 1979) and** *Rom* **(December 1979).**

▶ **Stan Lee's poetic prose and Jack Kirby's startling images combine to create a memorable page from the pioneering graphic novel** *The Silver Surfer* **(1978).**

Today, Marvel has solidified its position as the preeminent publisher of American comic books, with sales greater than those of all its competitors combined. In recent years a series of astute business decisions has provided the company with a new staff structure, a new distribution system and the opportunity to experiment with new formats. The company also acquired its own animation company. During the same period, an infusion of new talent has kept the company's classic super heroes fresh while simultaneously adding a host of new characters to their ranks.

A significant factor in creating the Marvel of today was Jim Shooter, who became the company's editor-in-chief on the first working day of 1978. A dynamic, sometimes controversial figure, Shooter stayed on the job for close to a decade, the longest tenure as creative spearhead of the company since Stan Lee held the post.

The Boy Wonder

Even in a business where starting young is commonplace, Jim Shooter was a prodigy: he became a professional comic book writer at the age of fourteen. Born in 1951, Shooter made his decision to work in comics when he was only twelve years old. While in a Pittsburgh hospital recuperating from minor surgery, he read comics, and was particularly taken with *The Amazing Spider-Man* #2 and its unusually persuasive depiction of a super hero's personal problems. He devoured other Marvel comics in the children's ward, and discovered that the copies were worn and dirty. "Obviously," he says, "all the kids had been reading these and ignoring the other comic books. And that's when the opportunity to make money blossomed in my mind. If I could learn how to do comics like the good ones, I could sell them to the *other* guys. And it worked!

"I spent about a year trying to figure out how Marvel did it," Shooter recalls. "My family needed money, and when you're thirteen years old, what can you do? Nobody will give you a job." So he studied his Marvel comics, and early in 1966 he sold his first three Superboy stories to DC Comics. The feat brought him national publicity, and he continued to free-lance for DC from his home, but "I always felt that if I ever got good enough, I would want to go

to Marvel."

In 1969, at age eighteen, Shooter finally arranged a meeting with Stan Lee, who hired him on the spot as a staff writer. "We pretty much had the same point of view," says Shooter, "because I'd learned it from him." Shooter immediately moved to New York, but lasted only three weeks in his new environment. "I was only eighteen, I didn't have a lot of money, I couldn't find a place to stay—it just wasn't working out." Shooter returned to Pittsburgh and an advertising job, but in 1976, offers from both companies brought him back into the business, and he returned to Marvel as an associate editor.

Learning the Ropes

During his two-year stint as associate editor, Jim Shooter wrote *Daredevil*, *The Avengers* and *Ghost Rider*, but his principal task was supervising plots and scripts, and serving as second in com-

mand to a series of editors-in-chief: first Marv Wolfman, then Gerry Conway, and finally Archie Goodwin. While he read stories, Shooter analyzed the company's structure. His job was to relieve pressure on the editor-in-chief, but he saw one man after another walk away from the editorial position because of its impossible demands. He also noticed dissatisfaction among free-lance writers and artists.

Meanwhile, he studied with publisher Stan Lee. "Stan was like a creative director," Shooter says. "I'd sit down with him and we'd go over the comics. It was very educational, and he got to know me a little and saw that I knew what I was doing. So after Archie Goodwin decided to leave, Stan figured it was my turn. And my turn lasted for over nine years."

Shooter's first order of business as editor-in-chief was to confer with Marvel's president, James Galton. "I had a lot of ideas I wanted to try," says Shooter, and in Galton he found an executive who was open to change and was planning innovations of his own. It was the start of a new era.

The Medium and the Message

While plans were being made to move Marvel into uncharted territory, two of the company's greatest talents embarked on an experiment of their own—one that ultimately had considerable impact. After years apart, longtime collaborators Stan Lee and Jack Kirby got back together to produce a one-hundred-page Silver Surfer story. Published in 1978 by the firm of Simon & Schuster, *The Silver Surfer* was, in fact if not in name, Marvel's first "graphic novel"—an extended, full-color narrative, printed on quality paper and presented as a real book rather than as a flimsy pamphlet. Never before had an original adventure of a character from comic books appeared in such a prestigious format, but within a few years the idea began to catch on.

Networking

In search of new opportunities for Marvel, president James Galton realized "there were areas that were not being exploited. We began to talk to movie producers, television producers and animation companies." After The Hulk became a hit on television in 1977, a number of actors found themselves impersonating Marvel heroes in prime-time movies. Nicholas Hammond starred in *Spider-Man* in 1977, and a few sequels followed in 1978. *Dr. Strange* arrived in 1978 with Peter Hooten in the title role. Finally, Reb Brown portrayed Captain America in two 1979 television films. None of these productions led to a regular series, but each succeeded in bringing Marvel characters to an audience of millions.

The show that started Marvel in a whole new direction was a new animated version of *The*

Fantastic Four that began on NBC in 1978. The scripts were written by top writers, including Stan Lee and Roy Thomas. The Human Torch was replaced with a cute little robot named Herbie because rights to the Torch were tied up for a possible movie project. "I was not happy with the robot," says Stan Lee, "but there seemed to be no other solution."

The 1978 *Fantastic Four* was produced by DePatie-Freleng Enterprises, an expert animation studio that had been responsible for The Pink Panther and many of the cartoons in the Looney Tunes series. Stan Lee began commuting between New York and California to work on the show and to promote other Marvel characters for films and television. All this activity gave president James Galton an idea: "Why don't we try to become an animation company? Instead of selling the rights to the characters, we could deal with the networks ourselves. I sent Stan out to the West Coast for a year to represent us. And then DePatie-Freleng decided to close their studio."

It was a perfect opportunity for Marvel to snap up David DePatie, who became president of the newly formed Marvel Productions Ltd. in 1980, with Stan Lee serving as vice president in charge of creative affairs. Lee has stayed in California, devoting his time to film and television projects and writing the Spider-Man newspaper strip.

Operating with a License

Even as Marvel's characters were being adapted for other media, Marvel began taking concepts from other companies and turning them into comic books. The *Star Wars* comic had been a tremendous success since its inception in 1977, so when *Battlestar Galactica*, a television series imitating *Star Wars*, was aired in 1979, it also became a Marvel title. And when the old television series *Star Trek* was reincarnated as a feature film in 1979, Marvel was right behind it with a *Star Trek* comic book in 1980. The process of employing established characters or properties is known as "licensing," and while few of the licensed titles were long-range successes, they did serve the purpose of providing short-term revenues and attracting new readers to Marvel.

▲ Actor Nicholas Hammond (or a stuntman) dons a familiar red-and-blue costume for the made-for-television movie *Spider-Man* (1977).

James Galton, Marvel's president from 1975 to 1990, oversaw the growth of the company through years of change.

Spinning Off

Perhaps the most unusual result of media cross-pollination was the idea, conceived by television executives, of creating female versions of the Marvel characters who were now becoming network stars. To protect the copyrights on these characters, Marvel was obliged to get them into print first. Thus Spider-Woman and She-Hulk were born.

The first issue of *Spider-Woman* (April 1978) was written by Marv Wolfman and drawn by Carmine Infantino, but the character had appeared earlier in a story by writer Archie Goodwin and artist Sal Buscema. Efforts were made to keep her distinguishable from Spider-Man: she had different powers, which resulted not from an accidental spider bite but from her father's scientific experiments. (Art seemed to be imitating life here, as Wolfman named the character, Jessica Drew, after his own daughter.) *Spider-Woman* lasted only five years in print, but fulfilled her original purpose

when her animated Saturday-morning television show made its debut on ABC in 1979.

She-Hulk was a different story. Her planned network appearance fell through, but the first issue of *The Savage She-Hulk* (February 1980) enjoyed tremendous sales, in large part because Stan Lee wrote it. She-Hulk was the first character the old master had created in years.

Jennifer Walters was the cousin of Bruce Banner (The Hulk's alter ego). She acquired her powers when Banner gave her an emergency blood transfusion, although the comparatively weak dose of gamma radiation she received enabled her to retain her own personality even in the Hulkish state. Lee's Hollywood commitments soon obliged him to leave the lovely She-Hulk in the lurch, and her original comic book lasted only twenty-five issues. Ultimately, the character endured and even prospered: She-Hulk became a prominent member of The Avengers, and even joined The Fantastic Four during one of that team's frequent fallings out. Writers and artists seemed to have a special fondness for the big, beautiful, bright green heroine, and her finest hour lay ahead.

Book Maker

Publisher Stan Lee was busy establishing a beachhead for Marvel on the West Coast, so Michael Z. Hobson was brought into the company in 1980 as vice president in charge of publishing. "They needed somebody to run the comic book operation," says Hobson, "because Stan was busy in a lot of other areas and wasn't able to do it himself on a day-to-day basis." Like president James Galton, Hobson had a background in books rather than comics. "I had been in children's publishing, with Scholastic's book clubs," says Hobson, "and I had no comic book experience at that point. But I had been a big comic book fan as a kid in the 1940s, and I remembered The Sub-Mariner, Captain America and The Red Skull very well." As it turned out, a different background was quite appropriate, as Marvel moved into a new decade that brought substantial changes to the industry. The company even experimented briefly with a line called Marvel Books, which published children's storybooks, coloring books and activity books. Featuring both Marvel characters and other licensed characters, these books were sold in toy stores, drugstores and supermarkets. Along with Galton and editor-in-chief Jim Shooter, Hobson was to be actively involved as Marvel created new formats, sought new markets, and worked to change its relationship with the free-lance talent.

Taking Care of Business

Unlike several of his predecessors, Jim Shooter took an active interest in the business side of Marvel, and he proposed several financial changes that he believed would be beneficial to the com-

MARVEL ANIMATES ITSELF

When Marvel Productions Ltd. was created in 1980, its primary goal was to produce animated versions of its parent company's characters. Success came almost immediately: *Spider-Man and His Amazing Friends* became a top-rated show on the NBC Saturday-morning lineup in September 1981, and it was soon joined by a cartoon version of *The Incredible Hulk*. Both programs were narrated by Stan Lee.

The studio quickly acquired a reputation for quality work in the field, with the somewhat ironic result that other companies and their characters soon came to dominate the company's schedule. Marvel Productions animated such successful syndicated shows as *Transformers*, *My Little Pony* and *G. I. Joe*, and for CBS did the popular *Dungeons and Dragons*, as well as the Emmy Award–winning *Muppet Babies*. Even the anthology program called *Marvel Action Universe*, which featured several cartoons, was most notable for its adaptation of the 1987 movie *RoboCop*. Marvel Productions has done extremely well with many different kinds of material; clearly the project of animating Marvel's heroes is no longer its only priority.

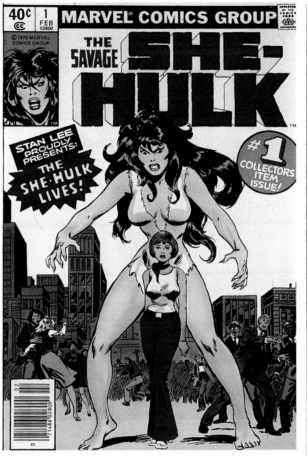

◀ Like Eve, who sprang from Adam's rib, these female characters were spin-offs from their male counterparts. The *Spider-Woman* #1 (April 1978) cover is by Joe Sinnott from John Romita's sketch; *The Savage She-Hulk* #1 (February 1980) cover is by John Buscema.

pany and its employees. He was concerned about conditions for artists and writers, and he was convinced that making some changes would ultimately increase sales.

As James Galton recalls it, "Jim Shooter felt it was very important that Marvel change its traditional way of handling talent, which was to pay on a flat page-rate basis, with no share of possible profits from sales." Shooter believed that better comics and bigger sales would result if talent shared in the success of a popular product. "Since I had come out of the book publishing industry," says Galton, "I was certainly conversant with other ways to compensate creative people. So when Jim suggested a new system, it seemed logical."

The difficulty lay in trying to come up with a plan that would give everyone an even break, since an artist working on a popular character like Spider-Man would obviously have an advantage over somebody drawing a newer character or an old one that needed a boost. "We went through a long and complicated exercise," says Shooter, "to try and work out some kind of system that would reward both talent and performance.

"The first thing I wanted to do was get the rates up," says Shooter. "We actually doubled the page rates, and then doubled them again. We also made sure everybody had medical insurance coverage. And I established an incentive program that rewarded the talent for staying with a series, which helped avoid continuity problems." All of this

involved a considerable outlay for Marvel, but it also had a positive effect on freelancers. Sales and profits continued to rise.

An Epic Undertaking

Epic Illustrated, which made its debut in the spring of 1980, was the last major project set in motion before publisher Stan Lee left New York. "It was something I always wanted to do," says Lee. "I always felt we should have a classier magazine." Oversize, with full-color artwork printed on glossy paper, *Epic Illustrated* was Marvel's most luxurious publication to date; it sold for two dollars at a time when an ordinary comic book cost fifty cents. A more serious attempt to reach older readers than the generally disappointing black-and-white magazines of a few years earlier, *Epic Illustrated* was billed as "adult fantasy and science fiction."

"*Epic Illustrated* was the first publication for which we bought rights, as opposed to work-for-hire," recalls Jim Shooter. In essence, this meant that artists retained the copyright to their work, selling Marvel only the right to publish it. This approach attracted work by a number of independent-minded artists like Jim Starlin, who had worked for Marvel in the 1970s, and Wendy Pini, whose self-published series *Elfquest* had an enthusiastic following. Although it was an artistic success for six years, the magazine never met

Michael Z. Hobson, vice president in charge of publishing, supervises Marvel's entire roster of publications.

▶ The glossy and expensive *Epic Illustrated,* which published creator-copyrighted comics, made its debut in 1980. Covers by Frank Frazetta (left) and Richard Corben (right).

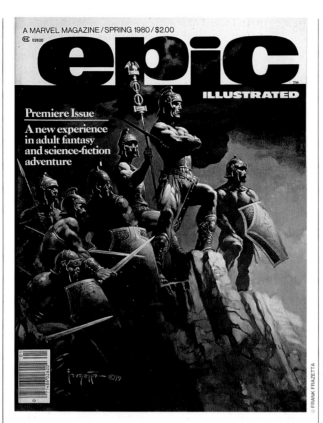

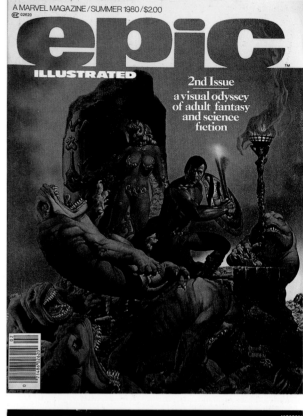

Marvel's expectations at the newsstand; it was expensive for kids and never overcame the American adult's resistance to comics.

The editor of *Epic Illustrated* was former Marvel editor-in-chief Archie Goodwin. His professionalism and rapport with artists eventually made the magazine the cornerstone of a whole new line of comics for Marvel. For the present, the mere fact that he was an editor, appointed to take some of the load off the editor-in-chief, signaled a change in company structure.

Sharing the Load

"Jim Shooter was terrific," recalls James Galton. "He gave the company a discipline it had not had before, and things just started clicking along very nicely. During the period when he was editor-in-chief, we expanded not only the number of publications, but the editorial staff as well."

Several of Shooter's predecessors had realized that Marvel was publishing more than any one person could edit, but they had responded to the problem by resigning. They were really only interested in the creative end of comics, not in making suggestions for restructuring the company. Shooter brought in Roger Stern and Bob Hall to serve under him as editors; along with Archie Goodwin, they constituted the core of the new editorial staff. "That was the beginning of it," says Shooter. "As we added more titles, we eventually had to add more editors." Ultimately, assistant editors were hired as well. Marvel, which Stan Lee had once supervised almost single-handedly, had become a very big business.

The new editorial system was not welcomed by

The cover of *King Conan* #1 (March 1980) was penciled by John Buscema and inked by Ernie Chan. Buscema, who has worked on just about every Marvel character, reports that he enjoys drawing Conan most.

Phoenix gets tough, even with the logo. Pencils: John Byrne. Inks: Terry Austin.

everyone, especially those creators who were accustomed to a lot of autonomy. A case in point was Roy Thomas, who was serving as writer-editor on several books, including *Conan the Barbarian*. When Thomas' contract came up for renewal in 1980 at the same time that the new *King Conan* book was launched, he and Shooter were unable to agree on terms regarding the degree of supervision required. Thomas left for DC Comics, and six years passed

before he returned to Marvel.

In the Dark

In 1980, The X-Men became involved in a long, multi-issue story sequence that became known to fans as the Dark Phoenix saga. One of the most complex, spectacular and emotional stories ever attempted in super hero comics, it evoked a tremendous response from the readers. At the same time, it became a test case for the editorial system that Marvel had put in place. "A lot of creative people were involved," says Jim Salicrup, who had recently become the editor of *The X-Men*, "each one contributing his interpretation of the story."

"Phoenix" was a new name for Jean Grey, the member of The X-Men known as Marvel Girl when she was first introduced in 1963. She had become Phoenix in 1976, when her identity merged with an incalculably powerful alien force so awesome that the fate of the universe was in her grasp. By 1980, Phoenix was raging out of control, and had become a megalomaniac with brief periods of lucidity. The story built to a crisis that was scheduled to be resolved in *The X-Men* #137, a special double-length issue for September 1980. The preparation of this issue created another sort of crisis at Marvel, one that was only resolved after much struggle and soul-searching.

Chris Claremont had been writing *The X-Men* for five years, and his interest in strong, complex female characters had come to fruition in the Dark Phoenix stories. His partner on the series since the end of 1977 had been John Byrne, whose subtle and polished penciling was attracting considerable attention. Sales were inching up. "By the time the Dark Phoenix saga drew to its climax," Claremont says, "we were defining the state of the art."

North Star

Born in England in 1950, John Byrne was raised in Canada, where he continued to live while work-

▲ Penciler John Byrne and inker Terry Austin depict Wolverine in action (above) and Cyclops in anguish (below) on two 1980 covers from the Dark Phoenix saga.

◄ On a whim, penciler John Byrne drew this single panel showing the destruction of a distant planet. As a result, The X-Men were transformed. Script: Chris Claremont. Inks: Terry Austin.

▶ **In the original, unpublished ending to the Dark Phoenix saga, shown penciled, scripted and lettered, Jean Grey was to have been drained of her overwhelming powers by an alien force. After much soul-searching, Marvel published another version (far right), in which she paid for her crimes with her life. Script: Chris Claremont. Pencils: John Byrne. Inks: Terry Austin.**

ing on *The X-Men*. "When I was a kid it was my favorite Marvel book," he says. Like many artists working in The Marvel Method, Byrne gradually started to contribute to plots. He and Claremont clashed at times, he admits, but "what came out was more than we both put in. There was tremendous enthusiasm on both sides, and we used to run up some phenomenal phone bills."

Byrne's influence brought the dangerous, enigmatic mutant Wolverine into greater prominence. "Chris had reached the point where he was about ready to write Wolverine out of the book, and I just sort of wrapped myself in the flag and said, 'No way do you get rid of the only Canadian character!' I had to make him interesting to Chris, so I pulled out all the stops." Byrne also created the youngest of The X-Men: Kitty Pryde, a thirteen-year-old with the power to pass through solid objects.

Byrne, who asserts that "fun" is the key word in comics, was never as serious about Phoenix as the more intense Claremont. In a burst of enthusiasm, Byrne drew a scene that was not in the agreed-upon plot: Phoenix went on a rampage and wiped out an entire inhabited world. "I went too far," he says, with more glee than remorse. "I had her cook the planet of the asparagus people."

Dark Victory

When editor-in-chief Jim Shooter saw that Jean Grey, one of The X-Men, had in effect become a

mass murderer, he told editor Jim Salicrup that "there had to be moral consequences." A Marvel hero could not kill with impunity. Shooter was unhappy with the upcoming issue that had already been drawn, in which an interplanetary tribunal scientifically exorcised the Dark Phoenix side of Jean's personality, and sent her safely home.

Shooter, Claremont and Byrne discussed the issue with Louise Jones, a new editor already assigned to relieve the busy Salicrup on *X-Men*. To satisfy Shooter's conviction that Jean Grey's cosmic crime could not logically be overlooked, various endings were suggested, but most were too complicated or unconvincing. An imminent deadline made a quick decision mandatory. When *The X-Men* #137 appeared, one of the most beloved characters in The Marvel Universe was dead. Phoenix had short-circuited her destructive tendencies by destroying herself.

The controversial story created a sensation, and *The X-Men* became the comic book to watch. Shooter, who maintains that he did not insist on a death sentence, notes that "if we had planned it that way, it would have been a brilliant strategy. It catapulted *The X-Men* to the top of the business."

Chris Claremont, who initially experienced some bitterness about the change in his story, now says, "I think Jim Shooter justified his salary with that one. It was brilliant." *The X-Men* became the book where anything might happen and, as Claremont proudly notes today, "*The X-Men* has been number one in the business, give or take an odd issue, for easily the last ten years."

Direct to the Top

While Marvel was creating the country's best-selling comic book, it was also discovering a new way to market its line. The idea was direct sales, and it revolutionized the industry.

The direct sales system started when a comic book fan and entrepreneur named Phil Seuling saw an opportunity in the growing market for rare back issues of old comic books. Several antique comics dealers were doing so well that they had opened retail shops, and Seuling realized that they could sell their customers new comics as well. He set up as a distributor, and approached publishers with the idea of servicing the comic book shops.

Ed Shukin was Marvel's vice president of sales from 1974 to 1985. "When direct sales started, the newsstand business was in the doldrums," he says. "Newsstands simply didn't know how to market comics, and returns of unsold books were high. Around 1976, I opened up direct sales to people who cared about the product and made it their principal business."

Direct sales started small, but represented a minimal risk for Marvel since the comic book shops were not allowed to return unsold copies. The distributor bought the books outright, and so, in turn, did the retailers. In exchange for this, Marvel offered a better discount.

"We just watched it grow," Shukin says. "Of course, we also had the right product. There were years when we doubled our business."

The direct sales market gradually turned into a giant. Phil Seuling had hoped to be sole distributor to the countless comics shops springing up around the country, but publishers ultimately did not grant him this exclusivity and some bitterness resulted. Yet Seuling certainly made his mark on comics. "He was a pioneer in our field," says Shukin. "The industry owes him a lot."

Between 1981 and 1982 the direct market had become the source for approximately half of Marvel's sales, and it was still expanding. Nonetheless, Ed Shukin says, "the best decision of my entire career at Marvel was hiring Carol Kalish. She was just an enormous enthusiast who also had a sense of business management. She understood the product and understood the people." Kalish started out as an assistant, advanced to direct sales manager, and today is vice president of new product development.

Kalish believes that direct sales have become the bulwark of the business because the specialty stores are catering to a discriminating clientele. "The direct market retailers are our best salespersons," she says. "There's no reason for someone to go into the business unless they really know and like comics. Going to a comic book store is like going to a private club. Friendships start among

the customers, and marriages have even occurred."

Editor-in-chief Jim Shooter took note of the phenomenon when he was first appointed, and says that eventually "the direct market started to influence publishing decisions. We even tried printing something for these stores exclusively. We offered *Dazzler* #1 (March 1981) direct to comic book stores only, and sold 428,000 copies."

Before long, several titles were being published exclusively for the direct market. *Moon Knight*, launched in November 1980, featured a mysterious nocturnal character created by writer Doug Moench. Although the book was popular enough to have a cult following, newsstand sales were weak. Offered at a slightly higher price for direct sales only, the title gained a new lease on life. Soon a wide range of innovative characters and formats were being offered to the new market of comic book shops and, meanwhile, many of Marvel's classic heroes were undergoing renovations of their own.

Mr. Fixit

In 1981 artist John Byrne left *The X-Men* to take on *The Fantastic Four*. "To me, *The Fantastic Four* is the cornerstone of The Marvel Universe," says Byrne, "and I felt the book had wandered away from the things that had made it special when I was a kid. That was really the first time 'Mr. Fixit' was born in me." To achieve his objective, Byrne decided to write the series as well as pencil and ink it, adopting the old one-man-band approach.

Byrne's approach worked, and it was a harbinger of things to come: throughout the 1980s popular artists turned into writer-artists and dedicated themselves to reaffirming the appeal of Marvel's classic characters. In the process, the writer-

Dazzler #1 (March 1981) presented a mutant who was a pop singer. Cover: Bob Larkin.

▼ *Moon Knight* #1 (November 1980) featured a hero who got his power from moonlight. Cover: Bill Sienkiewicz. For later issues, Sienkiewicz drew a striking series of black-and-white covers.

John Byrne was writer-artist of *The Fantastic Four* for its twentieth anniversary issue (November 1981).

John Byrne's cover for *Fantastic Four* #264 (March 1984) paid tribute to Jack Kirby's classic cover for *Fantastic Four* #1.

Canadian John Byrne portrayed a team of Canadian heroes, including the big beast Sasquatch, in *Alpha Flight* #1 (August 1983).

Writer-artist John Byrne has specialized in breathing new life into old characters.

Writer-artist Frank Miller shows readers the shadowy, sinister side of a super hero's life.

artists became superstars, capable of boosting the sales of whatever hero they worked on. The talent began to receive the kind of adulation once reserved for costumed characters.

Although Byrne's specialty is breathing new life into old formulas (he was even hired to revamp Superman for that DC character's fiftieth anniversary), he did create one series of his own: *Alpha Flight*. The first issue appeared in August 1983, and in it Byrne brought back a group of Canadian heroes who were originally invented as guest stars for an issue of *The X-Men*. *Alpha Flight* was a solid success that is still running. Byrne, however, dropped the book after two years. "For the most part," he admits, "I prefer to play with the toys that are already there."

Giving the Devil His Due

Few people have had more of an impact on the course that current comic books have taken than Frank Miller, who began drawing *Daredevil* in 1979, and took on the writing as well in 1981. Almost immediately, he began to attract attention with his terse tales of urban crime. Marvel had already made its editorial mark by showing the problems encountered by individuals who were unexpectedly gifted with bizarre powers, but Miller went a step further by probing the slightly mad motives that might cause a less obviously qualified citizen to choose a career as a vigilante. "It's not a normal pursuit for a human being to follow," he

says. "In the case of Daredevil, you've got a blind character whose passions are so deep that he takes ridiculous chances."

To make his point, Miller needed "a relatively grounded story line, considering that comics are about men in tights punching each other out." It was easy for Miller to cut back on fantasy since Daredevil's only improbable power was his heightened sensory awareness. He fought thugs and gangsters, not aliens or mad scientists, and his most implacable foe was the obese urban crime lord called The Kingpin. His most memorable opponent, however, was the female assassin known as Elektra.

The Cartoonist

At a time when many artists rendered myriad tiny details, and many writers filled each page with verbose prose, Frank Miller employed a stripped-down style. He intended to "work in such a way that every line told as much of the story as possible, in both the drawing and the writing. I wanted to use a style where the reader had to do a great deal of the work, where a pair of squiggles and a black shadow became an expressive face in the reader's mind." Some admirers have called his style "expressionism," but Miller finds that "a little lofty. The term I really like to use is 'cartoon.' It's a language in line; that's what my eye wants to see."

Although Miller has a reputation as a comic book auteur, he is quick to note that "in every case it's been collaborative." His drawings were embellished, inked and colored by Klaus Janson. "We were very much in tune," Miller says, "and the feel and look of it was very bold and very graphic." More recently, Miller has chosen to concentrate on writing, often collaborating with artists David Mazzucchelli and Bill Sienkiewicz, but he has not totally abandoned his drawing board.

After years of honing his craft on Marvel characters, Miller took the opportunity to work on DC's Batman, redefining him as the bitter, brooding "Dark Knight" in 1986. This version stirred up a storm, and paved the way for an immensely successful Batman movie in 1989, but Miller has returned to Marvel to do a Daredevil project again: "He's actually, of the two characters, the one that I enjoy writing more."

A Limited Success

Wolverine, perhaps the single most popular member of the mutant group X-Men, began to come into his own as a solo character in 1982, when artist Frank Miller and writer Chris Claremont joined forces to turn him loose. The setting for the story was Japan, where Wolverine was forced to judge himself and his actions against the samurai code of honor. "Until then, everybody had thought of him as a berserk killer," Claremont explains, "and what we did was reveal the man inside."

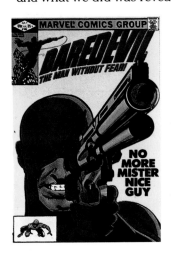

"Chris and I had a lot of fun working together," says Miller. "I was the guy who did the flying ninjas and the big fight scenes, and he brought the other, more literary values to it." The four-issue series was extremely popular, and it established the character with the built-in retractable claws as a presence independent of his group.

The limited series was a new concept made possible by the direct market and its faithful fan customers. Top talent could take time out for an unusual project when there was an end in sight, and, as Jim Shooter notes, "it was a good way to set special things apart. It was also a good way of testing." In the case of Wolverine, the limited series was a stop on the way to a successful solo series.

Sharing the Wealth

In 1982, Marvel initiated an incentive program that offered additional compensation to artists and writers based on the sales of their work. "Frankly,"

says vice president Michael Hobson, "we started it because DC started a program, but ours cost us a lot more money. Jim Shooter had always wanted to have the creators share in a book's success, and he has to be given a lot of credit for it."

Basically, the incentive plan means that the talent receives a share of revenues after sales pass the 100,000 copy mark, the point at which a comic book is considered to be enjoying good sales. "Almost none of DC's books qualified for the royalties," says Shooter, "but when Marvel did the same thing, almost every title qualified. It cost Marvel hundreds of thousands of dollars, but it didn't matter because we kept the good people we had, we attracted other good people, and the plan paid for

Frank Miller's version of Daredevil debates vigilante tactics with the less-scrupulous Punisher (above) in *Daredevil* #183 (June 1982). By the next issue (left), the blind hero was rethinking his priorities. Script and pencils: Frank Miller. Inks: Klaus Janson.

Elektra practices entrapment, meditates before battle and transcends mortality. Pencils: Frank Miller. Inks: Klaus Janson.

THE VILLAIN TO BEAT: ELEKTRA

"Elektra came into existence simply because I wanted Daredevil to have a femme fatale," says Frank Miller, and the character he came up with is one of Marvel's most fascinating villains. Elektra, daughter of an ambassador who was slain during a terrorist attack, was so embittered by the experience that she turned to a life of senseless crime. After extensive training in the martial arts, she returned to New York as a paid killer, unaware that the young man she had loved in more innocent days had since become Daredevil. Their subsequent clash seemed inevitable.

"The idea of the old girlfriend gone bad," says Miller, "was a lot different from what was coming out at the time." In fact, the idea went beyond the particulars of the plot and perhaps symbolized the battle of the sexes, which was in a particularly confrontational phase during the early 1980s. Elektra may have been an emblem of the independent modern woman, or perhaps she was a projection of male suspicion and hos-

tility. In any case, the deck was stacked against her—after all, she was a guest in Daredevil's comic book. Ultimately, she was killed by another criminal and died in her blind lover's arms.

Good bad guys are too valuable to toss away, however, and before long, Elektra was revived. Miller brought her back, working with artist Lynn Varley, in the best-selling graphic novel *Elektra Lives Again* (1990). He may have had no choice in the matter. "When I talk about Elektra," he confesses, "I tend to talk about things she demands and things she insists on. She's generally in control of the stories I write about her."

itself quickly."

For the people creating Marvel's most popular characters, the plan created incomes that previous generations in the business had only dreamed about. "It went a long way," says James Galton, "toward changing the attitudes of the artists and writers toward us as publishers. I like to think that they really believe we treat them fairly."

Comics for Creators

Marvel came up with yet another way to keep its talent happy when it launched Epic Comics, a spin-off of *Epic Illustrated* magazine. Archie Goodwin, the editor of the magazine, was put in charge of the new line; like its namesake, it would publish mature material on which the creator retained the copyright. "Archie really made Epic happen as far as I'm concerned," says Jim Shooter. "He knows his way around the comic book world and I was glad to have him there."

Goodwin realized that Epic Comics, a separate branch of Marvel, provided an opportunity to "find ways of doing offbeat material. The only place new things can come from is the creators, and unless you have

His first solo series. Pencils: Frank Miller. Inks: Josef Rubinstein.

deals that interest them, they're going to take their stuff elsewhere." In fact, it was a writer-artist, Jim Starlin, who provided much of the impetus for the new line. "He was very keen on doing more with some of the characters he had done for *Epic Illustrated*," Goodwin says. "So Starlin, Jim Shooter and Mike Hobson developed a model creator's contract, and out of that came *Dreadstar* (November 1982), the first Epic comic."

The earliest Epic comics were essentially variations on the super hero theme, but during Goodwin's Epic years (1982-90), a separate identity developed. One exceptionally entertaining series is Sergio Aragonés' *Groo the Wanderer*, which began its Epic run in March 1985. Groo is a dim-witted barbarian with a penchant for mindless violence and a lust for cheese dip, and the series parodies the sword and sorcery genre while returning the medium to its "comic" roots. Groo's exploits have been consistently hilarious, thanks in part to the writer-artist's dialogue assistant, Mark Evanier. "It's incredible," says Goodwin. "A funny comic book! What a concept!"

The Epic Style

Probably the greatest contribution of Epic Comics was to provide the opportunity for artists to experiment with nontraditional styles. Using glossy

WOLVERINE

In essence, Wolverine fits the pattern of the archetypal hero who appears out of nowhere, performs deeds nobody else would dare attempt, and yet by the very nature of those deeds is denied total integration into the community he serves. Outwardly, this small man is cocky, pushy and quarrelsome, but inwardly he is troubled by the rages that sometimes drive him to kill enemies without compunction. Yet as he learns to control his fury, he runs the risk that his ability to fight fiercely will be impaired; becoming fully human might cost him his life. He must walk forever on a razor's edge, and when all is said and done, he knows he must walk alone.

Wolverine is the mutant who walks alone. Marvel's mutants, the most popular comic book characters of the 1980s, tended to cluster together in groups; so far only Wolverine has broken out to carve a solo career for himself. Writer Len Wein and art director John Romita introduced him on his own in 1974, but he was almost immediately recruited to join The X-Men. Even as part of that team, however, his aggressive yet puzzling personality set him apart from the others, and eventually he was unleashed in his own series.

Wolverine's first costume, which he wore when he was the Canadian government's "Weapon X."

Wolverine's most visible attribute is a set of long, unbreakable metal claws. These dangerous weapons suggest that Wolverine is an expert at inflicting injuries, but in fact his special mutant ability is the power to endure unimaginable agony. Although he is gifted with a modified form of invulnerability, he doesn't have a tough hide: he can be hurt, and frequently is, but he heals with incredible speed. It was his innate capacity for tolerating pain that allowed an unidentified individual to implant the claws and a reinforced skeleton into Wolverine's body. The enormous shock of this strange and grotesque surgical procedure, which seems to have been designed to turn Wolverine into a living, breathing, walking weapon, was evidently strong enough to drive him temporarily out of his mind, and he was discovered living like an animal in a Canadian forest. Wolverine answers to the name of Logan, but beyond that nothing of his past is known.

▶ **The dreamlike atmosphere of *Moonshadow*, a limited series with painted panels, published by Epic from 1985 through 1987. Script: J. M. DeMatteis. Art: Jon J Muth.**

paper and costly photographic color separations, "Epic found a way to do successful painted comics," Goodwin says. "I thought it was wonderful that Marvel took a gamble on this."

Because painting a comic book page is so time-consuming, the limited series was an ideal format for *Moonshadow*, written by J. M. DeMatteis and illustrated by Jon J Muth. This wry yet delicate fantasy about an extraordinary child received glowing reviews from critics who ordinarily would not have looked at a comic book. "Artistically, I think *Moonshadow* is one of the best things that came out of Epic," says Goodwin.

Ironically, but perhaps inevitably, Epic's biggest sellers featured sophisticated versions of characters who were already familiar to Marvel fans. Frank Miller and Bill Sienkiewicz brought back one of the era's most popular villains in *Elektra: Assassin* (1986), an eight-issue series of savage political satire mixed with psychodrama.

"If we packaged a book right, so that it was worth a higher price, we didn't have to sell *X-Men* numbers in order to have a success," says Archie Goodwin. Nevertheless, Epic's most popular series featured two of Marvel's major mutants: *Havok and Wolverine* (1989). The script was by the husband-and-wife team Walter and Louise Simonson, with different painters handling Havok (Jon J Muth) and Wolverine (Kent Williams). The impetus for the project came from the artists, and the final result "was very much the four of us mixing the pot together," says Walter Simonson.

Dreadstar #1 (November 1982) was the first Epic Comics publication. Cover: Jim Starlin.

Coyote #1 (April 1983), the second Epic title. Script: Steve Englehart. Art: Steve Leialoha.

A Novel Approach

In 1982, the same year that Epic Comics started, Marvel published its first graphic novel, *The Death of Captain Marvel* by Jim Starlin. The same writer-artist who had jump-started Epic got the new graphic novel format off to a fine start, racking up one hundred thousand sales of a quality paperback book that cost $5.95. In fact, Jim Shooter was convinced that it would have made the national best-seller lists if comic book shops had been included in the best-seller list surveys.

Following in its wake have come dozens of graphic novels—oversize square-bound paperback books printed on slick paper—featuring the adventures of characters both old and new. Other paperback books are collections of all the issues from various limited series, or are reprints of noteworthy story sequences from the regular comic books. Recently, hardcover editions have become increasingly commonplace. Altogether, these more expensive formats now generate roughly twenty percent of Marvel's revenues, and have provided the medium with the prestige and dignity that ordinary comic books never enjoyed.

Michael Hobson has been responsible for approving new ways to present comics to the public, and acknowledges that the direct market made them possible: "I think that Marvel did more than anyone to make the direct market work, and the growth of that market has changed the business entirely. Without it, we wouldn't be publishing all these new formats." Even so, Hobson continues working to establish new outlets.

Recently, Marvel began placing its paperback and hardcover books in mainstream bookstores, and both the B. Dalton and Waldenbooks chains now sell the regular comic books. "Our biggest challenge in the future is to establish a mass market," Hobson says. "When you pick up your first comic book, you aren't going to have to go to a specialty store to get it."

Not To Be Toyed With

One of Marvel's biggest mass market successes came from out of the blue with *G. I. Joe* (June 1982). Hasbro, one of the largest toy companies in the country, was preparing to reintroduce its popular character G. I. Joe, and wanted a whole series of action figures to accompany him. "Hasbro's advertising agency approached us," says Michael Hobson, "with the idea for a three-pronged campaign that included the toys, an animated television show and a comic book. So we had our comic book advertised on national television and it really sold comics." A Marvel team, led by writer-artist Larry Hama, designed new characters, and even contributed the first and still major group of G.I. Joe villains, Cobra Command. In exchange, Marvel got one of its top sellers of the era, and in venues outside the direct sales market, *G.I. Joe* proved to be the most popular Marvel title of all.

Mutant Mania

Overall, nothing outsold *The X-Men*, and Jim Shooter believes the reason was writer Chris Claremont. "Chris has a couple of things he does extremely well," says Shooter. "He always makes you feel something important is going on: he puts the fate of the universe at stake. He also does some very nice little human things with the mutants. But the other important thing he does is care about the overall book—more than any other writer or artist. He does everything he can on every front, not just the writing, to make it good."

At a time when many writers and artists stuck with a title for only a year or two, Claremont has been a bulwark. "*The X-Men* has had consistently good art ever since Chris started working on it, and that's not an accident," says Shooter. "It's because Chris went out there and recruited." In the years since John Byrne moved on, *X-Men* artists have included Paul Smith, John Romita, Jr., Art Adams, Marc Silvestri and Jim Lee. Each has brought a different look to the book, and a new set of adjustments for Claremont to make. "It's a pain in the ass," Claremont says, "but in a way it's useful, especially in my case, because after fifteen years there is a tendency to take things for granted. Someone coming in with a fresh eye challenges my perceptions, my assumptions. Out of that I may come up with something completely different. Some pencilers are more comfortable with space opera than family drama. Others are more comfortable with classic super hero punch-outs. We have to find what works. No matter how much time passes, the series continues to renew itself."

The buffoonish barbarian Groo, created by Sergio Aragonés, allows the artist to mock both traditional comic book conflict and the brainless brutality that is an apparently inevitable component of the human condition. Panels from *Groo the Wanderer* #55 (September 1989).

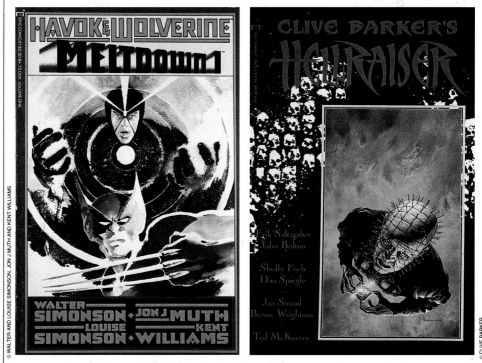

Havok and Wolverine (1989) presented *X-Men* characters in a new light and proved to be Epic's best-selling series. Cover: Jon J Muth and Kent Williams. *Hellraiser* #1 (1989) inaugurated a horror comic inspired by the stories of British writer Clive Barker. Cover: John Bolton.

at Marvel, handling the Conan books and *Star Wars*, as well as what proved to be a growing roster of mutant titles. "She is probably the best editor I've ever worked with," says Chris Claremont. "I've never seen anyone with as sure a hand at dealing with creative people, and with as solid a story sense."

Louise Simonson and Chris Claremont had a chance to show what they could do together when they learned that Jim Shooter wanted to launch a second mutant group. "I think he wanted a new *X-Men* title, but we came up with a batch of new characters and offered him *The New Mutants* instead," says Louise Simonson. "Chris came up with a lot of it, and I had some input, although I'm darned if I can remember what it was. Shooter had some input as well."

New Mutants

The New Mutants made its 1982 debut in an unusual way, as Marvel's fourth graphic novel. "We did a story that we thought was going to be the first issue," says Louise Simonson, "but there was a gap in the graphic novel schedule," which in fact was caused by her husband Walter running

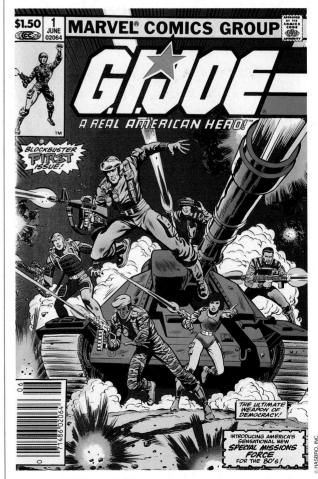

G. I. Joe **#1 (June 1982), based on a group of action toys from Hasbro, kicked off a series that turned out to be one of Marvel's biggest successes of the 1980s. Pencils: Herb Trimpe. Inks: Bob McLeod.**

▲ **The artists who have worked with writer Chris Claremont to maintain the tremendous popularity of The X-Men include Paul Smith (top left), John Romita, Jr. (top right), Art Adams (bottom left) and Marc Silvestri (bottom right).**

Ms. Mutant

Few people have contributed as much to the success of Marvel's mutants as Louise Jones, who became editor of *The X-Men* at the end of the Dark Phoenix saga in 1980. In that same year she married artist Walter Simonson, but continued to use her maiden name for a few more years before becoming known as Louise Simonson. In any case, most of her colleagues call her "Weezie." A professional with years of editorial experience at Warren Publishing, she quickly became invaluable

A super hero was dramatically retired in the first graphic novel published by Marvel: *The Death of Captain Marvel* **by Jim Starlin.**

late with his book *Starslammers*. So the team's origin story became a fill-in graphic novel, and *The New Mutants* #1 (March 1983) was really the second issue of the series.

Drawn by Bob McLeod, The New Mutants were a team of young teenagers assembled by Professor Xavier, the original teacher of The X-Men. "We felt that the series needed a school, and The X-Men were too old and experienced for that," Chris Claremont explains. "So we got Xavier some students, and it's evolved from there." The first batch of pupils included Karma, a Vietnamese girl who can control other people's minds; Wolfsbane, a Scottish girl who is, in effect, a good-natured werewolf; Psyche, a Cheyenne girl who projects illusory images; Sunspot, a Brazilian boy who absorbs solar power, and Cannonball, a Kentuckian boy who emits thermonuclear energy. Like their predecessors The X-Men, The New Mutants have added new members from time to time; perhaps the most consistently interesting is Warlock, created by Claremont and artist Bill Sienkiewicz in 1984. A childlike living machine from outer space, Warlock can alter his function and appearance at will, a tendency that allows for considerable visual humor.

The New Mutants immediately became one of Marvel's top sellers; after a few years, Chris Claremont moved on to other projects and Louise Simonson took over the writing. The series ended its run with issue #100, and its most popular characters became charter members of The X-Force, a new mutant group.

WET PAINT: BILL SIENKIEWICZ

"Working with Bill Sienkiewicz is like riding a bucking bronco. He's wild," says his frequent collaborator Frank Miller. Although other comic book artists have worked with paints, few have explored advanced techniques with the verve of Sienkiewicz. He mixes media, employing oils, acrylics and collages of objects ranging from photocopies to transistors, but his most significant contribution to comics is the intensity of his personal vision. Determined to paint things the way they feel rather than the way they look, Sienkiewicz at his best approaches abstract expressionism.

Sienkiewicz established his professional ability with his early work on *Moon Knight* in 1980, but he was dissatisfied with conventional comic book drawing and left the field to spend time studying in Paris. He came back determined to bring modern painting styles into the comic book medium, and has succeeded in a small but significant body of work, including *Elektra: Assassin*, the graphic novel *Daredevil in Love and War* and the four-issue *Stray Toasters*, a tale of love, murder and the relationship between people and small appliances. "I think that artists, in general, have a responsibility in our society to expose people to new ways of seeing things," Sienkiewicz says. "Comics artists have that responsibility too."

A series of terrifying, disorienting images depict the emotions of a psychotic killer in these paintings by Bill Sienkiewicz for *Daredevil in Love and War* **(1986). Script: Frank Miller.**

PHOTO BY ELIOT R. BROWN

Chris Claremont, who has written the *X-Men* series for more than fifteen years.

Kid Stuff

"Jim Shooter, aware that his editors were horribly overloaded, hired a whole batch of new editors, cut everybody's work load in half, and I got bored." So runs Louise Simonson's explanation for her creation of the unique super group featured in *Power Pack* (August 1984). The members are all children, siblings who are granted amazing abilities by a friendly alien. The idea, intended for a limited series, worked well enough to spawn a regular monthly comic book.

Simonson worked with June Brigman, an artist who was new to comics. "June came up with some wonderful drawings that in some ways strengthened the characterizations," says Simonson. Although *Power Pack* was pretty much ignored by typical comic book readers—action-hungry males on the verge of puberty—it found favor with younger readers and also with adults who bought the books for their children. Tapping into this young audience for somewhat gentler fantasies was an idea whose time was coming.

Myth Master

Walter Simonson, another major writer-artist, came into his own at Marvel when he went to work on *Thor* in 1983. "I've always been interested in Norse myth. Perhaps it's my Norwegian heritage. I was familiar with that stuff before I ever bought a Marvel comic," Simonson says. "*Thor* was the first Marvel comic I ever bought, when I was in college in the mid 1960s, and I became an avid fan."

Simonson had studied paleontology, and his fascination with fossils is shown in his signature—the letters form a dinosaur. After graduating from Amherst, he enrolled at The Rhode Island School of Design; his senior degree project there later provided the basis for his 1982 graphic novel *Starslammers*. His early work at Marvel included layouts on *Thor*, and a long stint on *Battlestar Galactica* that culminated when his editor and future wife encouraged him to contribute scripts as well as artwork. Shortly thereafter, editor Mark Gruenwald offered Simonson the chance to write, pencil and ink *Thor*. "The book was not doing well commercially," says Simonson. "I'd like to think I pulled it back from the brink." In fact, his first issue (November 1983) sold out.

Simonson's dynamic approach was embodied in his initial cover, which depicted a monster dressed in Thor's costume, wielding the hero's hammer to bring the letters of the logo crashing down. "I wanted to make as great a leap from the previous issues as I could," says Simonson. "So the first thing I did was create a character who would be worthy to pick up Thor's hammer, but he had to look like a monster." This was Beta Ray Bill, a brave and honorable alien who usurped Thor's power to save his own race. The stories that resulted exemplified Simonson's approach: "It's the conflict of that mythical background with a kind of science fiction."

All Together Now

As editor-in-chief, Jim Shooter kept an eye on fan letters, and noticed that "one thing was consistent in the mail. Every day a bunch of readers would say, 'Why don't you have one big story with all the

▲ *The New Mutants*, a graphic novel in 1982 (left), became a regular series in March 1983 (center). Covers: Bob McLeod. By May 1985 (right), Bill Sienkiewicz was the artist and Warlock a star.

Louise Simonson created a young hero group in *Power Pack* #1. Pencils: June Brigman. Inks: Bob Wiacek.

characters in it together?'" Marvel's first attempt to respond to this clamor was the *Marvel Super Heroes Contest of Champions*, Marvel's first limited series, which was published in 1982. However, the ultimate character crossover occurred when Mattel Toys decided to manufacture a set of Marvel action figures, and asked for a publishing tie-in. "They came up with the title," says Shooter, who ended up writing the twelve-issue limited series called *Marvel Super Heroes Secret Wars*.

Secret Wars, as it was generally known, featured pencils by Mike Zeck and inks by John Beatty. It got its start in May 1984, and featured Spider-Man, The Hulk, Thor, Captain America, Iron Man, Wolverine, and all of The Avengers, The X-Men and The Fantastic Four. Also in the cast were a mob of Marvel's most menacing villains, from Galactus to Dr. Doom. All of them were transported into outer space by an immensely powerful being called The Beyonder, who ordered them into battle to satisfy his curiosity about earth creatures.

A few cynics thought the busy *Secret Wars* was too much, but readers loved it and circulation approached 750,000 copies per issue for the duration of the series. These numbers were reminiscent of the Golden Age of the 1940s, so *Secret Wars II* (1985) was inevitable. Despite pencils by Al Milgrom and inks by Steve Leialoha, it

A STAR IS BORN

When Marvel started the Star Comics line in 1985, the company was making a conscious effort to reach an almost forgotten audience: young kids. Super heroes had come to dominate the industry to such an extent that other types of material had been virtually abandoned. Star brought back humor, child protagonists and talking animals.

Michael Hobson set up Star, and appointed, as editor of the line, Sid Jacobson, a veteran comic book pro with extensive experience at Harvey Comics working on characters like Richie Rich and Casper the Friendly Ghost. The ambitious Star program was a combination of new creations (*Top Dog*, *Planet Terry*, *Wally the Wizard*), and licensed properties already familiar in other media (*Heathcliff*, *Strawberry Shortcake*, *The Muppet Babies*, *Fraggle Rock*). Within a few months it was obvious that the licensed characters were the ones that sold best; more recently, *Alf*, *Barbie*, *Mighty Mouse* and *Count Duckula* have been added. Marvel eventually let the Star trademark lapse, along with its in-house creations.

Despite the changes, Marvel remains committed to the concept of publishing

Barbie #1 (January 1991) seeks to get young girls interested in comic books. Cover: John Romita.

comics for children. Circulation figures may not reach super hero levels, but as Michael Hobson says, "we feel comics for kids are an important thing to do."

► Walter Simonson's determination to reinvigorate Thor led to an alien in a god's clothing (November 1983), a new logo designed by Alex Jay (January 1985), a god changed into a frog by a magic spell (April 1986) and one of the few super heroes ever to wear a beard (May 1986).

◄ In response to reader requests, editor-in-chief Jim Shooter brought a horde of super heroes together for a crowd-pleasing limited series that began with *Secret Wars* #1 (May 1984). Pencils: Mike Zeck. Inks: John Beatty.

▶ **Marvel Comics appear in forty countries, on six continents and in seventeen different languages. Michelle Gagnon, Marvel's vice president of international licensing, reports that the latest nations to become part of The Marvel Universe are Poland and Hungary. Countries in this display include (top row) Denmark, Finland, Germany, Spain and (bottom row) France, Brazil, Italy and Holland.**

did not sell as well as its predecessor. All in all, however, the *Secret Wars* books delighted fans, earned a lot of money, and brought into even tighter focus the notion of The Marvel Universe, where the destinies of countless characters were intertwined. The massive undertaking of *Secret Wars* was the apex of Shooter's long tenure as editor-in-chief.

Going Through Changes

One of the most striking results of the *Secret Wars* story line was a drastic change in the appearance of Spider-Man, who over the years had developed into Marvel's corporate symbol. Back from beyond in a new black outfit known as "the alien costume," Spidey looked more like a ninja than his old self, and years passed before he reverted to his familiar togs of red and blue.

The idea of transformation was in the air. Writer Peter David returned The Hulk to the original gray color that had previously been seen only in the character's first appearance in 1962. And Marvel's hero teams, from The X-Men to The Avengers to The Fantastic Four, seemed to be undergoing constant membership modifications. "My theory was that we should be a creative house," says Jim Shooter. "No matter how crazy an idea was, I would always say, 'Okay, how can we make that work?' I thought, 'This is Marvel Comics—we

should be wild, we should do everything.'"

The Marvel Universe was becoming so complex that you couldn't tell the players apart without scorecards. Marvel was ready to provide them.

Keeping Score

In 1983, Marvel inaugurated two projects that provide information about its characters and comic books: one about the past and one about the present. The record of the past was *The Official Handbook of The Marvel Universe*, which began its fifteen-issue run in January 1983. In the same format as a comic book, the *Handbook* was actually an encyclopedia with alphabetical entries on the company's host of heroes and villains. The daunting task of assembling and writing this information fell to Mark Gruenwald, who had come to Marvel as an assistant editor during the staff expansion begun in 1978. By 1983 he was a full-fledged editor handling such titles as *Thor*, *Iron Man*, *Captain America* and *The Avengers*.

"One of the things I was able to do with the *Handbook*," Gruenwald says, "was to put facts down in an easily accessible place where other writers could get basic information." In short, it was detailed enough for in-house use, yet it also proved immensely popular with fans who wanted to know everything from a hero's place of birth to his height, weight and eye color. *Marvel Universe*

Jim Shooter, who served as Marvel's editor-in-chief from 1978 to 1987.

was totally revised and expanded in 1985, and this version was also printed as a ten-volume set of quality paperbacks. An update followed in 1989, and a newly revised version published as comic-book size file cards began appearing in 1990. Marvel projects a five-year schedule for the update's complete revision, at which time it will stand as the most thorough character catalog ever produced.

For timely tidbits about the present, Carol Kalish of direct sales launched a little magazine in April 1983 called *Marvel Age*, which promised to "tell you everything you want to know about what's going on in the hallowed halls of Marvel." Jim Salicrup took over as editor with *Marvel Age* #6, and he's still on the job. "I just want this to be around," he says. "This is the most direct forum we have to talk to people about the books, and the mail response is quite high. It's as if we're guiding the fans through The Marvel Universe." An enthu-siastic fan in his youth, Salicrup seems to know what readers want, from previews of upcoming art to a monthly list of which villains will be appearing where. He even persuaded Stan Lee to revive his "Stan's Soapbox" column. To the uninitiated, *Marvel Age*, which is essentially a publication of house-promotion advertising with healthy sales and a fan following of its own, may seem baffling, but it demonstrates, like *The Official Handbook of The Marvel Universe*, the intensity of interest that Marvel inspires.

The Team Spirit

The consistent popularity of *The Fantastic Four* and *The Avengers*, coupled with impressive sales for *The X-Men* and *The New Mutants*, offered strong evidence that the demand for super hero teams was still growing. Marvel responded by launching three new series in the space of a few months, although not before each team had been first tested in a guest appearance in another book or in a "market-testing" limited series. The final results were *Cloak and Dagger* #1 (July 1985), *The West Coast Avengers* #1 (October 1985) and *X-Factor* (February 1986).

Created by writer Bill Mantlo and artist Ed Hannigan, *Cloak and Dagger* depicted the exploits of two teenage runaways transformed into super heroes. One was able to project a terrifying dark-ness and the other an overwhelming light, and the pair became vigilantes, protecting the young from urban corruption. Mantlo's fervid condemnation of street crime was a sign of the times.

If *The West Coast Avengers* featured any social problem, it was the housing shortage. So many heroes had served with the all-star Avengers that a splinter group was formed and sent to California to alleviate crowding. The leader was Hawkeye, the improbably popular archer with a bad temper and no super powers; other members included Iron Man and Tigra (formerly The Cat), but in what was becoming the established Marvel tradition, heroes came and went at will.

The Official Handbook of The Marvel Universe #1 (January 1983). Pencils: Ed Hannigan. Inks: Josef Rubinstein.

Marvel Age #1 (April 1983) kicked off a long-running company newsmagazine. Cover: Walter Simonson.

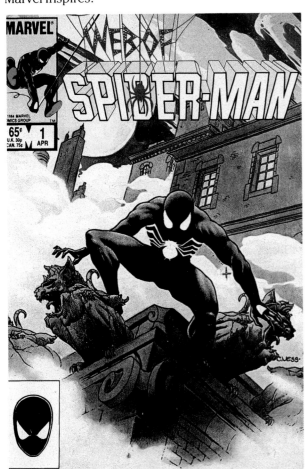

◄ Marvel kept interest high with changes in its characters. Charles Vess provided a striking study of the black costume, which Spidey wore for several years, on the cover of *Web of Spider-Man* #1 (April 1984). The Hulk reverted to his original gray for many months, as shown on this powerful cover by Jeff Purves for *The Incredible Hulk* #358 (August 1989).

The blockbuster of the new groups was *X-Factor*, another mutant group that streaked up the sales chart and has stayed at the top ever since. *X-Factor* could have been subtitled "The Old Mutants," since the roster consisted of the original X-Men created by Lee and Kirby in 1963 who were eventually squeezed out of the team by new recruits. *X-Factor* included Cyclops, The Angel, Iceman, The Beast (now actually a furry animal-man, not just an agile human) and Marvel Girl. The latter, of course, had years before become Phoenix and then died, but hardworking writers had explained all that away before *X-Factor* was ever born. The Marvel Universe was becoming very tricky terrain, but readers relished all the complications.

A Home for Heroes

A few months after its debut, *X-Factor* found a new writer in Louise Simonson, who had given up editing to go free-lance. Soon she was writing *The New Mutants* as well. Her knowledge of the characters and her experience in editing *The X-Men* were considerable assets. As Chris Claremont says, "One advantage the X-books have had is that for five years only two people wrote them, me and Weezie. There's a coherence of vision."

X-Factor became even more of a family affair at the end of 1986, when Walter Simonson took over the art. The collaboration between husband and wife was a first for Marvel, and for the Simonsons as well. Despite the potential problems, they worked together happily at home. "There's that initial period of trying to figure out how much information to give the artist so he's comfortable with it," says Louise. "Walter likes things very loose, so I would sit down and write up a minimal plot. If he didn't understand something or had a better idea, he'd come upstairs and say so. And often he'd do loose layouts that were sort of scribbled, and I would write the script from that."

"I get to live with one of the best editors Marvel ever had," says Walter, "and I've made full use of that. You can talk about your work around the house, and you both speak the same language."

"You also understand about deadlines," says Louise, who notes that marathon sessions to complete work on time have "created some friction in several marriages. But we understand. With creative types, it's not just a nine-to-five job."

Changing Hands

In 1986, Marvel celebrated the twenty-fifth anniversary of the company's modern incarnation, which had been ushered in by the debut of *The Fantastic Four* in 1961. Several celebratory publishing events were planned, but perhaps none of them was as significant as the purchase of Marvel by New World Pictures. The motion picture company had been created by producer-director Roger Corman, who sold it in 1982. New World's new owners planned to expand the operation, and Marvel was slated to play a key role.

"The new New World bought us for several reasons," explains James Galton. "We were a profitable company in our own right; we had an animation studio that was synergistic with their television production company; and we had a lot of

▼ **Super hero teams continued to find favor. Rick Leonardi and Terry Austin did the cover for *Cloak and Dagger* #1 (July 1985); Al Milgrom and Joe Sinnott did the honors for *West Coast Avengers* #1 (October 1985); Walter Simonson and Josef Rubinstein launched *X-Factor* #1 (February 1986).**

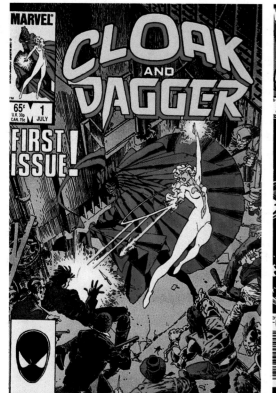

The husband-and-wife team of Walter and Louise Simonson provided art and script for *X-Factor* #24 (January 1988), in which mutants come under fire and The Angel suffers a cruel fate.

Louise Simonson, a writer-editor who helped put Marvel's mutants over the top.

characters that had not been exploited for either television or theatrical films." In short, Marvel had become a very desirable company, and during the 1980s, when the buying and selling of corporations was all the rage, its acquisition was almost inevitable. In fact, it would be sold again before the decade was over.

Just Punishment

The United States experienced a rise in violent crime during the 1980s, and there was a public perception that the legal system was no longer handling the problem properly. In this atmosphere of anger and resentment, The Punisher came into his own. This no-nonsense enemy of the underworld had been around since 1974, when writer Gerry Conway conceived him as a quasi-villain for Spider-Man. The Punisher had usually been presented as a dark and somewhat undesirable character, a contrast to Marvel's more humane and ethical heroes. By 1986, however, the time seemed right to unleash him with both guns blazing.

Writer Steven Grant and penciler Mike Zeck were convinced there was untapped potential in Marvel's most ruthless crime-fighter, and they found an ally in editor Carl Potts. The result was *The Punisher*, a limited series that struck a nerve. In it, the protagonist started out in a brutal prison and then got himself into some really hot water;

before things settled down, the pages were littered with criminals who would never bother anyone again. The idea of a one-man war on crime, waged by a character who took no prisoners, may have been a fantasy, but it had very real appeal.

In short order, editor Potts ushered in a monthly series for the character: *The Punisher* #1 appeared in July 1987. This time the writer was Mike Baron and the artist was Klaus Janson, and again sales were explosive. A second regularly published series, *The Punisher War Journal*, was added in November 1988; this time Carl Potts provided the scripts himself, and also did layouts that were fully rendered by artist Jim Lee. So many versions of The Punisher were appearing so quickly that a touch of rivalry grew up among the various teams as to whose was the definitive treatment of the character, but fortunately no shots were fired. Was The Punisher a menace or a martyr? Was he a lunatic or the one sane person in an insane world? Everything was controversial except the sales, which rivaled those of Marvel's mutants.

Things Change

By the time The Punisher was going full blast, Jim Shooter had left Marvel. In nearly a decade as editor-in-chief, Shooter had shown more interest in the business side of the business than most of his predecessors, and the 1986 sale of Marvel to New

Walter Simonson, a writer-artist whose work alone and with his wife made a strong impression.

The 'Nam #1 (December 1986) presented a common foot soldier's view of a controversial war, written by Vietnam veteran Doug Murray. Cover: Michael Golden.

► Night in the jungle, captured by artist Michael Golden and writer Doug Murray for *The 'Nam* #2 (January 1987).

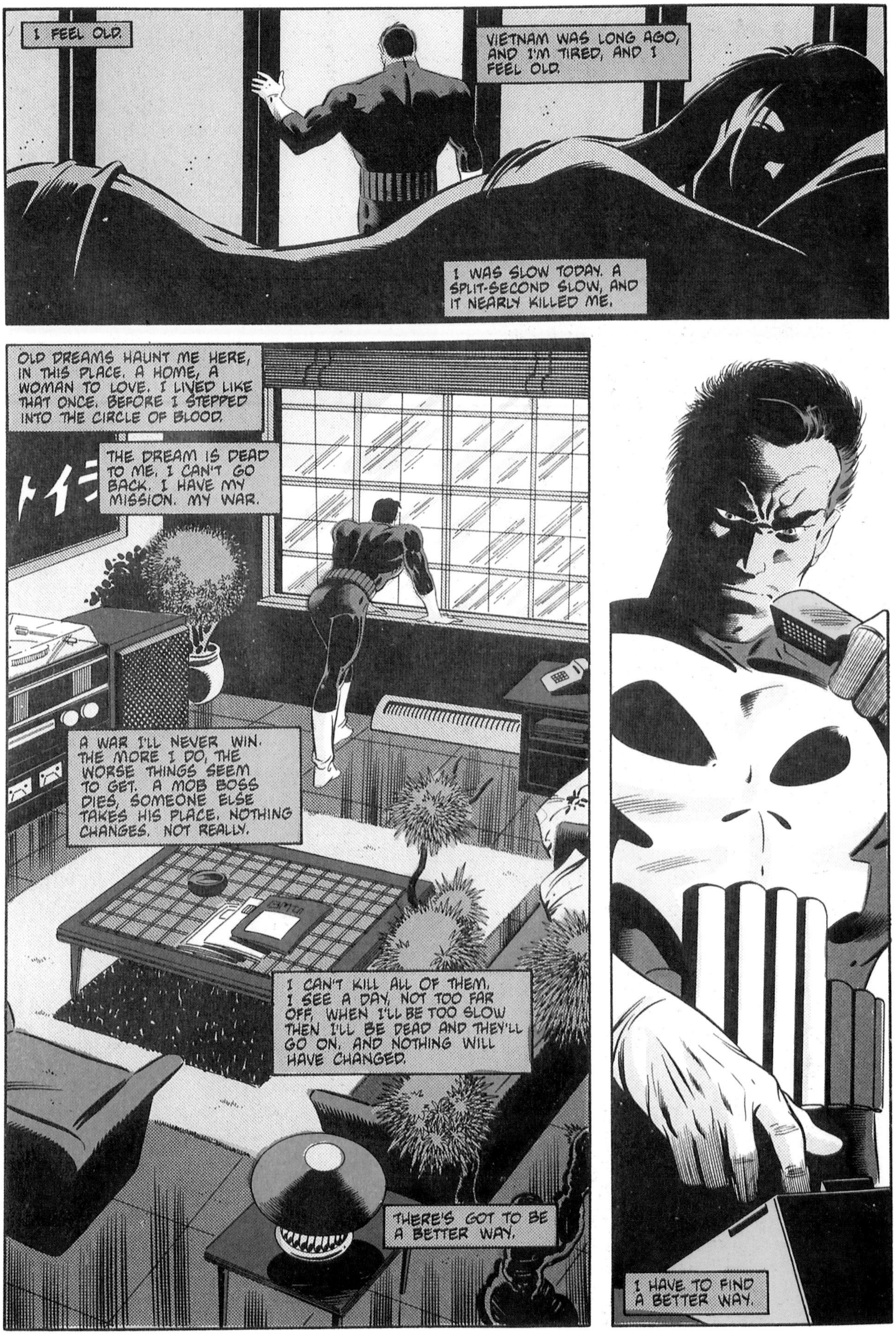
I FEEL OLD.
VIETNAM WAS LONG AGO, AND I'M TIRED, AND I FEEL OLD.
I WAS SLOW TODAY. A SPLIT-SECOND SLOW, AND IT NEARLY KILLED ME.
OLD DREAMS HAUNT ME HERE, IN THIS PLACE. A HOME, A WOMAN TO LOVE. I LIVED LIKE THAT ONCE. BEFORE I STEPPED INTO THE CIRCLE OF BLOOD.
THE DREAM IS DEAD TO ME. I CAN'T GO BACK. I HAVE MY MISSION. MY WAR.
A WAR I'LL NEVER WIN. THE MORE I DO, THE WORSE THINGS SEEM TO GET. A MOB BOSS DIES, SOMEONE ELSE TAKES HIS PLACE. NOTHING CHANGES. NOT REALLY.
I CAN'T KILL ALL OF THEM. I SEE A DAY, NOT TOO FAR OFF, WHEN I'LL BE TOO SLOW. THEN I'LL BE DEAD AND THEY'LL GO ON, AND NOTHING WILL HAVE CHANGED.
THERE'S GOT TO BE A BETTER WAY.
I HAVE TO FIND A BETTER WAY.

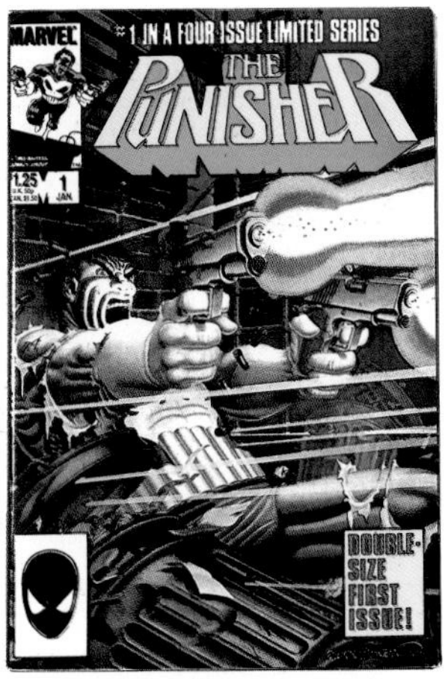
MARVEL
#1 IN A FOUR ISSUE LIMITED SERIES
THE PUNISHER
DOUBLE-SIZE FIRST ISSUE!

This wild cover got The Punisher's limited series off to a strong start in January 1986. Airbrushed painting by Phil Zimelman from a drawing by Mike Zeck.

◄Caught in an endless battle thousands of miles from Vietnam, The Punisher contemplates his options in the second issue of his limited series (February 1986). Script: Steven Grant. Pencils: Mick Zeck. Inks: John Beatty.

The New Universe, an ambitious attempt to introduce eight new comic book series simultaneously, all of them tied together and none of them related to the classic characters who inhabit The Marvel Universe. It got its start in 1986 but never quite got off the ground, perhaps because Marvel had, in effect, gone into competition with itself by creating another universe.

THE NEW UNIVERSE

In 1986, after The Marvel Universe had been around for a quarter century, the company took a chance on an idea called The New Universe. The plan was to create a group of interrelated comic books that would not interact with Marvel's established heroes. The concept came from editor-in-chief Jim Shooter: "Use the real world, introduce a couple of carefully controlled anomalies, and then play them out." The idea was to show the effect of a weird "White Event" that gave certain ordinary individuals paranormal powers.

The planning team included several top writers and editors: Shooter, Tom DeFalco, Archie Goodwin, Mark Gruenwald, Eliot Brown and John Morelli. There were high hopes for the project, but it never really caught on, and in 1989 The New Universe was canceled.

"We were horrendously late, and they were rushed out," says Archie Goodwin. "And if readers are not entertained by the first few issues, it's hard to convince them that things will get better." Perhaps the premise wasn't wild enough for fans, or perhaps they were already too involved in the vast fictional construct called The Marvel Universe. Despite some excellent work, The New Universe never quite came to life.

In *Thor* #387, the giants keep getting bigger. Script: Tom DeFalco. Pencils: Ron Frenz. Inks: Brett Breeding.

World seemed to exacerbate some areas of disagreement. By early 1987 divergent philosophies of publishing led to a parting of the ways.

"He was very competent and very hardworking," says publisher Stan Lee. In addition to his editorial duties, Shooter played a part in a number of changes, from pay scales to staff organization, that ultimately benefited both the company and its creative contributors. In his enthusiasm to make changes and get things moving, Shooter may have stepped on a few toes, but his work overall helped make Marvel the giant it is today. In 1989 he became president and editor-in-chief of his own comic book company, Voyager Communications.

An Unrelenting Juggernaut

"When Jim Shooter left," says James Galton, "Tom DeFalco was the logical person to succeed him. And when Tom came on, he hardly missed a beat. Actually, since Tom has been editor-in-chief, we've enjoyed the most profitable period in the existence of Marvel Comics."

"Marvel is an unrelenting juggernaut," says Tom DeFalco. "It's constantly rolling forward, and the job of the editor-in-chief is to keep it on track. I edit the editors. You could ask me what's happening in this month's issue of, say, *Iron Man*, and I can't always tell you. But I can tell you the long-range plan for *Iron Man*. I try to establish a tone that will keep everybody happy and yet challenged creatively, and I'm not necessarily the most effective when I'm sitting in the office working on a piece of paper. When I'm sitting with my feet up on the desk, staring at the ceiling, that's when the company's really getting its money's worth."

DeFalco got his early training at Archie Comics, then became a free-lance writer for various publishers, and in 1980 was offered a full-time contract to write exclusively for Marvel. A few months later he was promoted to editor, handling such characters as Spider-Man and Ghost Rider. He showed his resourcefulness almost at once, bringing a very late book in on schedule by hiring several inkers, a different one for each page of pencils. Within a few years he was involved in the development of the Star Comics line, and not long after that he was named executive editor, Jim Shooter's second in command. He even edited Shooter's work on the blockbuster *Secret Wars* series. On April 15, 1987, he became Marvel's tenth editor-in-chief.

DeFalco continues to write, working with artist Ron Frenz on *Thor*. He does his writing under the supervision of another editor, Ralph Macchio. "It's a lot of fun," says DeFalco. "A good editor is a fabulous safety net and a great spark plug." In fact, DeFalco attributes much of his success to his staff, which he calls "the most talented editorial team the universe has ever seen."

The Keeper of the Flame

When Tom DeFalco became editor-in-chief, he appointed Mark Gruenwald executive editor. Gruenwald, who spearheaded the *Official Handbook of The Marvel Universe* project, is the resident expert on Marvel's imaginary history, and the ultimate arbiter on questions concerning characters, costumes and crossovers. He reads every Marvel comic before it's published to make sure it remains true to the accumulated lore of countless past issues. "I'm also a clearinghouse for names," he says, "which we don't want to duplicate needlessly. Before I took on this job, for example, Marvel had seven characters called The Destroyer."

One of Gruenwald's most daunting tasks was to coordinate the logistics for a number of massive crossovers, which ran in multiple books, and in some cases involved almost every major Marvel character. "The crossovers are very popular," he says, "but very difficult." Such epics as "Inferno," "Acts of Vengeance" and "The Evolutionary Wars" taxed the concept of The Marvel Universe to its limit. A typical example, the 1989 "Atlantis Attacks," ran in fourteen oversize summer annual issues. Dozens of writers, artists and editors worked on the story, inevitably resulting in headaches and a few loose ends along the way.

Gruenwald has also continued as a writer, working on *Captain America* and doing a little house-

▲ Mark Gruenwald's villain-killer Scourge cleaned up in Captain America #319 (July 1986). Cover: Paul Neary and Joe Sinnott. In 1988, Gruenwald depicted Captain America deprived of his classic costume, committing a crime to save his country.
Pencils: Kieron Dwyer.
Inks: Al Milgrom.

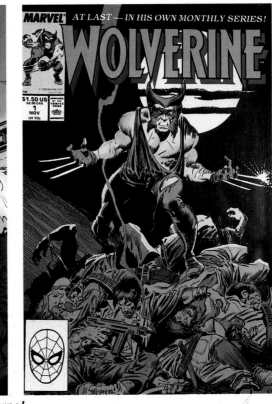

Tough guys get their own series: *The Punisher* (Cover: Klaus Janson); *The Punisher War Journal* (Cover: Carl Potts and Jim Lee); *Wolverine* (Cover: John Buscema and Al Williamson).

AS THE WEB SPINS: SPIDEY'S SOAP OPERA

"I felt we had to marry off Peter Parker someday," says Stan Lee, "because it would give us a whole new angle for the stories." Matrimony was the last thing on young Peter's mind when he received a radioactive spider bite in 1962, but over the ensuing years (in which he and his cohorts aged more slowly than mere mortals), Spider-Man and his webbing became entangled with a number of eligible young women. When Lee refers to Marvel's "soap opera," he is doubtless including Spider-Man's mixed-up love life.

Our hero's first female crush was high school classmate Liz Allen, but she eventually married the son of his hated foe, The Green Goblin. Peter became more deeply involved with Betty Brant, a colleague at *The Daily Bugle*, where he was employed as a news photographer, but he broke off the relationship when he realized that she disliked and feared the much-maligned Spider-Man. Meanwhile, in 1964, Lee and artist Steve Ditko began a running gag in which Peter's old Aunt May incessantly attempted to introduce him to a neighbor's niece named Mary Jane Watson.

"We had a lot of fun with that," says Lee, "poor Peter living in fear that someday he might actually have to meet her." It was 1966 before John Romita finally drew the first picture of Mary Jane: she turned out to be a gorgeous redhead, but one whose frivolous behavior frequently rubbed Peter the wrong way.

While attending Empire State University, a fictional New York school, Peter fell for a sweet, quiet, dependable student named Gwen Stacy. "We always intended that Gwen would be the one Peter would marry," says Lee, "but for some reason or other, Mary Jane always seemed to have the most personality."

By 1973, Gerry Conway was writing Spidey's scripts with major plotting input provided by John Romita. They both felt that "Gwen was a stiff, actually," Conway says. So they made her one for real by having The Green Goblin knock her off the George Washington Bridge. Conway insists that Lee approved the idea, but Lee denies vehemently that he was an accomplice to the heartless killing.

At this point, a union with Mary Jane seemed imminent, especially after she discovered Spidey's secret identity, but both were afraid of commitment. So while Mary Jane pursued her career as an actress and model, Peter embarked on a dalliance with a somewhat shady character, a reformed costumed criminal called The Black Cat.

It was 1987 before Peter and Mary Jane finally got together. Lee decided that a marriage would make his newspaper strip "more realistic and adult," then passed the word to Spider-Man's editor, Jim Salicrup, who hastily arranged a wedding for the year's summer annual issue. "The strip doesn't have the same storyline as the comic book," explains Lee, "but we managed the marriage at the same time in both places."

There was even a third, real-life ceremony: two appropriately dressed actors (Spidey in his classic blue and red, the bride in a gown by designer Willi Smith) exchanged vows on June 5, 1987, before a cheering throng of 55,000 baseball fans at New York's Shea Stadium. Stan Lee officiated, massive publicity ensued and after fifteen years of hairbreadth escapes, Spider-Man was finally caught.

▲ Liz Allen, Spidey's high school crush, drawn by Steve Ditko.

▲ Betty Brant, Spidey's office romance, drawn by Steve Ditko.

▲ Mary Jane Watson, wild card, drawn by John Romita.

▲ The death of Spidey's college sweetheart Gwen Stacy (drawn by Gil Kane), and his subsequent fling with the adventuress known as The Black Cat (drawn by Al Milgrom).

▶ Mary Jane Watson and Spidey tied the knot in 1987. John Romita drew the cover for the comic book event, which was reenacted by costumed performers in New York.

SPIDEY'S INFLATED REPUTATION

Spider-Man's reputation as an integral part of American popular culture was validated in 1987 when he was chosen to be one of the huge inflated icons that hover over the Macy's Thanksgiving Day Parade. Kept afloat with 9,522 cubic feet of helium, the massive Spider-Man balloon is seventy-eight feet long and thirty-six feet wide.

The designer of the lighter-than-air Spidey was Marvel's art director, John Romita. "I got a charge out of doing that," he says. "At the initial meeting they were teaching me aerodynamics, saying the bulk had to be in the upper part—you usually need a big head filled with helium to keep these balloons upright. But I was thinking of a crawling character, so I needed his rump and his thighs to be a volume area. They made a plaster model from my sketch, and I crouched and twisted and bent to paint onto that four-foot figure the exact pattern of the webbing, and the eyes, and where the boots and the gloves go. They made the balloon from that model. To see it go from sketch to fruition was just a terrific feeling."

The giant Spidey is seen "in person" each November by roughly two million people, while eighty million more watch him on television.

Bigger than life and much more buoyant, the giant Spider-Man balloon crawls over New York City crowds and floats past the Empire State Building each Thanksgiving Day.

PHOTO BY RICHARD CHEVALIER

---

cleaning with a character he created called Scourge. Because The Marvel Universe was cluttered with minor villains whom no one took seriously, Gruenwald convinced many of his fellow writers to have Scourge make surprise appearances in various books, each time bumping off bad guys and shouting, "Justice is served!" In one appearance alone, Scourge rid Marvel of seventeen extraneous evildoers. "I guess I've killed more characters than anybody else," admits Gruenwald, "but I've created more than I've killed, so ultimately I give back more than I take."

In a somewhat more serious vein, Gruenwald has succeeded in keeping Captain America fresh. "He was always one of my favorites," says Gruenwald. "He's such an archetype. I've been writing him now for longer than anybody except Stan Lee, and I'm going for the record." Gruenwald created quite a stir with a storyline in which Steve Rogers, the original Captain America, was deprived of his title by an overbearing government agency that accused him of excessive independence. The red, white and blue uniform was handed over to a unscrupulous bully named John Walker, who became Captain America for months. "I had a lot of people convinced that we were not going back to the status quo," says Gruenwald, "and I wasn't

certain myself. I really didn't know how it was going to wind up."

The Cutting Edge

It was perhaps inevitable that the most popular of Marvel's mutants would get his own monthly comic book, and it finally happened with *Wolverine* #1 (November 1988). A hot seller from its first issue, *Wolverine* brought out a new side in writer Chris Claremont. Removed from the complicated plotting and complex emotional relationships that characterized *The X-Men*, Wolverine's solo adventures had a dark, gritty, hard-boiled quality that suited the menacing, enigmatic hero. Eschewing his uniform, Wolverine set up shop in the lawless Oriental city of Madripoor, narrating his own adventures in a clipped, cynical style. "It's different," says Claremont, "but it's a different aspect of the same guy."

One of Marvel's old masters, John Buscema, provided the pencils for *Wolverine*; the inks were by another veteran, Al Williamson. Buscema's first work for the company was done in 1948, and he has been working regularly for Marvel since 1966. An artist's artist, Buscema has received offers from other companies, but he always replies, "Where

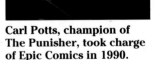

Carl Potts, champion of The Punisher, took charge of Epic Comics in 1990.

PHOTO BY ELIOT R. BROWN

▲ **Tom DeFalco, Marvel's tenth and current editor-in-chief, provides the vision that keeps a universe alive.**

▲ **"Atlantis Attacks," one of Marvel's most spectacular super-crossovers, involved dozens of super heroes in an epic tale that ran through fourteen summer annuals.**

were you when I needed you?"

Tough characters like Wolverine and The Punisher are in vogue, believes editor-in-chief Tom DeFalco, because "it's a way of dealing with society's frustrations. These days, people are upset with the way the law works, upset with politicians, upset with everything. They want to see someone actively solving problems instead of just talking about them. The characters that are popular are the ones people need at the time."

More Mutants

"Hard-boiled isn't that tough to do," says Chris Claremont. "Humor is much harder." Regardless, he took on the challenge of creating a mutant team with a touch of comedy. The result was *Excalibur*, which began as a paperback and made its debut as a series six months later in October 1988.

The central figure in *Excalibur* was Captain

Britain, a hero Claremont had created in the mid-1970s for Marvel's British division. British artist Alan Davis had devoted a lot of time to the character, and Claremont says *Excalibur* was born because, "I wanted to work with Alan, and this seemed like a really neat way to do it. *The X-Men* was a hard-edged series, and we wanted to create something a little more lighthearted and absurdist." Former X-Men with a touch of humor, like Nightcrawler and Kitty Pryde, were added to the British-based group, and another hit was born. Claremont has since left the scripting of the series in the capable hands of his collaborator Alan Davis.

"I've tried to get people back into the idea of having fun with comics," says editor-in-chief Tom DeFalco, and in fact humor has been making a comeback in books other than *Excalibur*, even while grim characters pushed their way into the spotlight. Still, mutants—funny or not—are best-

sellers, and *Excalibur* joined *X-Men*, *X-Factor*, *The New Mutants* and *Wolverine* at the top of the charts. Sales figures fluctuate, but it has been estimated that Marvel's mutants alone outsell the entire output of any other comic book publisher.

The Queen of Green

One of Marvel's most impressive forays into comedy occurred when writer-artist John Byrne took a new approach to an old character in *The Sensational She-Hulk* #1 (May 1989). This female Hulk had originally been created for copyright purposes, and she had always had a faint touch of absurdity, which Byrne exploited when he revived her. Byrne credits writer Roger Stern with the idea that She-Hulk could be "somebody who was having fun being seven feet tall and green. And it was such a logical extrapolation," says Byrne, "to carry that wackiness to the extreme and say she knows

she's in a comic book." In short order, Byrne was producing the best parody of comic books in decades. "Little did I know," confesses Byrne, "that it would get totally berserk."

She-Hulk talked to her readers, talked back to her artist and talked to herself about the indignities of life as a comic book character. She endured all the comic book conventions, but took them with a grain of salt: when she flew through space, it was in a 1959 Dodge. In typical Marvel style, Byrne provided a Golden Age guest star: The Blonde Phantom, who hadn't been seen in comics in forty years and was desperate to get back into the medium because comic book characters never aged and she had become elderly while out of work. As the strangest sidekick in comics, the little old Blonde Phantom stuck around to show She-Hulk the ropes. By his fifth issue, Byrne was deconstructing the medium, allowing She-Hulk to rip through the pages of her book to reach the

▲ Mark Gruenwald, Marvel's executive editor, scans the New York streets for signs of super heroes.

▲ The "Atlantis Attacks" extravaganza that ran through fourteen summer annuals commemorated The Sub-Mariner's fiftieth anniversary. It was so overwhelming an effort that such super-crossovers may become a thing of the past, despite their usual sensational sales.

▲ A Spidey figure that sticks anywhere (Marvel).

▲ Anthologies of classic comic book adventures (Marvel).

▼ Limited edition ceramic bisques of popular heroes (Marvel).

► Super hero adventures for videocassette collectors.

▲ The Spider-Man Dragster, with lift-up hatch, for living room races (Toy Biz).

◄ Neon skateboards for sidewalk heroes (Dynacraft Industries).

▲ Silver Surfer video game (Mastertronic) and Spider-Man Gameboy cartridge (Acclaim) for Nintendo warriors.

▼ PVC figures poised for play (Marvel).

PHOTOS BY DAVID ARKY

Super Hero Souvenirs

Marvel began as a publishing enterprise and sells eleven million comic books each month. Today, the Marvel super heroes have become so popular that they are readily available in a variety of forms.

Eighty American companies currently license the rights to manufacture Marvel-themed merchandise. These products appear in a variety of locations: some are sold in mass merchandise stores like K-Mart and Wal-Mart; others appear in high-ticket locations like New York City's upscale gadget store, Hammacher Schlemmer; still others are sold in limited editions to individual collectors through direct mail offerings.

When comic books alone are not enough, Marvel collectibles are available for everyone from serious investors to kids looking for a good time.

▲ *Cloisonné lapel pins (Planet Studios).*

▲ *A thirteen-inch Spider-Man figurine stands tall. (Hamilton Gifts).*

▲ *A Marvel heroes and villains chess set of pewter. For this special limited edition set, the heroes are dipped in 14K gold (Gallo Pewter).*

▲ *Tin lapel pins identify fans with their favorite heroes (One-Stop Posters). Pencil and pen toppers make homework more fun (Applause).*

▶ Writer Chris Claremont gives Marvel's mutants a humorous slant in *Excalibur*. The team featured his creation Captain Britain, along with ex-X-Men Nightcrawler and Kitty Pryde. Covers: Alan Davis and Paul Neary.

▶ John Byrne's *Sensational She-Hulk*, which got its start in May 1989, showed its star threatening comic book collectors and displaying doubt about the concept of crossovers.

Writer Steve Gerber saw Howard the Duck as a suitable companion for the new She-Hulk. Cover by Mark Texeira and Harry Candecario.

She-Hulk, confronted by a team of minor villains, turns on writer-artist John Byrne. Inks: Bob Wiacek.

villain she knew was lurking on the other side.

Alas, it couldn't last, and in fact may have contained the seeds of its own destruction. In less than a year, after some disagreement with his editor, Byrne left the book. Still, by redefining a character and challenging comics conventions, Byrne had accomplished a lot in a short time.

He found a worthy successor in writer Steve Gerber, a comedy expert who joined artist Bryan Hitch to keep *The Sensational She-Hulk* going strong. "I've been able to take what Byrne did and run with it to do my own kind of stories," says Gerber. "It's the most fun I've had writing in years." He even found a place for his favorite character, Howard the Duck, who, being utterly out of place, couldn't have been more at home.

SKETCH BY JOHN BYRNE

Big Business

Early in 1989, New World Pictures sold the Marvel publishing division for $82.5 million. The comic book company had come a long way from the days, thirty years earlier, when virtually its only asset was a desk with Stan Lee sitting behind it. Marvel's new owner is Andrews Group Incorporated, a subsidiary of MacAndrews & Forbes Group, Incorporated, a corporate holding company with diverse interests.

In 1990, having guided Marvel through the tran-

MARVEL'S MOST SENSIBLE SERIES

Mass destruction has been a byproduct of the super hero business for years, but nobody seemed to know what to do about it until writer Dwayne McDuffie came up with *Damage Control,* a miniseries that first appeared in 1989. Another followed, and in both, McDuffie envisioned a construction company with advanced techniques and resourceful employees that makes big bucks cleaning up the messes left behind after a typical Marvel brawl. After death rays have done their worst, after giant robots have crashed to the ground, Damage Control is there to pick up the pieces and collect a fee.

With art by cocreator Ernie Colon, *Damage Control* is an eminently logical extrapolation, a tribute to the free-enterprise system that is also an extremely funny comic book. Located in New York City's Flatiron Building, Damage Control serves clients ranging from The Avengers to The X-Men, most of whom pay their bills by making claims on their Extraordinary Activity Assurance policies. Those who haven't been paying their premiums apply for federal aid, of course. In The Marvel Universe, where villains never really die and the battle between good and evil never ends, the only clear winner is Damage Control. Could this be the way The Marvel Universe will end, in a sea of insurance forms, building code regulations and applications for matching funds? Probably nothing else could stop it.

When The Avengers save New York by stopping a giant robot in its tracks, Damage Control arrives on the scene to mop up. From *Damage Control* #1 (May 1989). Script: Dwayne McDuffie. Pencils: Ernie Colon. Inks: Bob Wiacek.

© MARVEL ENT. GROUP AND NEW WORLD

© MARVEL ENT. GROUP AND 21ST CENTURY PRODUCTIONS

MARVEL IN THE MOVIES

Despite Marvel's continuing dominance of the comic book field and Hollywood's recent enthusiasm for fantasy in general and comics in particular, no film yet produced has really captured the Marvel style. The closest approximation so far has come in the television adaptations of The Hulk, who returned in three 1989–90 television movies from New World Pictures. The best of the bunch, *The Death of The Incredible Hulk*, was directed with considerable flair by co-star Bill Bixby.

Lack of commitment to the comic book original took its toll on the film of *The Punisher* (1989), an adaptation set in New York but shot in Australia by director Mark Goldblatt. Oscar winner Lou Gossett appeared, and muscular Dolph Lundgren had the title role, but the title was almost the only Marvel element used. Devoid of his distinctive costume

and his unique methods, The Punisher became just another angry guy with a gun. The film was released theatrically abroad, but went straight to video in the United States.

Captain America (1990) stayed somewhat closer to its source, but betrayed a certain coyness about showing the hero in costume and in action. Director Albert Pyun seemed inhibited by a rather modest budget, and perhaps the most interesting thing about the actor playing Captain America is the fact that he is the son of noted novelist J. D. Salinger.

Hope springs eternal, however, and many Marvel characters are under option, in development or preparing for production. Stan Lee is actively working to push these projects through, and calls effective dramatization the company's "next plateau." The definitive Marvel movie is waiting to be made.

sition period, president James Galton announced his intention to step aside from the company's day-to-day operations and assume the position of chairman of the board of the Marvel Entertainment Group. Since 1975, Galton had kept Marvel on a firm financial footing, and his efforts were instrumental in making the company the giant of the comic book industry. Marvel's newest president, as of 1990, is Terry Stewart, an avid comic book collector with a background in international business and marketing. Stewart says his mission is "to oversee Marvel's emergence as a comprehensive entertainment company, enhancing its growth in television, feature films, theme parks and other leisure-time arenas."

The Old Guard

Recently, Marvel has been reviving a number of its classic characters that were either temporarily on vacation or in use as guest stars, but were not featured in their own monthly titles. "Sometimes we look around," says editor-in-chief Tom DeFalco, "and notice a character we haven't been using for a while, and we try to build a series around it." Recent comebacks include *The Silver Surfer* (July 1987), *Dr. Strange* (November 1988), *Moon Knight* (June 1989), *Nick Fury, Agent of S.H.I.E.L.D.* (September 1989) and *Ghost Rider* (May 1990). Even Marvel Boy, a minor hero from 1950, achieved a new incarnation as *Quasar* (October 1989).

The fiftieth anniversary of the publication of *Marvel Comics* was celebrated in 1989, and this brought renewed interest in Marvel's first heroes, The Sub-Mariner and The Human Torch. Two limited series recapitulating the highlights of their careers were written by Roy Thomas, who had recently returned to the company and remains its most enthusiastic expert on the Golden Age. At the same time, writer-artist John Byrne brought both characters back into the limelight in regularly scheduled books. The original Human Torch, comatose for decades and long supplanted by the younger Torch from The Fantastic Four, nonetheless popped up in the renamed *Avengers West Coast* #50 (November 1989), and he's been on the scene ever since. Soon thereafter, Byrne brought back the undersea monarch in *Namor The Sub-Mariner* (April 1990), the character's first solo series since the year after his creator Bill Everett's death in 1973. "Marvel said they wanted to do him as a big-business man," says Byrne, "which is something I'd been thinking about myself." Backed by treasure from the ocean floor, Namor is now an action-oriented, international tycoon.

The Non-Mutant Super Hero

For years now, Marvel's list of best-sellers has been dominated by various mutants and by The Punisher. They have had one rival for the top spot, however, and that has been the perennially popular

SHE-HULK

For years Marvel has searched for a female star intriguing enough to sustain a long career like the ones enjoyed by numerous male super heroes. Currently the most promising contender is She-Hulk. Introduced by writer Stan Lee and artist John Buscema in 1980 as an effort to copyright the concept for a television project that never materialized, over the years She-Hulk has developed her own distinctive personality. The agonizing associated with her cousin The Hulk is not her style—she has a sense of humor.

Jennifer Walters was a defense attorney when a transfusion from her blood relative, Bruce Banner, changed her life forever. Now she has become so much less defensive that she's a prosecutor instead, working for the Manhattan District Attorney when she's not out protecting The Marvel Universe from desperadoes. She luxuriates in her strength and striking appearance, and after she discovered that she could make the physical switch between Jennifer and She-Hulk at will, and without changing her personality, she rarely took the trouble to look commonplace. A cheerful nonconformist, she merely shrugged when exposure to radiation left her a green giant with no option to change back into normal form. For her, it's easy being green. Marvel's maladjusted male heroes may feel almost guilty about their powers, but She-Hulk revels in hers. This is one Marvel character who does not have an identity crisis.

The original She-Hulk of 1980 had a savage streak.

She-Hulk's essential affability has allowed Marvel to indulge in some good-humored kidding of the super hero genre. The character herself acknowledges the inherent absurdity of her situation, and her current series is an ingenious concoction of satire and nonsense that is also a running commentary on the very nature of the comic book form. In an era that sometimes seems to be dominated by grim heroes and tragic storylines, She-Hulk is a welcome reminder that humor is one of the things comics do best.

▶ Fifty years after his first
appearance, the original
Human Torch bursts
into flame again in
Avengers West Coast #50
(November 1989).
Cover: John Byrne.

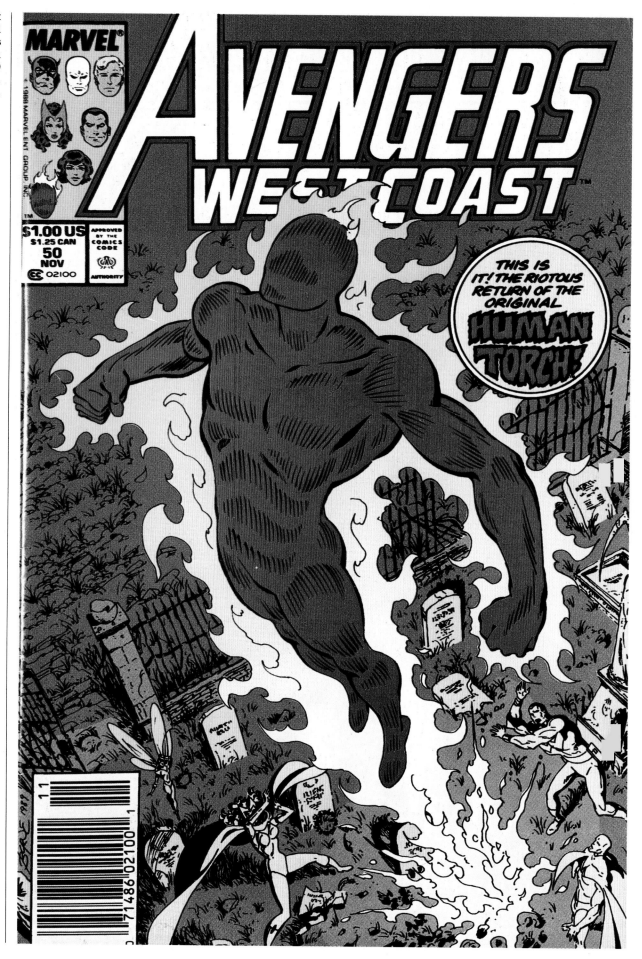

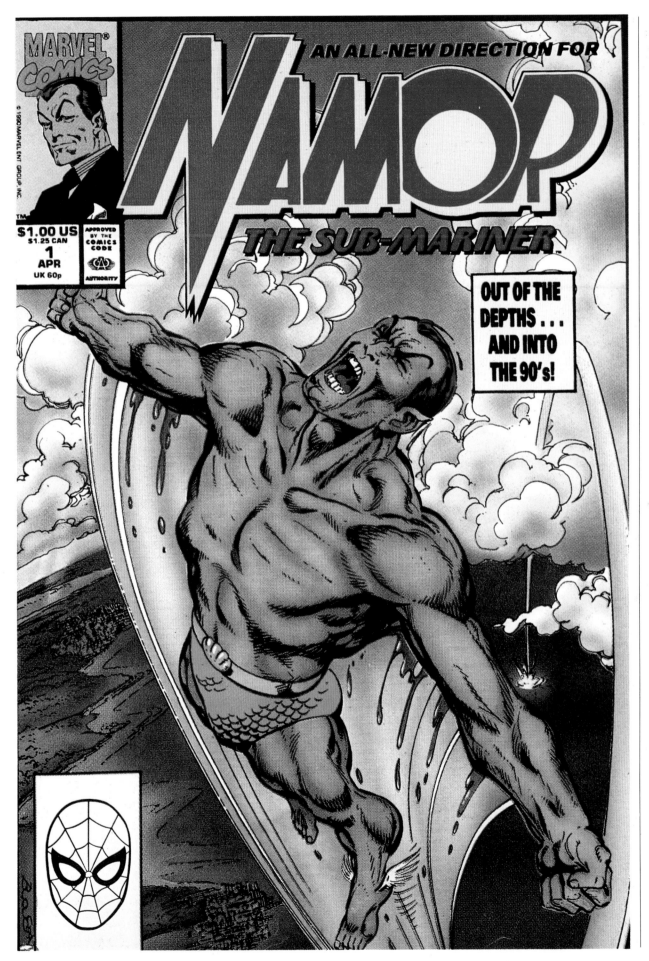

◄Part of a matched set of comic book bookends, The Sub-Mariner soars out of the sea in writer-artist John Byrne's cover for *Namor The Sub-Mariner* #1 (April 1990).

▶ Comic book comebacks: *The Silver Surfer* #1 (July 1987). Cover: Marshall Rogers and Josef Rubinstein. *Dr. Strange* #1 (November 1988). Cover: K. C. Nowlan. *Moon Knight* #1 (June 1989). Cover: Carl Potts, Sal Velluto and K. C. Nowlan. *Nick Fury* #1 (September 1989). Cover: Bob Hall and Kim DeMulder. *Ghost Rider* #1 (May 1990). Cover: Javier Saltares. A new version of the 1950s hero Marvel Boy came back in *Quasar* #1 (October 1989). Cover: Paul Ryan.

Marvel's first licensed character was back on the job too, in *Mighty Mouse* #1 (October 1990). Cover: Ernie Colon.

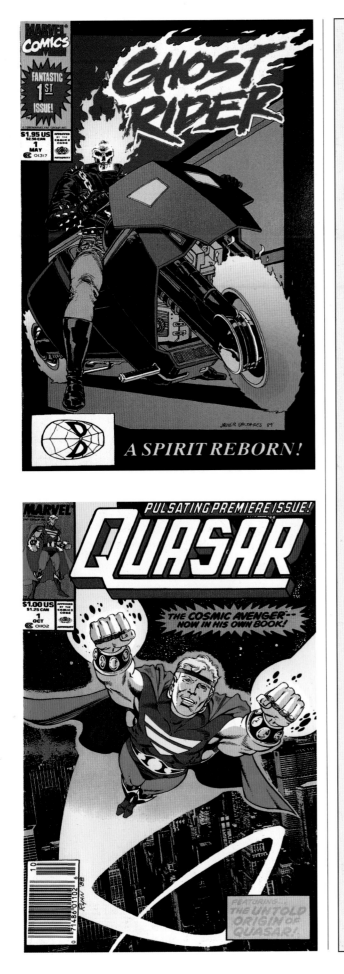

MARVEL FAN MAIL

Marvel receives hundreds of letters from readers every week. Loyal fans send compliments, criticisms and story ideas. Invariably, they catch minor errors that creep into the books—typographical errors, mistakes in the coloring of costumes, illogical plot details. Most often though, fans write to tell the editors, writers and artists how much they enjoy the comics.

When fourteen-year-old Billy Fraser, a devoted fan and collector, read in *Marvel Age* that this book was in preparation, he offered to contribute an essay about why he loves comics. Billy owns more than five hundred comics, most of them Marvel books. "I went through a Hulk phase," he explains, "but now I'm most enthusiastic about Spider-Man, because he is so realistic and believable. For example, it's *really* interesting that he and Mary Jane are thinking about starting a family."

Like many fans his age, Billy would like to grow up to be a Marvel editor or writer —he is afraid that his drawing isn't good enough to qualify him to be an artist. But whatever happens, Billy's commitment to comics is firm. "I hope I never grow out of comics," he says. "My father grew up with Spidey and now I am too. Spidey is really cool—that's what matters."

```
                    Why I Like Comics

     I think that comics are great.  Where else can you get
action, excitement, fantasy and an intriguing plot all rolled
into one?

     Did you ever just stop and think what it would be like to be
able to fly?  It would be INCREDIBLE.  Comics make it possible
for me to see what it would be like to lift a truck, to have
telepathy, to be indestructible.  With comics, the possibilities
are endless.  That is what makes them so great:  You can do
anything in a comic.

     And when comics get exciting, they get REAL exciting.  I
mean, blood-flowing, heart-racing, eye-popping excitement.  Like,
"Is he dead?" or "Will the hero win or lose?" or just plain, "How
will the story end?"

     I particularly like stories where super heroes meet and
clash.  One of my most serious investments was for Amazing
Spider-Man #201, where The Punisher and Spidey have a temporary,
but awful misunderstanding.  It's a cool book.

     And I also like the different characters in comics.  They
each have their own personalities, their own way of dealing with
problems and their own lives.  Some are stubborn, some are easy-
going, some are loners and some are team-workers.

     Plus I LOVE comic book art.  Rippling muscles, dramatic
poses, detailed facial expressions.  All of it.  A character's
pose can make a scene look important, but it can also make that
same scene look like an everyday get-together.  Expressions and
muscles can make a character look deranged, angered or pained.
The colors in the artists's pictures can also set the mood;
bright colors represent happiness, while darker ones represent
gloominess.

     All of these things are reasons I like comics.  And as long
as those are around, I'll be a collector.

                                        Billy Fraser
                              Billy Fraser, age 14
                              Damariscotta, Maine
```

Terry Stewart, Marvel's new president, took charge of the company in 1990.

Artist Todd McFarlane, whose winning way with a web has made Spider-Man more popular than ever.

Spider-Man's black costume was the disguise for a villain in *Amazing Spider-Man* #316 (June 1989). Cover: Todd McFarlane.

▶ Spidey returns to his classic fashion statement and acquires a wild new look in *Amazing Spider-Man* #300 (May 1988). Pencils and inks: Todd McFarlane.

Spider-Man. Editor Jim Salicrup, who took charge of all Spider-Man books in 1987, dubbed him in print, "The Non-Mutant Super Hero," and in conversation calls him "the super hero of the baby boom generation."

Editing Spider-Man is particularly tricky for Salicrup because story lines have to be kept consistent in three monthly books—*The Amazing Spider-Man*, *The Spectacular Spider-Man* and *Web of Spider-Man*—while they simultaneously tie in with the rest of The Marvel Universe. "Ideally there would be one writer, but that's not practical," says Salicrup. "We've managed pretty good consistency though. I'm lucky to have Gerry Conway writing two of the books."

A former editor-in-chief who produced his first Spider-Man story almost twenty years ago, Conway has been writing *Web* (with art by Alex Saviuk) and *Spectacular* (with art by Sal Buscema) since his recent return to Marvel. "I've written more Spider-Man stories since 1986 than I wrote my first time around," says Conway. "I understand the character a lot better now than I did when I was nineteen. And one of the nice things about the Marvel characters is that you can keep them fresh by changing them just a bit."

David Michelinie has been writing *Amazing,* and he, Conway and Salicrup confer regularly. Conway's stories concentrate on Spider-Man's job as Peter Parker, news photographer, while Michelinie emphasizes Parker's private life. "The three books are separate," says Conway, "but there is cross-referencing whenever possible."

The Emperor's Old Clothes

As of May 1988 the artist on *Amazing Spider-Man* was Todd McFarlane, a young Canadian born in 1961, the year The Marvel Age began. McFarlane, only one year older than Spider-Man, had worked on several major characters for various publishers, and was just hitting his stride when he got his first assignment to draw Spider-Man. McFarlane was no fan of the character's black costume, however, and notes that "before I took the book, I knew they were going back to the old one. Otherwise I wouldn't have done it."

Editor Jim Salicrup wanted the old costume back, and so did editor-in-chief Tom DeFalco, even though he had written the best stories about the black alien outfit that had gradually developed a mind of its own. The old red-and-blue Spidey suit returned in issue #300 (May 1988). At the same time, McFarlane got his first chance to ink his own pencils, and the combination of the

old Spider-Man with a new art style took the fans by storm.

"They got to see my artwork the way I wanted to present it," says McFarlane, "and I think most people liked the traditional costume anyway. But I didn't go back to the same look they were used to—I threw in the big eyes and the different webbing and everything else. It was a new look for the old look." In fact, McFarlane's style introduced the most spiderish Spider-Man ever, a character who contorted himself into what the artist calls "weird, funky positions. My intention was that even if you posed the character in silhouette, so you couldn't see the costume, you would still know that it was Spider-Man." McFarlane also festooned the hero with intricate spaghettilike webbing, and seemed to relish every line of it. "No way!" says the artist. "I hate doing those lines! But that's Spider-Man, you know?"

McFarlane also had a winning way with Spidey's wife Mary Jane, and together with writer Michelinie, he produced a splendid series of stories about a villain named Venom who was garbed in the old black Spidey suit. Yet McFarlane

◄ *Spider-Man* #1
(August 1990), with script,
pencils and inks by
Todd McFarlane, broke
every comic book sales
record, and made Spidey
the world's champion
super hero.

► Spidey keeps the streets safe in Todd McFarlane's pencils for a two-page spread from *Spider-Man #1*.

► The published pages, with their black borders, innovative design and detailed drawing, exemplify the style that has made McFarlane the hottest artist of a new decade. Script, pencils and inks: Todd McFarlane.

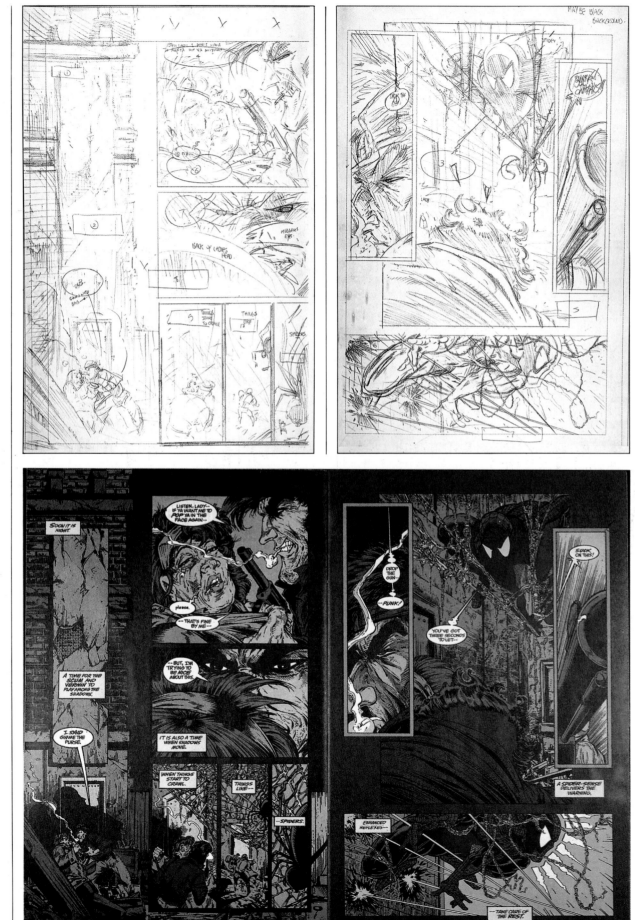

pulled out of *Amazing Spider-Man* with issue #325, and was replaced by artist Erik Larsen. Plans were afoot for yet another Spider-Man series.

The Hottest Hero

Spider-Man #1, a new title with no qualifiers, made its debut in August 1990 and immediately drew the attention of the national media. The reason was simple: *Spider-Man* #1 was the best-selling comic book in the history of the United States. The initial press run was 2.35 million, and 500,000 additional copies were later printed to handle the demand. The first issue was a phenom-enon that put even Golden Age sales to shame.

Marvel's marketing department undoubtedly had a hand in these stupendous sales. This first issue, the kind collectors hoard, was printed with several different covers in a variety of colors, some of them sealed in plastic so they could be preserved. Beyond the gimmicks, however, was a recognition of Spider-Man as a fabulous character and of Todd McFarlane as the hottest talent in the business. Marvel's tradition of putting flexible heroes into the hands of innovative artists had paid off in spades.

"For the first issue," says McFarlane, "I wanted to make an impact visually." He took on the writing as well so he could have "the freedom to draw what I want to draw. I'm trying to break people of reading a comic book the way they've been used to for the last twenty years. I try to play with the storytelling, graphics and design of the pages,

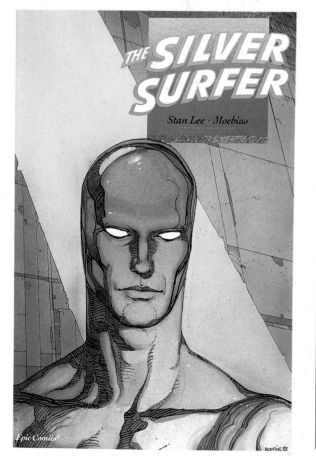

Panels from a computer-generated Iron Man graphic novel, *Crash* (1988). Artist and writer: Mike Saenz. Producer and programmer: William Bates.

because people are acclimated to a certain style and I'm trying to keep them on their toes, if I can."

McFarlane's pages, driven by image rather than plot, were intended to revitalize the medium, but he acknowledges that such efforts are part of an ongoing process. "The next kid will come along and be the next big hot shot," he says, "and as long as he's true to what strikes his fancy, he's got a good chance of making a name for himself."

The Future Lies Ahead

"This medium has grown up tremendously in the last few years," says editor-in-chief Tom DeFalco, "and I think this is just the beginning. As society becomes more visual, someone is going to notice how well pictures and words work together, and that someone will say, 'I've just discovered a new invention, and it's called a comic book.' Comics were originally intended for adults, not kids, and we're slowly getting back to that again."

Publisher Stan Lee, who in his half a century with the company has contributed more than anyone else to The Marvel Universe, was named chairman of Marvel Comics in 1990, but he is not resting on his laurels. Lee continues to negotiate movie deals for Marvel's heroes, and from time to time writes new adventures for his favorites among the myriad characters he has created. Still going strong after fifty years with Marvel, Lee remains optimistic about the company's future. "The past is behind us," says Lee, "and the future, with all its mysterious wonders, is ever unfolding. There are countless stories for us to tell, and we never tire of telling them.

"So we'll continue to probe the endless pos-sibilities of our wonderful comic book world, knowing it has no limits other than imagination itself. And wherever the flight of fantasy may take us, one truth remains as steadfast today as in the past—we and our readers will be sharing the excitement together."

'Nuff said.

◀Publisher Stan Lee, who continues to write stories featuring the idealistic Silver Surfer, collaborated with the renowned French artist "Moebius" (Jean Giraud) on this 1988 graphic novel.

Creating a Comic Book:
The Marvel Method

The procedure for the creation and production of comic books is an unstreamlined, labor-intensive process that requires many hours and many hands. In addition to the writer, three artists—a penciler, an inker and a colorist—participate in the creation of every panel; still another person letters the speech balloons and sound effects. This system, developed in the formative years of comics, remains essentially unchanged to this day.

The most significant innovation has been the introduction of The Marvel Method, a procedural system in which the artist works from a plot rather than from a fully-written script. In the Marvel system, the artist draws the story before the writer contributes dialogue. This approach, which dramatically increases the artist's role in the creation of the storyline, takes full advantage of the medium and capitalizes on the collaborative nature of the art form.

A single page from *Ghost Rider* #13, a current Marvel best-seller, is used here to illustrate the creative process.

1 THE EDITORIAL CONFERENCE

Writer Howard Mackie and editor Bobbie Chase meet to throw around possible ideas for an upcoming issue of *Ghost Rider*. Once they have settled on an idea, the writer produces a plot, a brief, general summary of the bare outlines of the story that will serve as a guideline for the artist.

Sometimes the writer and artist are the same person, in which case the plot may be only a very rough approximation of the story's action. At other times the plot may be created by one writer and the final script by still another writer, in which case the plot summary will be written in much greater detail.

▲ The plot for page one of *Ghost Rider* #13, including a personal note and instructions from the writer to the artist.

GHOST RIDER #13
"You'll Never See What's Coming!"/Mackie

Mark--

I'm going to try and not overwrite the stories we do together. I have full trust in your excellent storytelling abilities. Please take the liberty, where ever you feel the situation presents itself, of doing full page splashes and/or double page spreads.

As we've discussed in the past, I really want to continue to give the book a more moody/mysterious/grim/scary/horrific feeling. Also, anytime you have any suggestions that you feel may improve the story, or have a particular character you'd like to use, or any input into the future storylines—I'd love to hear them!

—Howard

PAGE ONE/SPLASH
(Please leave room for top copy, title credits and the Marvel indicia at the bottom.)

• The painful transformation into **GHOST RIDER** has begun.

• **DAN KETCH** is straddling his bike. The gas cap is glowing.

• **DAN**'s mouth is opened in a silent scream.

• Nothing else on this page.

• In the background only darkness.

PENCILING THE PAGE

Artist Mark Texeira pencils the story. He sketches out each comic page on an 11" x 17" art board, making decisions as he works about how big each panel will be, how many panels will be devoted to each section of the plot, what perspective each panel will be "seen" from. This overall process of decision-making, including the general determination of the pace at which the story moves, the degree of emphasis on specific characters and incidents, the amount of background detail to be included, and the mood and "look" of the story, is referred to as "story-telling." Pencilers are evaluated by their colleagues and comic book readers on both their drawing skill and their storytelling ability.

▲ Pencils by Mark Texeira for page one, known traditionally as the "splash page" because it opens a story with a splash.

▲ The finished script page and the penciled and lettered page.

LETTERING THE PAGE

3

The penciled pages are returned to the writer, who uses them as a guide to write the final script. The script is then delivered to the letterer, sometimes a Marvel staff employee and sometimes a free lancer. Here Janice Chiang letters dialogue for the next issue of the *Ghost Rider* series; she will also draw the panel frames, the word balloons and the sound effects.

INKING THE PAGE

4

The lettered page is passed along to the inker, who in this case is also the penciler, Mark Texeira. (More often, the penciler and the inker are two different people.) Experienced readers can look at a page and identify both the penciler and the inker — without credits.

▲ The inked and lettered page.

COLORING THE PAGE

The inked page, after approval by the editor, is photocopied and reduced to fit the finished comic book page size (6 11/16" x 10 1/4"). Using Dr. Martin's watercolor dyes, colorist Gregory Wright paints the photocopied page. The colorist's choices can contribute significantly to the mood of the finished page. After painting, he assigns a code number to each colored area as a guide for the color separator who prepares the film from which the printer will make printing plates.

TAKING CARE OF DETAILS

Artist Mark Texeira and executive art director John Romita confer about details of a page-in-progress. Because the creation of comic books is such a specialized skill, many creators have learned their craft by apprenticing themselves to older hands. Romita supervises the design and production of all comic book covers, and assists young talent with tricky problems. He is also available to facilitate communication between artists and editors, because the visual and verbal communities often speak very different languages.

▲ The colored and coded page.

▲ In the belly of the beast, where there's lots of action.

7 THE MARVEL BULLPEN

The physical hub of the Marvel offices is the bullpen, where staff artists and production technicians do lettering and make minor corrections on the work of free-lance artists. The bullpen staff, many of whom aspire to careers as Marvel creators, also assist the editors in trafficking the pages through the various steps of production.

◀ The huge Flexographic web press at World Color in Sparta, Illinois, which handles the majority of Marvel's comics.

8 PRINTING THE COMICS

The inked pages, together with the colorist's painted guide and technical instructions, are sent to the color separator who creates color film for each page. The pages are then sent to the printer, who makes printing plates for each page and then prints, binds and ships the finished books. Approximately four weeks time is needed to complete the color separations and the printing for each issue of a comic book.

▲ The colors of the printed page are less vivid than the painted guide because of the printing process used and the nature of the paper on which most comics are printed.

▶ Jim Hanley's Universe in New York City.

9 THE PRINTED PAGE

The first page of issue #13 of *Ghost Rider*, officially published in May 1991 but actually shipped in early March to wholesale distributors, who in turn ship the comics to newsstands and comic book shops all over the country. To allow time for distribution, and in accordance with traditional advance dating customs in the magazine industry, the books are shipped two months ahead of their cover date. The entire process of creation, color separation, printing and distribution of a single comic book issue requires, on average, about six months.

10 THE COMIC BOOK SHOP

More than half of all comic books are now purchased in the 4000 individually owned comic book shops that cater to comics fans. In addition to comics, these stores often sell other books as well: science fiction, fantasy, mystery and horror. Additionally, many of the stores carry various "related" materials, e.g., trading cards, posters, T-shirts and licensed merchandise featuring comic book characters.

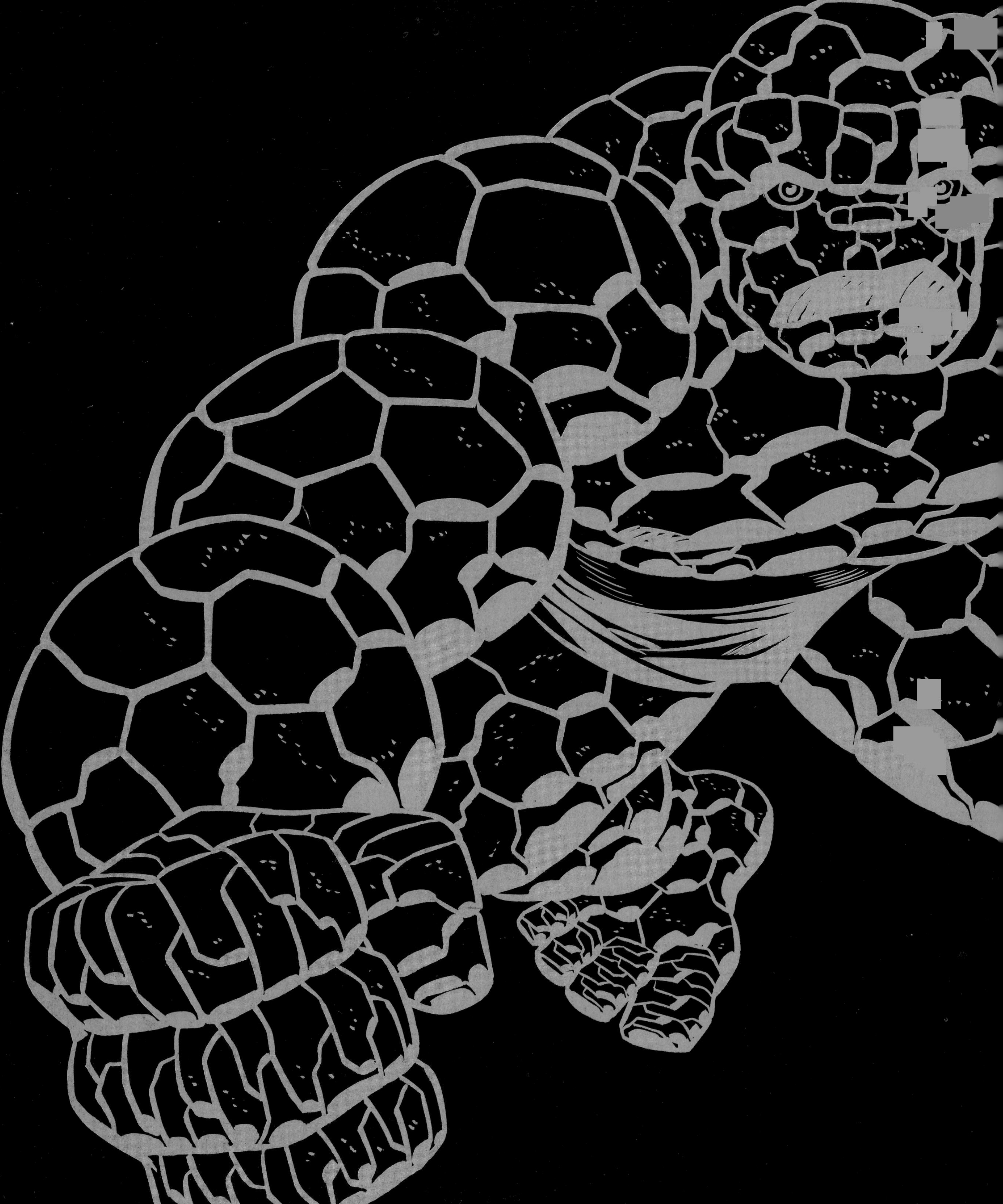

Classic Marvel Stories

The ultimate demonstration of Marvel's appeal lies in the comic book stories that have entertained millions over the years. Here are four of the best. They exemplify the visual and narrative techniques that have brought life to a universe of troubled but finally triumphant heroes.

"Vengeance" originally appeared in *Sub-Mariner* #35 (August 1954). Bill Everett, who wrote and drew this story fifteen years after creating the original Marvel super hero, had by this time developed a smooth cartooning style in which simple but pleasing caricatures were elegantly rendered. As the opening "splash" panel reveals, Everett's tales were still full of rambunctious fun, pitting the protagonist of this short piece against a madman, a monster and an army of robots as well.

Namor is a fish out of water, banished from his undersea kingdom and consequently deprived of the great strength he derives from contact with the ocean. Thus he falls easy victim to the machinations of the gnomish scientist, whose isolation and insanity are emphasized by the panel in which he appears as a tiny figure against a blank background.

The two female characters are color-coded in a commonplace kind of visual shorthand: The Sub-Mariner's long-suffering and virtuous companion, Betty Dean, is blonde, while the nameless wicked woman is brunette. She's also much more energetic and entertaining.

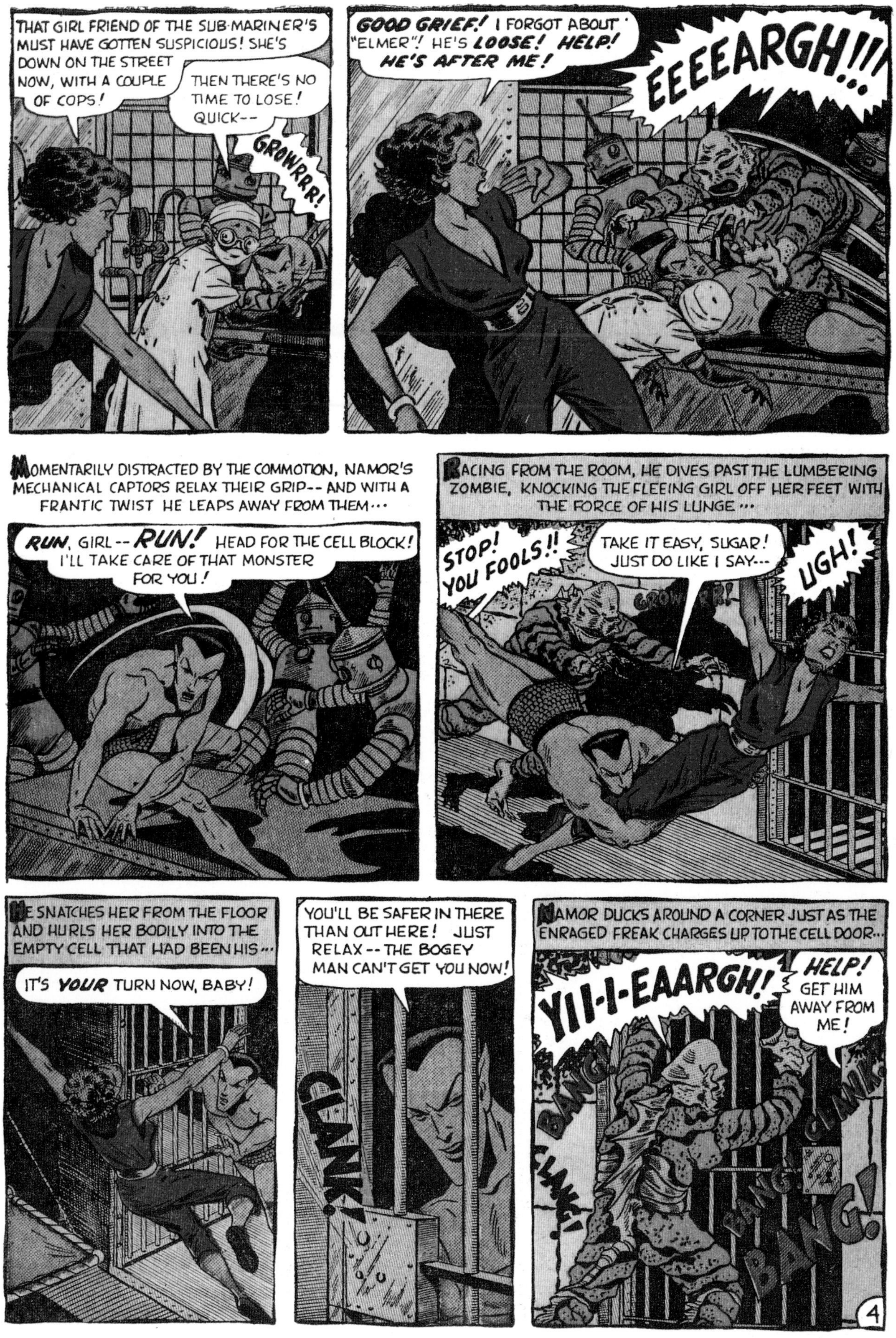
THAT GIRL FRIEND OF THE SUB-MARINER'S MUST HAVE GOTTEN SUSPICIOUS! SHE'S DOWN ON THE STREET NOW, WITH A COUPLE OF COPS!
THEN THERE'S NO TIME TO LOSE! QUICK--
GROWRRR!
GOOD GRIEF! I FORGOT ABOUT "ELMER"! HE'S LOOSE! HELP! HE'S AFTER ME!
EEEEARGH!!!
MOMENTARILY DISTRACTED BY THE COMMOTION, NAMOR'S MECHANICAL CAPTORS RELAX THEIR GRIP-- AND WITH A FRANTIC TWIST HE LEAPS AWAY FROM THEM...
RUN, GIRL-- RUN! HEAD FOR THE CELL BLOCK! I'LL TAKE CARE OF THAT MONSTER FOR YOU!
RACING FROM THE ROOM, HE DIVES PAST THE LUMBERING ZOMBIE, KNOCKING THE FLEEING GIRL OFF HER FEET WITH THE FORCE OF HIS LUNGE...
STOP! YOU FOOLS!!
TAKE IT EASY, SUGAR! JUST DO LIKE I SAY---
UGH!
HE SNATCHES HER FROM THE FLOOR AND HURLS HER BODILY INTO THE EMPTY CELL THAT HAD BEEN HIS...
IT'S YOUR TURN NOW, BABY!
YOU'LL BE SAFER IN THERE THAN OUT HERE! JUST RELAX -- THE BOGEY MAN CAN'T GET YOU NOW!
CLANK!
NAMOR DUCKS AROUND A CORNER JUST AS THE ENRAGED FREAK CHARGES UP TO THE CELL DOOR...
YII-I-EAARGH!
HELP! GET HIM AWAY FROM ME!
BANG!
CLANK!
BANG!
4

"Sufferin' Shad!" Prince Namor, who displayed an inelegant fondness for slang in his early adventures, indulges in his favorite epithet during his moment of greatest peril. Everett emphasizes his hero's fall graphically by breaking up the standard page layout with a large, vertical panel. In the topsy-turvy world of comic books, the *deus ex machina* arrives not from the heavens, but from below.

If the monster "Elmer" looks familiar, it's because Everett clearly derived its design from the title character of the 1954 film *The Creature from the Black Lagoon.* And if the creature's fear of water makes him pathetic, it's possible that Everett found the movie monster just a weak imitation of Namor, the "amphibious man" he had created fifteen years before in 1939.

"Yipe!" Elmer's dying cry underscores the essentially comical nature of Everett's fish story, while the repetition of the large vertical panel suggests that Elmer and Namor are brothers under the skin. Yet when all is said and done, only a "crazy fool" would try to replace The Sub-Mariner.

"Duel to the Death with The Vulture" originally appeared in *The Amazing Spider-Man* #2 (May 1963). This is a key story in the development of Spider-Man, who had previously fought crooks and spies but now must test himself against his first super villain. Writer Stan Lee and artist Steve Ditko used the full splash page as a poster to advertise a battle of good against evil (and youth against age) set high above the rooftops of New York's skyscrapers.

Peter Parker's glasses were discarded in January 1964, broken and never replaced because, apparently, his super powers made them unnecessary. They did last long enough as comic book symbols to peg him as an intellectual, and throughout his career his wits have served him as well as his spider strength.

Peter's Aunt May performs an inestimable service by giving him a camera and thus providing him with the means for a livelihood. The camera is also a legacy from Uncle Ben, whom Peter inadvertently failed, and a symbol of Peter's commitment to protecting and supporting his aging aunt.

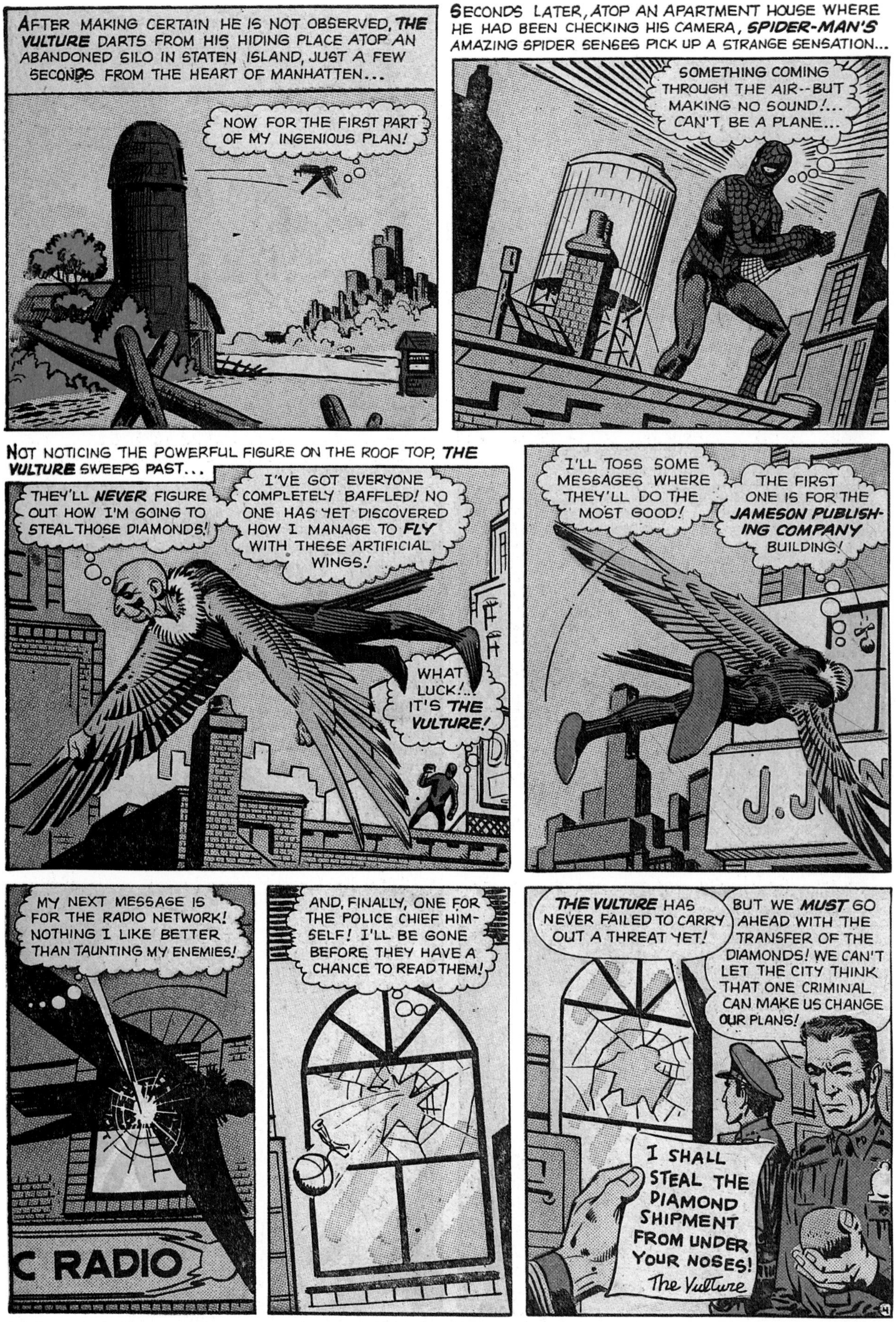
AFTER MAKING CERTAIN HE IS NOT OBSERVED, THE VULTURE DARTS FROM HIS HIDING PLACE ATOP AN ABANDONED SILO IN STATEN ISLAND, JUST A FEW SECONDS FROM THE HEART OF MANHATTEN...
NOW FOR THE FIRST PART OF MY INGENIOUS PLAN!
SECONDS LATER, ATOP AN APARTMENT HOUSE WHERE HE HAD BEEN CHECKING HIS CAMERA, SPIDER-MAN'S AMAZING SPIDER SENSES PICK UP A STRANGE SENSATION...
SOMETHING COMING THROUGH THE AIR--BUT MAKING NO SOUND!... CAN'T BE A PLANE...
NOT NOTICING THE POWERFUL FIGURE ON THE ROOF TOP, THE VULTURE SWEEPS PAST...
THEY'LL NEVER FIGURE OUT HOW I'M GOING TO STEAL THOSE DIAMONDS!
I'VE GOT EVERYONE COMPLETELY BAFFLED! NO ONE HAS YET DISCOVERED HOW I MANAGE TO FLY WITH THESE ARTIFICIAL WINGS!
WHAT LUCK!... IT'S THE VULTURE!
I'LL TOSS SOME MESSAGES WHERE THEY'LL DO THE MOST GOOD!
THE FIRST ONE IS FOR THE JAMESON PUBLISHING COMPANY BUILDING!
J.J
MY NEXT MESSAGE IS FOR THE RADIO NETWORK! NOTHING I LIKE BETTER THAN TAUNTING MY ENEMIES!
C RADIO
AND, FINALLY, ONE FOR THE POLICE CHIEF HIMSELF! I'LL BE GONE BEFORE THEY HAVE A CHANCE TO READ THEM!
THE VULTURE HAS NEVER FAILED TO CARRY OUT A THREAT YET!
BUT WE MUST GO AHEAD WITH THE TRANSFER OF THE DIAMONDS! WE CAN'T LET THE CITY THINK THAT ONE CRIMINAL CAN MAKE US CHANGE OUR PLANS!
I SHALL STEAL THE DIAMOND SHIPMENT FROM UNDER YOUR NOSES! The Vulture

Steve Ditko's pencils and inks, while actually quite sophisticated, had a certain rough-hewn feeling, reminiscent of woodcuts. This stylistic device made his work feel more down-to-earth and realistic than the slicker techniques that were in vogue before the onset of The Marvel Age.

In this tough spot, as in so many more to come, Spider-Man's brawn is useless without his brain.

In another historic scene, Peter refines the scientific gimmicks that enable him to function as Spider-Man. His webbing, which he created, defines his persona more than the super powers he acquired accidentally.

Peter makes his first sale to the obnoxious J. Jonah Jameson. He has worked for Jameson's newspaper, *The Daily Bugle*, ever since. Jim Shooter, Marvel's editor-in-chief from 1978 to 1987, read this story when he was a boy, and shortly thereafter embarked on a career as a teenage comic book writer. Shooter doubts there was a direct connection between his career move and Peter Parker's, but the possibility remains tantalizing.

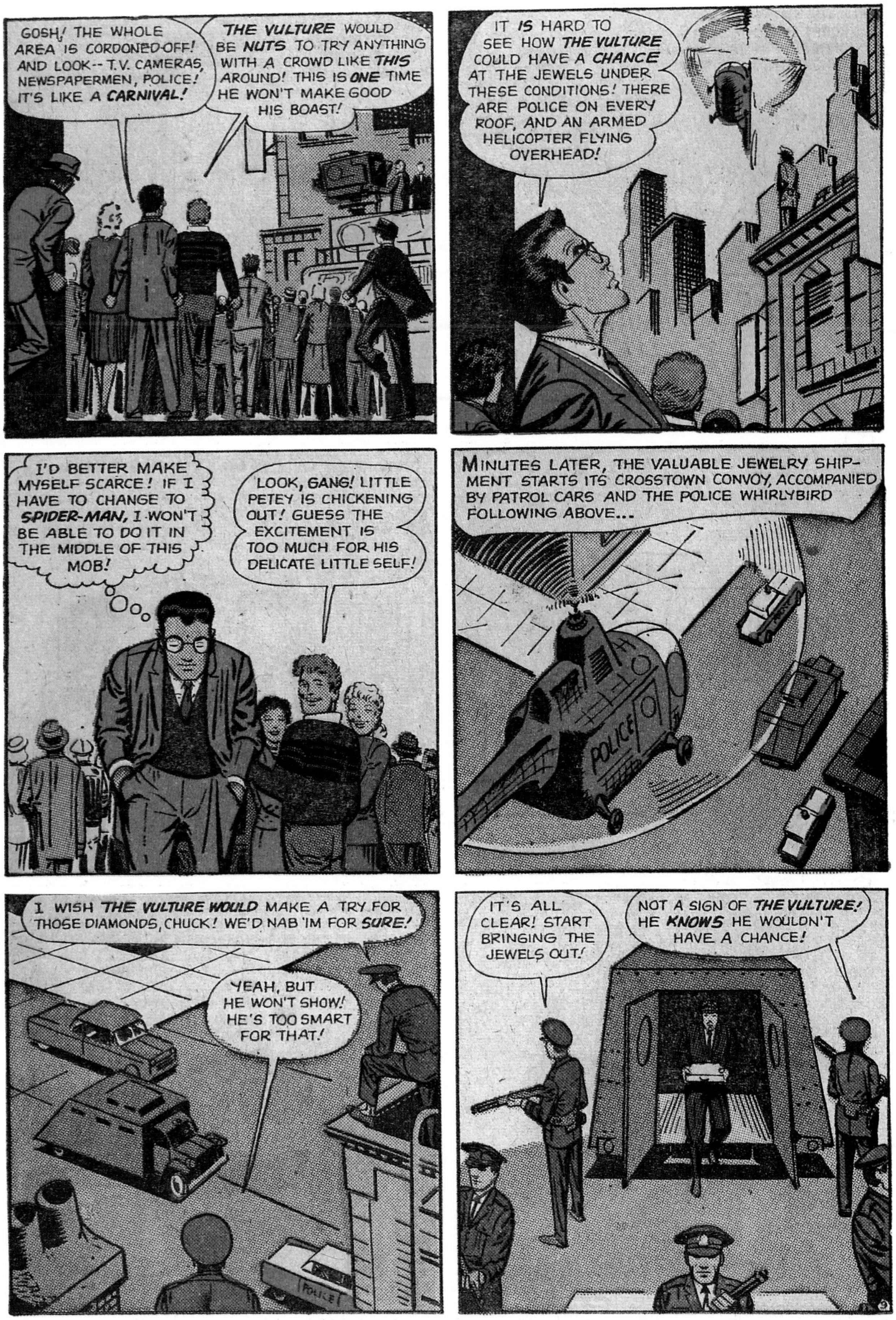
GOSH! THE WHOLE AREA IS CORDONED-OFF! AND LOOK-- T.V. CAMERAS, NEWSPAPERMEN, POLICE! IT'S LIKE A CARNIVAL!
THE VULTURE WOULD BE NUTS TO TRY ANYTHING WITH A CROWD LIKE THIS AROUND! THIS IS ONE TIME HE WON'T MAKE GOOD HIS BOAST!
IT IS HARD TO SEE HOW THE VULTURE COULD HAVE A CHANCE AT THE JEWELS UNDER THESE CONDITIONS! THERE ARE POLICE ON EVERY ROOF, AND AN ARMED HELICOPTER FLYING OVERHEAD!
I'D BETTER MAKE MYSELF SCARCE! IF I HAVE TO CHANGE TO SPIDER-MAN, I WON'T BE ABLE TO DO IT IN THE MIDDLE OF THIS MOB!
LOOK, GANG! LITTLE PETEY IS CHICKENING OUT! GUESS THE EXCITEMENT IS TOO MUCH FOR HIS DELICATE LITTLE SELF!
MINUTES LATER, THE VALUABLE JEWELRY SHIPMENT STARTS ITS CROSSTOWN CONVOY, ACCOMPANIED BY PATROL CARS AND THE POLICE WHIRLYBIRD FOLLOWING ABOVE...
POLICE
I WISH THE VULTURE WOULD MAKE A TRY FOR THOSE DIAMONDS, CHUCK! WE'D NAB 'IM FOR SURE!
YEAH, BUT HE WON'T SHOW! HE'S TOO SMART FOR THAT!
POLICE
IT'S ALL CLEAR! START BRINGING THE JEWELS OUT!
NOT A SIGN OF THE VULTURE! HE KNOWS HE WOULDN'T HAVE A CHANCE!

In an ingenious plot twist, The Vulture attacks from below rather than above. The sewer, while actually a practical place to hide, appears often in popular culture as a suitable, logical habitat for undesirable elements.

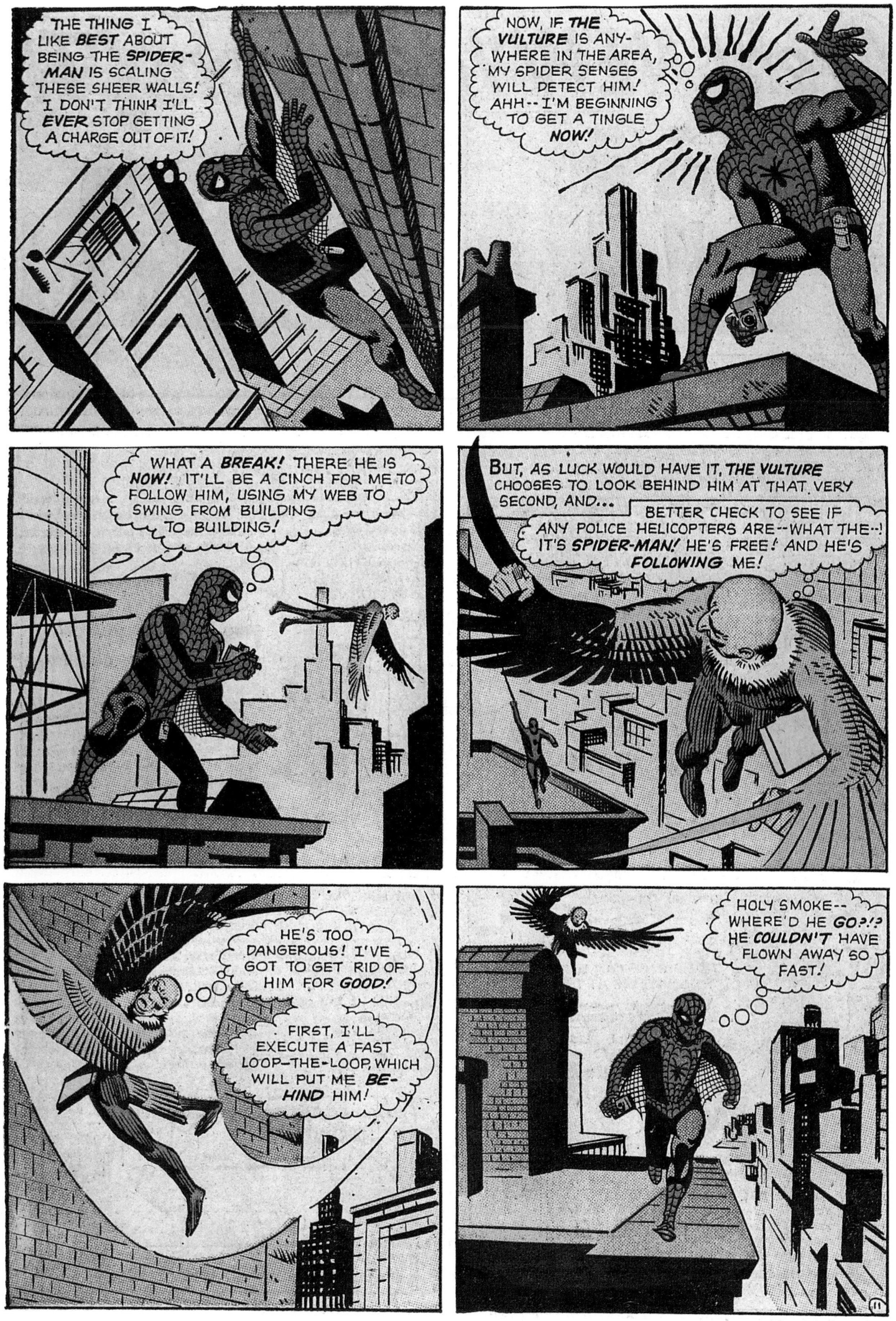
THE THING I LIKE BEST ABOUT BEING THE SPIDER-MAN IS SCALING THESE SHEER WALLS! I DON'T THINK I'LL EVER STOP GETTING A CHARGE OUT OF IT!
NOW, IF THE VULTURE IS ANYWHERE IN THE AREA, MY SPIDER SENSES WILL DETECT HIM! AHH-- I'M BEGINNING TO GET A TINGLE NOW!
WHAT A BREAK! THERE HE IS NOW! IT'LL BE A CINCH FOR ME TO FOLLOW HIM, USING MY WEB TO SWING FROM BUILDING TO BUILDING!
BUT, AS LUCK WOULD HAVE IT, THE VULTURE CHOOSES TO LOOK BEHIND HIM AT THAT VERY SECOND, AND...
BETTER CHECK TO SEE IF ANY POLICE HELICOPTERS ARE--WHAT THE--! IT'S SPIDER-MAN! HE'S FREE! AND HE'S FOLLOWING ME!
HE'S TOO DANGEROUS! I'VE GOT TO GET RID OF HIM FOR GOOD!
FIRST, I'LL EXECUTE A FAST LOOP-THE-LOOP, WHICH WILL PUT ME BE-HIND HIM!
HOLY SMOKE-- WHERE'D HE GO?!? HE COULDN'T HAVE FLOWN AWAY SO FAST!

Once again Spider-Man's courage and special abilities play their part, but his intelligence is what saves the day. The actual gimmick employed is less important than the idea that Peter Parker, even before his transformation into Spider-Man, possessed talents that went unnoticed and unappreciated.

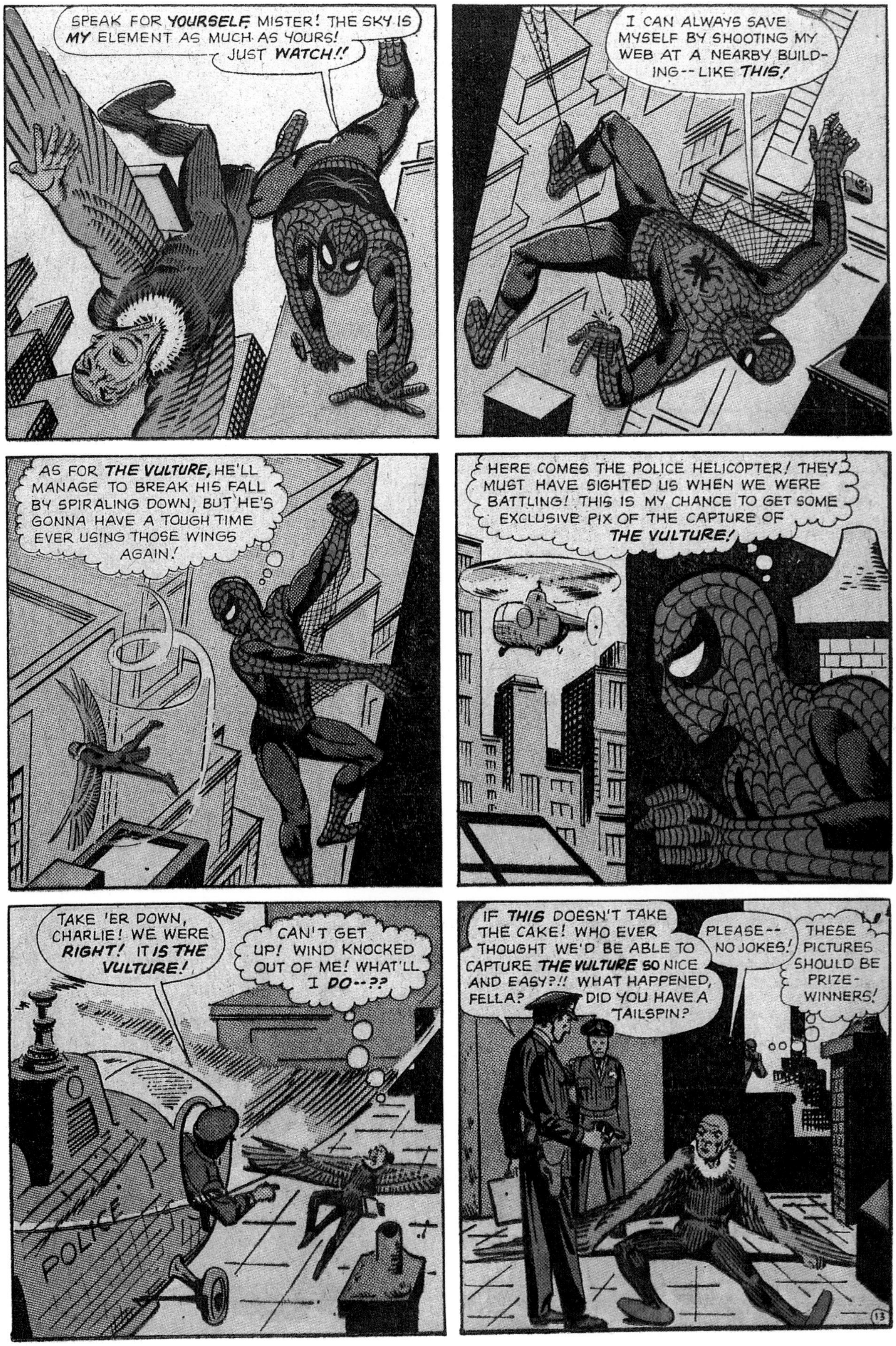
SPEAK FOR YOURSELF, MISTER! THE SKY IS MY ELEMENT AS MUCH AS YOURS! JUST WATCH!!
I CAN ALWAYS SAVE MYSELF BY SHOOTING MY WEB AT A NEARBY BUILDING-- LIKE THIS!
AS FOR THE VULTURE, HE'LL MANAGE TO BREAK HIS FALL BY SPIRALING DOWN, BUT HE'S GONNA HAVE A TOUGH TIME EVER USING THOSE WINGS AGAIN!
HERE COMES THE POLICE HELICOPTER! THEY MUST HAVE SIGHTED US WHEN WE WERE BATTLING! THIS IS MY CHANCE TO GET SOME EXCLUSIVE PIX OF THE CAPTURE OF THE VULTURE!
TAKE 'ER DOWN, CHARLIE! WE WERE RIGHT! IT IS THE VULTURE!
CAN'T GET UP! WIND KNOCKED OUT OF ME! WHAT'LL I DO--??
POLICE
IF THIS DOESN'T TAKE THE CAKE! WHO EVER THOUGHT WE'D BE ABLE TO CAPTURE THE VULTURE SO NICE AND EASY?!! WHAT HAPPENED, FELLA? DID YOU HAVE A TAILSPIN?
PLEASE-- NO JOKES!
THESE PICTURES SHOULD BE PRIZE-WINNERS!
13

"Go out and buy yourself some twist records!" Stan Lee's seemingly simple dialogue brings Jameson into sharp relief. With this brief phrase, the publisher attempts to appear generous and genial, but he is all too obviously issuing a curt dismissal that simultaneously reveals his complete failure as a judge of people. In any case, there is a happy ending for the frequently frustrated Spider-Man.

"This Man . . . This Monster" originally appeared in *Fantastic Four* #51 (June 1966). This story, coming immediately after the classic trilogy that introduced Galactus and The Silver Surfer, epitomizes an incredibly fruitful period in the collaboration between writer Stan Lee and artist Jack Kirby. Joe Sinnott, a distinguished inker with an extraordinary sensitivity to a penciler's style, also makes his presence felt.

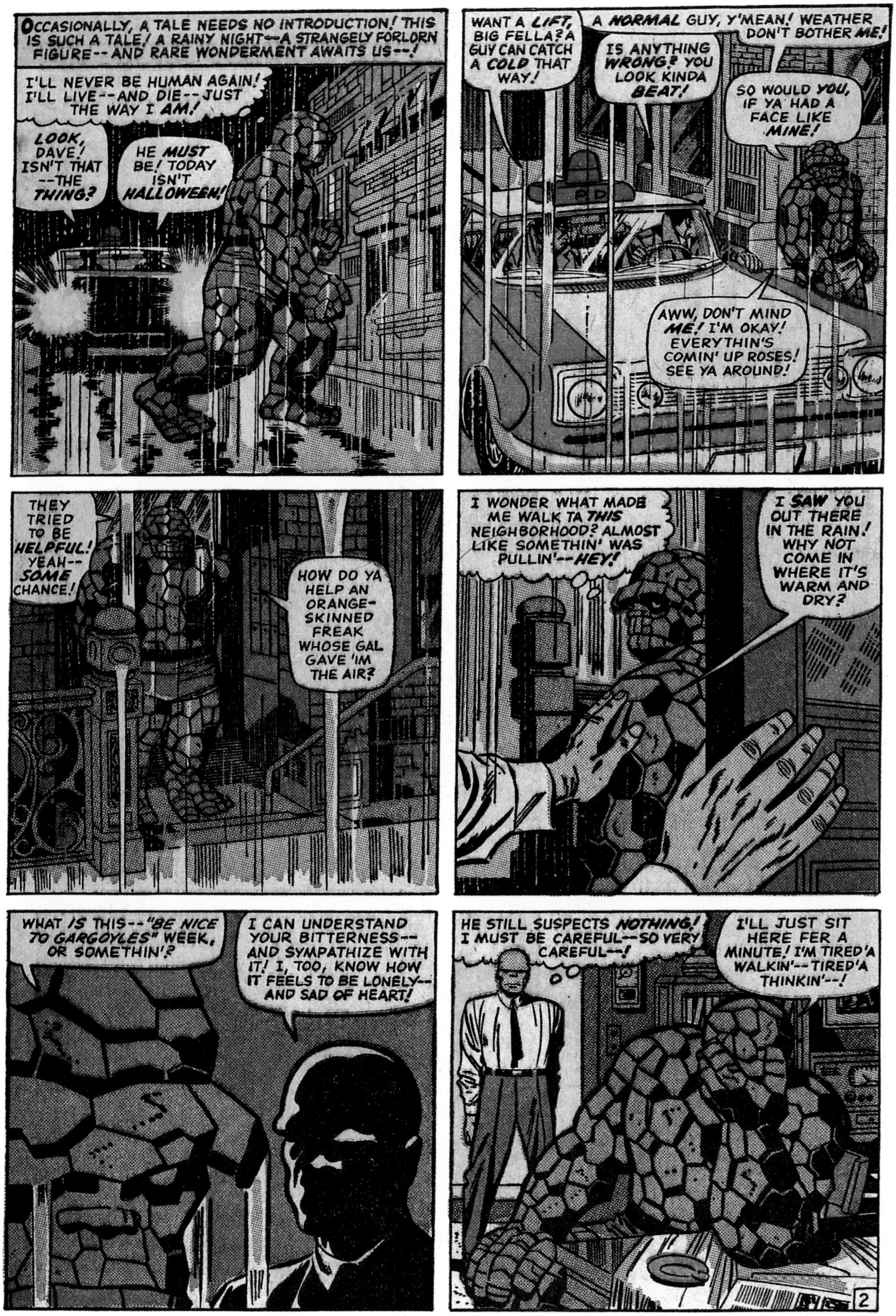
OCCASIONALLY, A TALE NEEDS NO INTRODUCTION! THIS IS SUCH A TALE! A RAINY NIGHT--A STRANGELY FORLORN FIGURE--AND RARE WONDERMENT AWAITS US--!
I'LL NEVER BE HUMAN AGAIN! I'LL LIVE--AND DIE--JUST THE WAY I AM!
LOOK, DAVE! ISN'T THAT --THE THING?
HE MUST BE! TODAY ISN'T HALLOWEEN!
WANT A LIFT, BIG FELLA? A GUY CAN CATCH A COLD THAT WAY!
A NORMAL GUY, Y'MEAN! WEATHER DON'T BOTHER ME!
IS ANYTHING WRONG? YOU LOOK KINDA BEAT!
SO WOULD YOU, IF YA HAD A FACE LIKE MINE!
AWW, DON'T MIND ME! I'M OKAY! EVERYTHIN'S COMIN' UP ROSES! SEE YA AROUND!
THEY TRIED TO BE HELPFUL! YEAH--SOME CHANCE!
HOW DO YA HELP AN ORANGE-SKINNED FREAK WHOSE GAL GAVE 'IM THE AIR?
I WONDER WHAT MADE ME WALK TA THIS NEIGHBORHOOD? ALMOST LIKE SOMETHIN' WAS PULLIN'--HEY!
I SAW YOU OUT THERE IN THE RAIN! WHY NOT COME IN WHERE IT'S WARM AND DRY?
WHAT IS THIS--"BE NICE TO GARGOYLES" WEEK, OR SOMETHIN'?
I CAN UNDERSTAND YOUR BITTERNESS--AND SYMPATHIZE WITH IT! I, TOO, KNOW HOW IT FEELS TO BE LONELY--AND SAD OF HEART!
HE STILL SUSPECTS NOTHING! I MUST BE CAREFUL--SO VERY CAREFUL--!
I'LL JUST SIT HERE FER A MINUTE! I'M TIRED'A WALKIN'--TIRED'A THINKIN'--!
2

The Thing, the one member of The Fantastic Four whose super powers are a curse as well as a blessing, is jealous because his blind sweetheart, Alicia, has been impressed by the noble Silver Surfer. The Thing also resents his brilliant colleague Reed Richards, and is thus spiritually akin to the nameless villain who represents his darker side.

"This Man . . . This Monster" is an example of an "evil twin" story. As such, it could have been a commonplace tale of a type all too familiar in popular culture, but Lee and Kirby rise above the obvious and renovate the cliché.

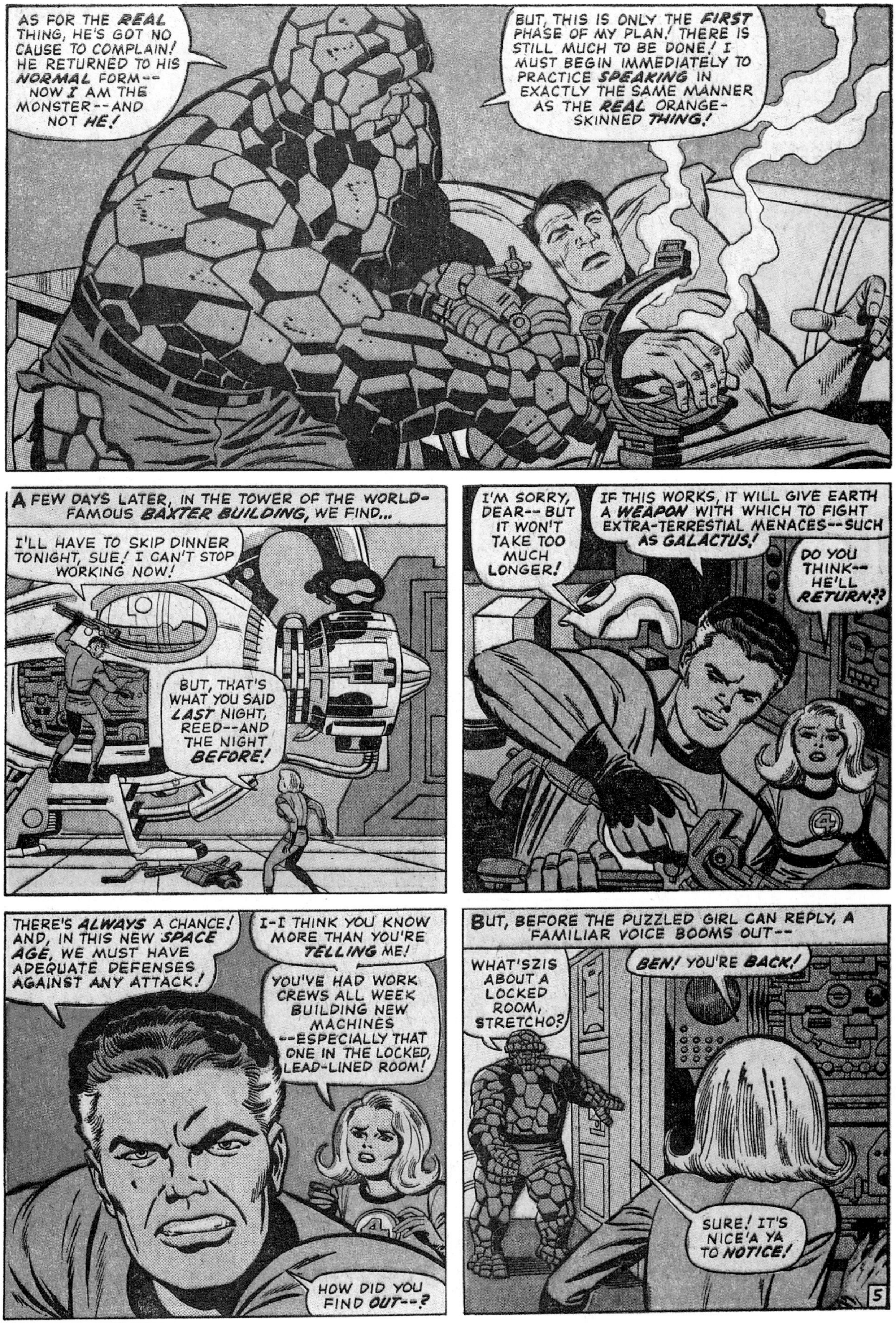
AS FOR THE REAL THING, HE'S GOT NO CAUSE TO COMPLAIN! HE RETURNED TO HIS NORMAL FORM-- NOW I AM THE MONSTER--AND NOT HE!
BUT, THIS IS ONLY THE FIRST PHASE OF MY PLAN! THERE IS STILL MUCH TO BE DONE! I MUST BEGIN IMMEDIATELY TO PRACTICE SPEAKING IN EXACTLY THE SAME MANNER AS THE REAL ORANGE-SKINNED THING!
A FEW DAYS LATER, IN THE TOWER OF THE WORLD-FAMOUS BAXTER BUILDING, WE FIND...
I'LL HAVE TO SKIP DINNER TONIGHT, SUE! I CAN'T STOP WORKING NOW!
BUT, THAT'S WHAT YOU SAID LAST NIGHT, REED--AND THE NIGHT BEFORE!
I'M SORRY, DEAR-- BUT IT WON'T TAKE TOO MUCH LONGER!
IF THIS WORKS, IT WILL GIVE EARTH A WEAPON WITH WHICH TO FIGHT EXTRA-TERRESTIAL MENACES--SUCH AS GALACTUS!
DO YOU THINK-- HE'LL RETURN?!?
THERE'S ALWAYS A CHANCE! AND, IN THIS NEW SPACE AGE, WE MUST HAVE ADEQUATE DEFENSES AGAINST ANY ATTACK!
I-I THINK YOU KNOW MORE THAN YOU'RE TELLING ME!
YOU'VE HAD WORK CREWS ALL WEEK BUILDING NEW MACHINES --ESPECIALLY THAT ONE IN THE LOCKED, LEAD-LINED ROOM!
HOW DID YOU FIND OUT--?
BUT, BEFORE THE PUZZLED GIRL CAN REPLY, A FAMILIAR VOICE BOOMS OUT--
WHAT'SZIS ABOUT A LOCKED ROOM, STRETCHO?
BEN! YOU'RE BACK!
SURE! IT'S NICE'A YA TO NOTICE!
5

This memorable story from 1966 made an impression on a number of youngsters who later became comic book professionals, including writer-artists John Byrne and Walter Simonson and writer-editor Jim Shooter. "If this is an art form," says Byrne, "if we can be that lofty, then Stan Lee and Jack Kirby have created a masterpiece there."

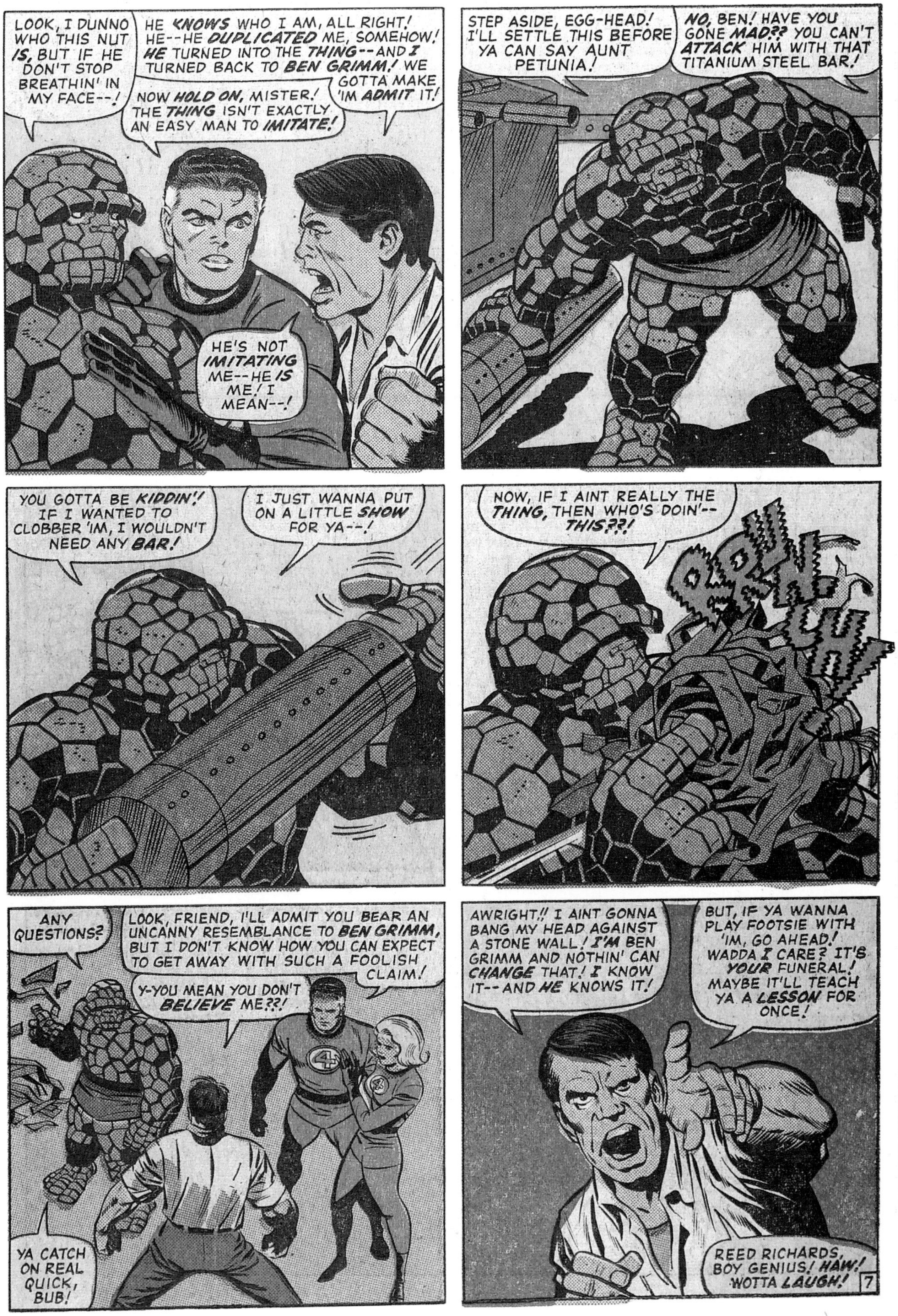
LOOK, I DUNNO WHO THIS NUT *IS*, BUT IF HE DON'T STOP BREATHIN' IN MY FACE--!
HE *KNOWS* WHO I AM, ALL RIGHT! HE--HE *DUPLICATED* ME, SOMEHOW! *HE* TURNED INTO THE *THING*--AND *I* TURNED BACK TO *BEN GRIMM!* WE GOTTA MAKE 'IM *ADMIT* IT!
NOW *HOLD ON*, MISTER! THE *THING* ISN'T EXACTLY AN EASY MAN TO *IMITATE!*
HE'S NOT *IMITATING* ME--HE *IS* ME! I MEAN--!
STEP ASIDE, EGG-HEAD! I'LL SETTLE THIS BEFORE YA CAN SAY AUNT PETUNIA!
NO, BEN! HAVE YOU GONE *MAD??* YOU CAN'T *ATTACK* HIM WITH THAT TITANIUM STEEL BAR!
YOU GOTTA BE *KIDDIN'!* IF I WANTED TO CLOBBER 'IM, I WOULDN'T NEED ANY *BAR!*
I JUST WANNA PUT ON A LITTLE *SHOW* FOR YA--!
NOW, IF I AINT REALLY THE *THING*, THEN WHO'S DOIN'-- *THIS??!*
ANY QUESTIONS?
LOOK, FRIEND, I'LL ADMIT YOU BEAR AN UNCANNY RESEMBLANCE TO *BEN GRIMM*, BUT I DON'T KNOW HOW YOU CAN EXPECT TO GET AWAY WITH SUCH A FOOLISH CLAIM!
Y-YOU MEAN YOU DON'T *BELIEVE* ME??!
YA CATCH ON REAL QUICK, BUB!
AWRIGHT!! I AINT GONNA BANG MY HEAD AGAINST A STONE WALL! *I'M* BEN GRIMM AND NOTHIN' CAN *CHANGE* THAT! *I* KNOW IT--AND *HE* KNOWS IT!
BUT, IF YA WANNA PLAY FOOTSIE WITH 'IM, GO AHEAD! WADDA *I* CARE? IT'S *YOUR* FUNERAL! MAYBE IT'LL TEACH YA A *LESSON* FOR ONCE!
REED RICHARDS, BOY GENIUS! *HAW!* WOTTA *LAUGH!*
7

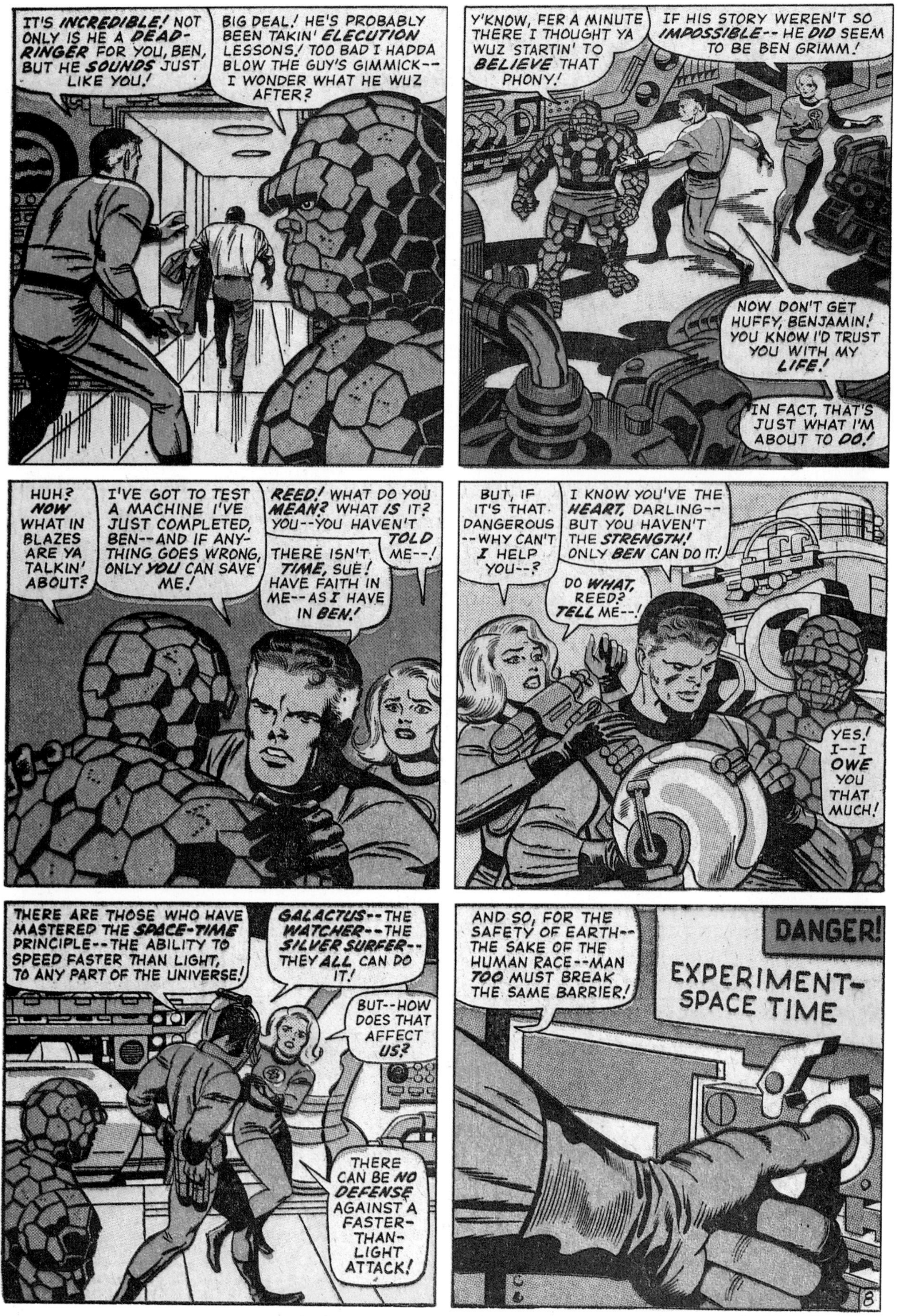
IT'S INCREDIBLE! NOT ONLY IS HE A DEAD-RINGER FOR YOU, BEN, BUT HE SOUNDS JUST LIKE YOU!
BIG DEAL! HE'S PROBABLY BEEN TAKIN' ELECUTION LESSONS! TOO BAD I HADDA BLOW THE GUY'S GIMMICK-- I WONDER WHAT HE WUZ AFTER?
Y'KNOW, FER A MINUTE THERE I THOUGHT YA WUZ STARTIN' TO BELIEVE THAT PHONY!
IF HIS STORY WEREN'T SO IMPOSSIBLE-- HE DID SEEM TO BE BEN GRIMM!
NOW DON'T GET HUFFY, BENJAMIN! YOU KNOW I'D TRUST YOU WITH MY LIFE!
IN FACT, THAT'S JUST WHAT I'M ABOUT TO DO!
HUH? NOW WHAT IN BLAZES ARE YA TALKIN' ABOUT?
I'VE GOT TO TEST A MACHINE I'VE JUST COMPLETED, BEN--AND IF ANYTHING GOES WRONG, ONLY YOU CAN SAVE ME!
REED! WHAT DO YOU MEAN? WHAT IS IT? YOU--YOU HAVEN'T TOLD ME--!
THERE ISN'T TIME, SUE! HAVE FAITH IN ME--AS I HAVE IN BEN!
BUT, IF IT'S THAT DANGEROUS --WHY CAN'T I HELP YOU--?
I KNOW YOU'VE THE HEART, DARLING-- BUT YOU HAVEN'T THE STRENGTH! ONLY BEN CAN DO IT!
DO WHAT, REED? TELL ME--!
YES! I--I OWE YOU THAT MUCH!
THERE ARE THOSE WHO HAVE MASTERED THE SPACE-TIME PRINCIPLE--THE ABILITY TO SPEED FASTER THAN LIGHT, TO ANY PART OF THE UNIVERSE!
GALACTUS--THE WATCHER--THE SILVER SURFER-- THEY ALL CAN DO IT!
BUT--HOW DOES THAT AFFECT US?
THERE CAN BE NO DEFENSE AGAINST A FASTER-THAN-LIGHT ATTACK!
AND SO, FOR THE SAFETY OF EARTH-- THE SAKE OF THE HUMAN RACE--MAN TOO MUST BREAK THE SAME BARRIER!
DANGER!
EXPERIMENT-SPACE TIME
8

Jack Kirby delighted a generation with the wild, warped machinery he envisioned. This full-page "radical cube" is one of his best efforts.

The sub-plot involving The Human Torch's college career may seem irrelevant, especially since The Torch (unlike Spider-Man) soon dropped out to resume his full-time job as a super hero. Yet this sequence, in which The Torch flicks his thumb on like a pocket lighter, is thematically significant. It's the only time any of the story's four heroes uses super powers, and it's presented as a joke. Lee and Kirby have crafted their tale so carefully that personalities, not powers, determine the action.

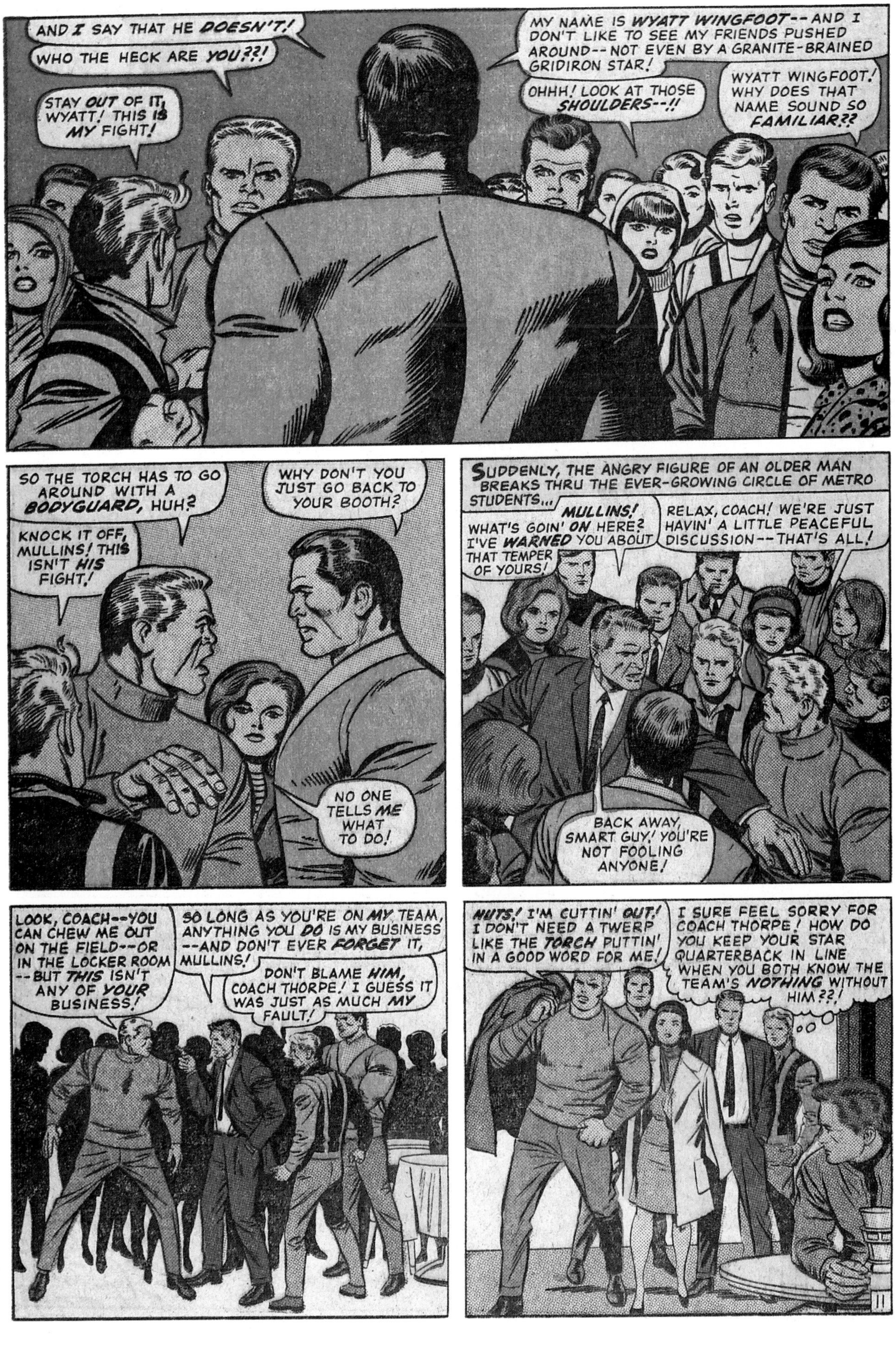
AND I SAY THAT HE DOESN'T!
WHO THE HECK ARE YOU??!
STAY OUT OF IT, WYATT! THIS IS MY FIGHT!
MY NAME IS WYATT WINGFOOT-- AND I DON'T LIKE TO SEE MY FRIENDS PUSHED AROUND-- NOT EVEN BY A GRANITE-BRAINED GRIDIRON STAR!
OHHH! LOOK AT THOSE SHOULDERS--!!
WYATT WINGFOOT! WHY DOES THAT NAME SOUND SO FAMILIAR??
SO THE TORCH HAS TO GO AROUND WITH A BODYGUARD, HUH?
WHY DON'T YOU JUST GO BACK TO YOUR BOOTH?
KNOCK IT OFF, MULLINS! THIS ISN'T HIS FIGHT!
NO ONE TELLS ME WHAT TO DO!
SUDDENLY, THE ANGRY FIGURE OF AN OLDER MAN BREAKS THRU THE EVER-GROWING CIRCLE OF METRO STUDENTS...
MULLINS! WHAT'S GOIN' ON HERE? I'VE WARNED YOU ABOUT THAT TEMPER OF YOURS!
RELAX, COACH! WE'RE JUST HAVIN' A LITTLE PEACEFUL DISCUSSION--THAT'S ALL!
BACK AWAY, SMART GUY! YOU'RE NOT FOOLING ANYONE!
LOOK, COACH--YOU CAN CHEW ME OUT ON THE FIELD--OR IN THE LOCKER ROOM --BUT THIS ISN'T ANY OF YOUR BUSINESS!
SO LONG AS YOU'RE ON MY TEAM, ANYTHING YOU DO IS MY BUSINESS --AND DON'T EVER FORGET IT, MULLINS!
DON'T BLAME HIM, COACH THORPE! I GUESS IT WAS JUST AS MUCH MY FAULT!
NUTS! I'M CUTTIN' OUT! I DON'T NEED A TWERP LIKE THE TORCH PUTTIN' IN A GOOD WORD FOR ME!
I SURE FEEL SORRY FOR COACH THORPE! HOW DO YOU KEEP YOUR STAR QUARTERBACK IN LINE WHEN YOU BOTH KNOW THE TEAM'S NOTHING WITHOUT HIM??
11

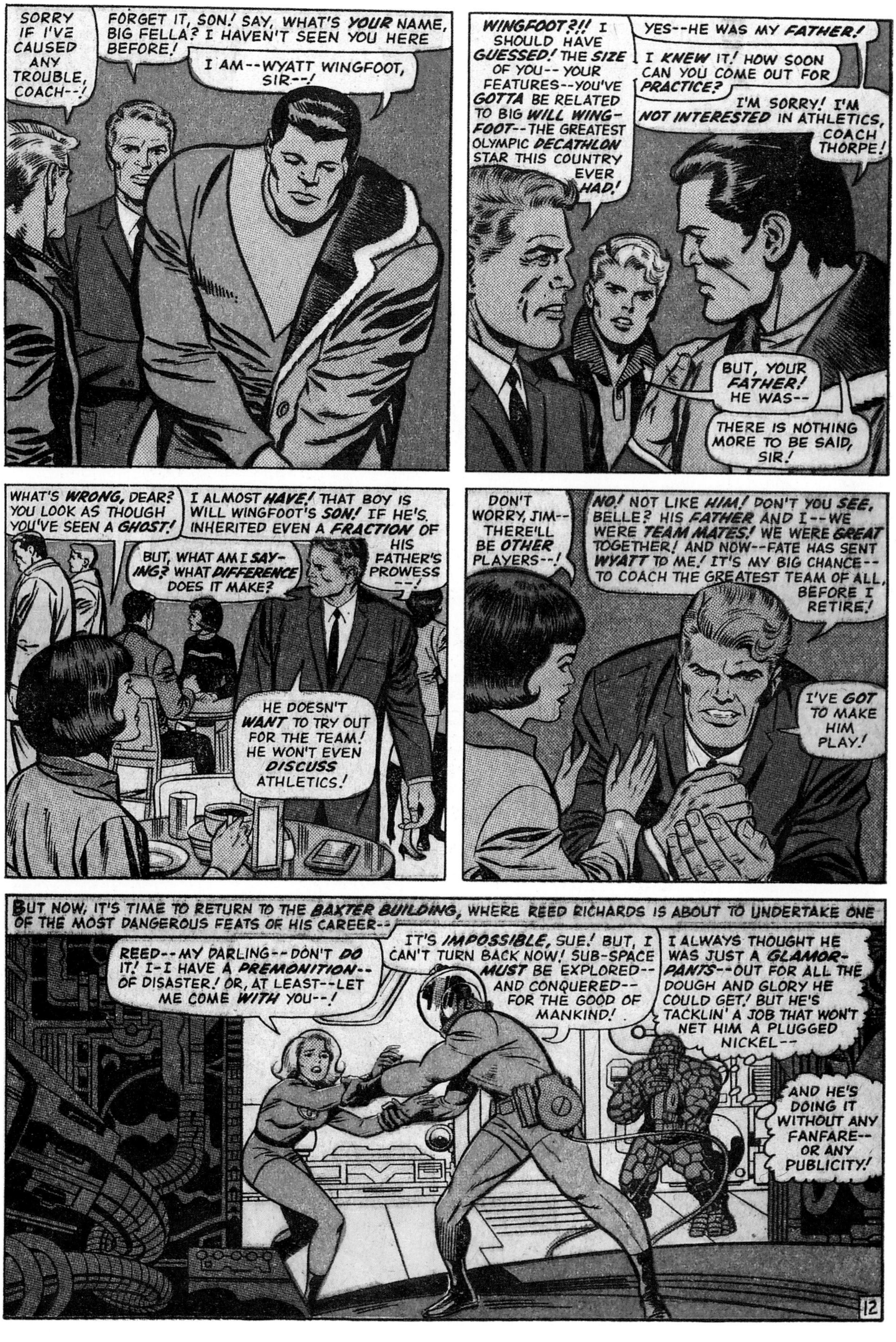
SORRY IF I'VE CAUSED ANY TROUBLE, COACH--!
FORGET IT, SON! SAY, WHAT'S YOUR NAME, BIG FELLA? I HAVEN'T SEEN YOU HERE BEFORE!
I AM--WYATT WINGFOOT, SIR--!
WINGFOOT?!! I SHOULD HAVE GUESSED! THE SIZE OF YOU-- YOUR FEATURES--YOU'VE GOTTA BE RELATED TO BIG WILL WINGFOOT--THE GREATEST OLYMPIC DECATHLON STAR THIS COUNTRY EVER HAD!
YES--HE WAS MY FATHER!
I KNEW IT! HOW SOON CAN YOU COME OUT FOR PRACTICE?
I'M SORRY! I'M NOT INTERESTED IN ATHLETICS, COACH THORPE!
BUT, YOUR FATHER! HE WAS--
THERE IS NOTHING MORE TO BE SAID, SIR!
WHAT'S WRONG, DEAR? YOU LOOK AS THOUGH YOU'VE SEEN A GHOST!
I ALMOST HAVE! THAT BOY IS WILL WINGFOOT'S SON! IF HE'S INHERITED EVEN A FRACTION OF HIS FATHER'S PROWESS--!
BUT, WHAT AM I SAYING? WHAT DIFFERENCE DOES IT MAKE?
HE DOESN'T WANT TO TRY OUT FOR THE TEAM! HE WON'T EVEN DISCUSS ATHLETICS!
DON'T WORRY, JIM-- THERE'LL BE OTHER PLAYERS--!
NO! NOT LIKE HIM! DON'T YOU SEE, BELLE? HIS FATHER AND I--WE WERE TEAM MATES! WE WERE GREAT TOGETHER! AND NOW--FATE HAS SENT WYATT TO ME! IT'S MY BIG CHANCE-- TO COACH THE GREATEST TEAM OF ALL, BEFORE I RETIRE!
I'VE GOT TO MAKE HIM PLAY!
BUT NOW, IT'S TIME TO RETURN TO THE BAXTER BUILDING, WHERE REED RICHARDS IS ABOUT TO UNDERTAKE ONE OF THE MOST DANGEROUS FEATS OF HIS CAREER--
REED--MY DARLING--DON'T DO IT! I-I HAVE A PREMONITION-- OF DISASTER! OR, AT LEAST--LET ME COME WITH YOU--!
IT'S IMPOSSIBLE, SUE! BUT, I CAN'T TURN BACK NOW! SUB-SPACE MUST BE EXPLORED-- AND CONQUERED-- FOR THE GOOD OF MANKIND!
I ALWAYS THOUGHT HE WAS JUST A GLAMOR-PANTS--OUT FOR ALL THE DOUGH AND GLORY HE COULD GET! BUT HE'S TACKLIN' A JOB THAT WON'T NET HIM A PLUGGED NICKEL--
AND HE'S DOING IT WITHOUT ANY FANFARE-- OR ANY PUBLICITY!
12

The concept of "sub-space" was an integral part of the "cosmic" approach with which Marvel opened up comic books of the 1960s.

During the 1960s Jack Kirby experimented with photo collages as a device for altering the look of comic books. The idea never really caught on, but it influenced the work of later artists from Jim Steranko to Todd McFarlane.

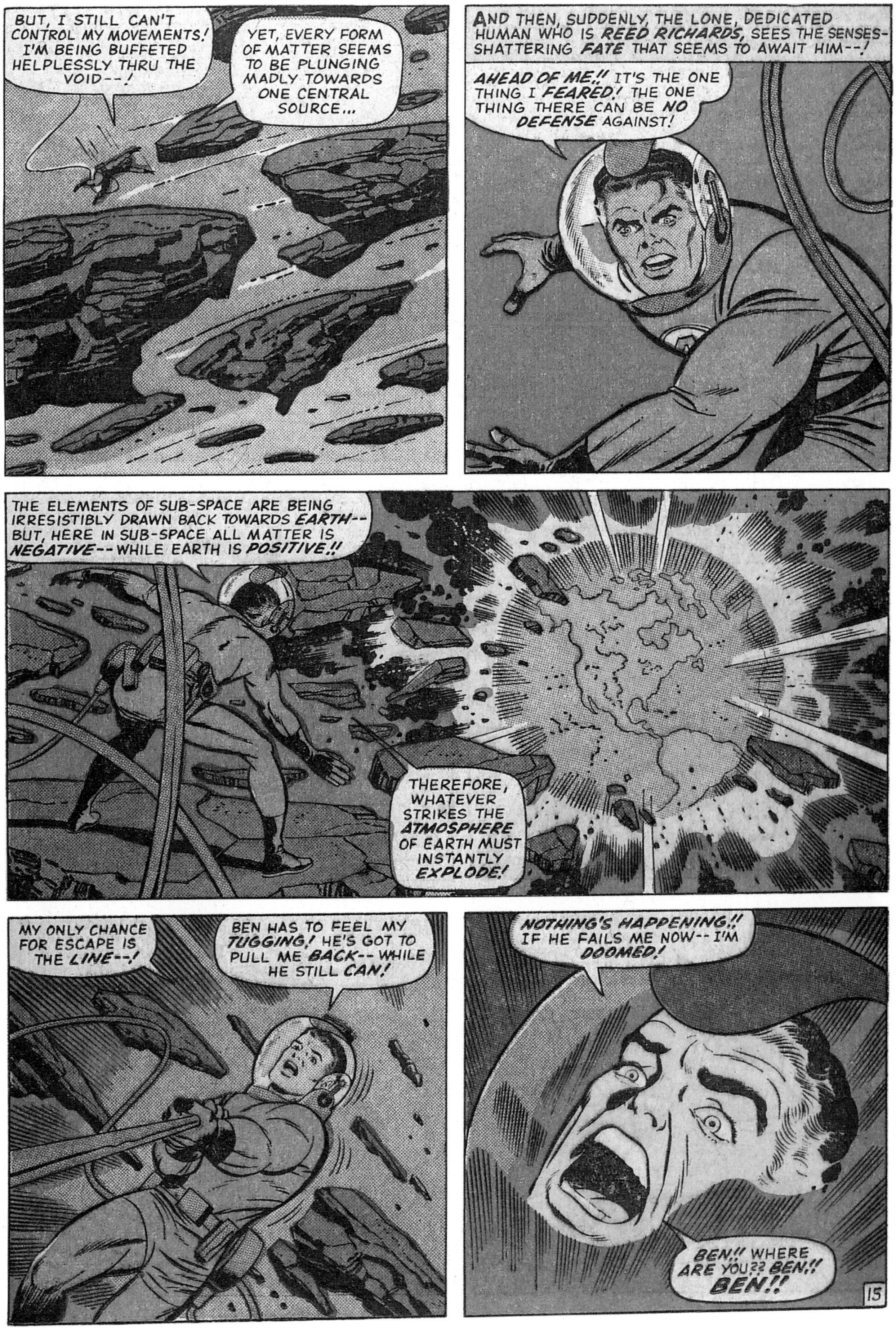
BUT, I STILL CAN'T CONTROL MY MOVEMENTS! I'M BEING BUFFETED HELPLESSLY THRU THE VOID--!
YET, EVERY FORM OF MATTER SEEMS TO BE PLUNGING MADLY TOWARDS ONE CENTRAL SOURCE...
AND THEN, SUDDENLY, THE LONE, DEDICATED HUMAN WHO IS REED RICHARDS, SEES THE SENSES-SHATTERING FATE THAT SEEMS TO AWAIT HIM--!
AHEAD OF ME!! IT'S THE ONE THING I FEARED! THE ONE THING THERE CAN BE NO DEFENSE AGAINST!
THE ELEMENTS OF SUB-SPACE ARE BEING IRRESISTIBLY DRAWN BACK TOWARDS EARTH-- BUT, HERE IN SUB-SPACE ALL MATTER IS NEGATIVE-- WHILE EARTH IS POSITIVE!!
THEREFORE, WHATEVER STRIKES THE ATMOSPHERE OF EARTH MUST INSTANTLY EXPLODE!
MY ONLY CHANCE FOR ESCAPE IS THE LINE--!
BEN HAS TO FEEL MY TUGGING! HE'S GOT TO PULL ME BACK-- WHILE HE STILL CAN!
NOTHING'S HAPPENING!! IF HE FAILS ME NOW-- I'M DOOMED!
BEN!! WHERE ARE YOU?? BEN!! BEN!!
15

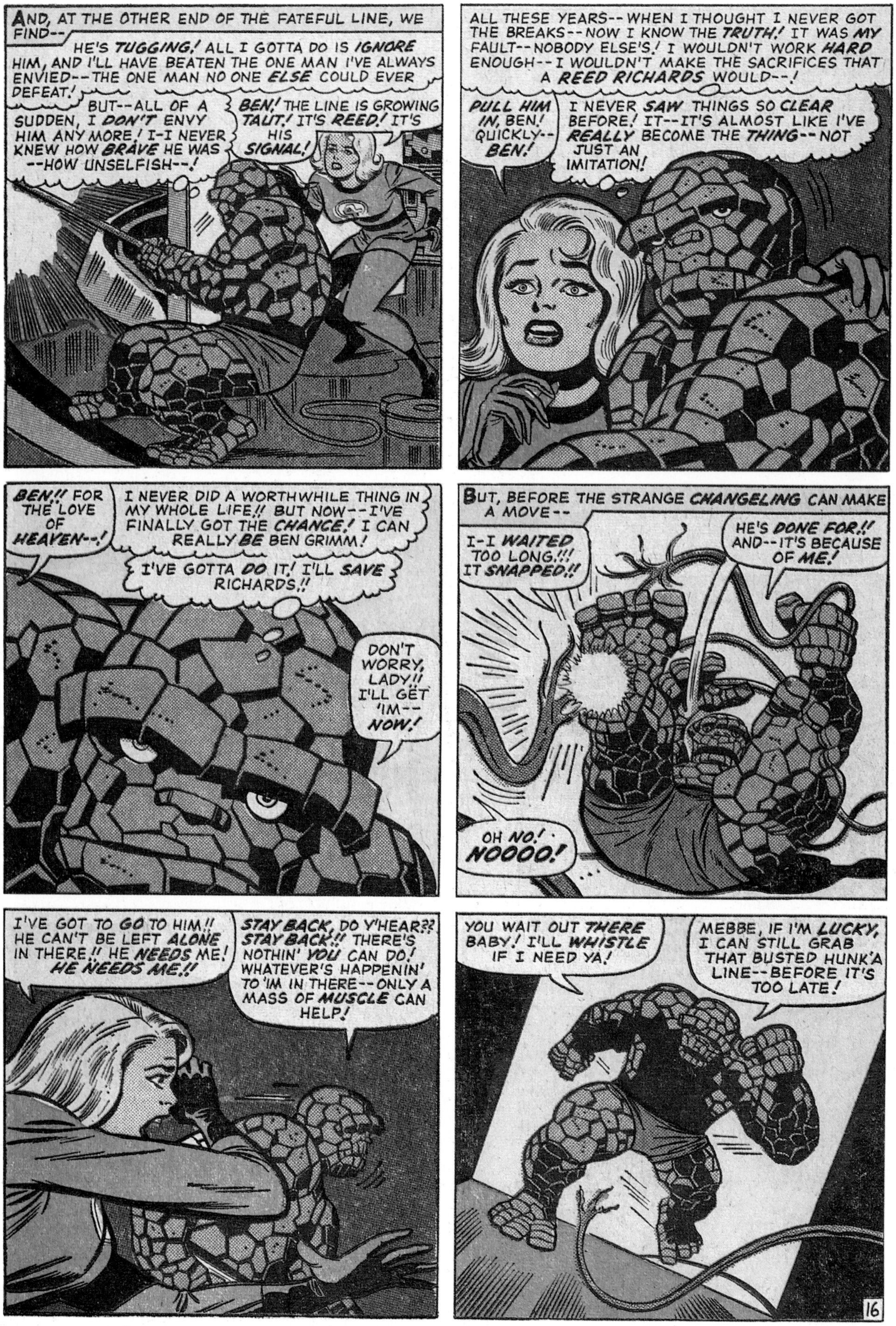
AND, AT THE OTHER END OF THE FATEFUL LINE, WE FIND--
HE'S TUGGING! ALL I GOTTA DO IS IGNORE HIM, AND I'LL HAVE BEATEN THE ONE MAN I'VE ALWAYS ENVIED--THE ONE MAN NO ONE ELSE COULD EVER DEFEAT!
BUT--ALL OF A SUDDEN, I DON'T ENVY HIM ANY MORE! I-I NEVER KNEW HOW BRAVE HE WAS --HOW UNSELFISH--!
BEN! THE LINE IS GROWING TAUT! IT'S REED! IT'S HIS SIGNAL!
ALL THESE YEARS--WHEN I THOUGHT I NEVER GOT THE BREAKS--NOW I KNOW THE TRUTH! IT WAS MY FAULT--NOBODY ELSE'S! I WOULDN'T WORK HARD ENOUGH--I WOULDN'T MAKE THE SACRIFICES THAT A REED RICHARDS WOULD--!
PULL HIM IN, BEN! QUICKLY--BEN!
I NEVER SAW THINGS SO CLEAR BEFORE! IT--IT'S ALMOST LIKE I'VE REALLY BECOME THE THING--NOT JUST AN IMITATION!
BEN!! FOR THE LOVE OF HEAVEN--!
I NEVER DID A WORTHWHILE THING IN MY WHOLE LIFE!! BUT NOW--I'VE FINALLY GOT THE CHANCE! I CAN REALLY BE BEN GRIMM!
I'VE GOTTA DO IT! I'LL SAVE RICHARDS!!
DON'T WORRY, LADY!! I'LL GET 'IM--NOW!
BUT, BEFORE THE STRANGE CHANGELING CAN MAKE A MOVE--
I-I WAITED TOO LONG!!! IT SNAPPED!!
HE'S DONE FOR!! AND--IT'S BECAUSE OF ME!
OH NO! NOOOO!
I'VE GOT TO GO TO HIM!! HE CAN'T BE LEFT ALONE IN THERE!! HE NEEDS ME! HE NEEDS ME!!
STAY BACK, DO Y'HEAR?? STAY BACK!! THERE'S NOTHIN' YOU CAN DO! WHATEVER'S HAPPENIN' TO 'IM IN THERE--ONLY A MASS OF MUSCLE CAN HELP!
YOU WAIT OUT THERE BABY! I'LL WHISTLE IF I NEED YA!
MEBBE, IF I'M LUCKY, I CAN STILL GRAB THAT BUSTED HUNK'A LINE--BEFORE IT'S TOO LATE!
16

Lee and Kirby confound expectations here. Instead of offering up the easy climax of the hero defeating his evil twin, they allow the villain to achieve nobility by example and by osmosis. "He did what The Thing would have done himself," says Kirby. "He became one of The Fantastic Four."

The pathetic sight of the imitation Thing, huddled on his little rock as he hurtles toward his doom, conjures up emotions deeper than the ones comic books were expected to provide.

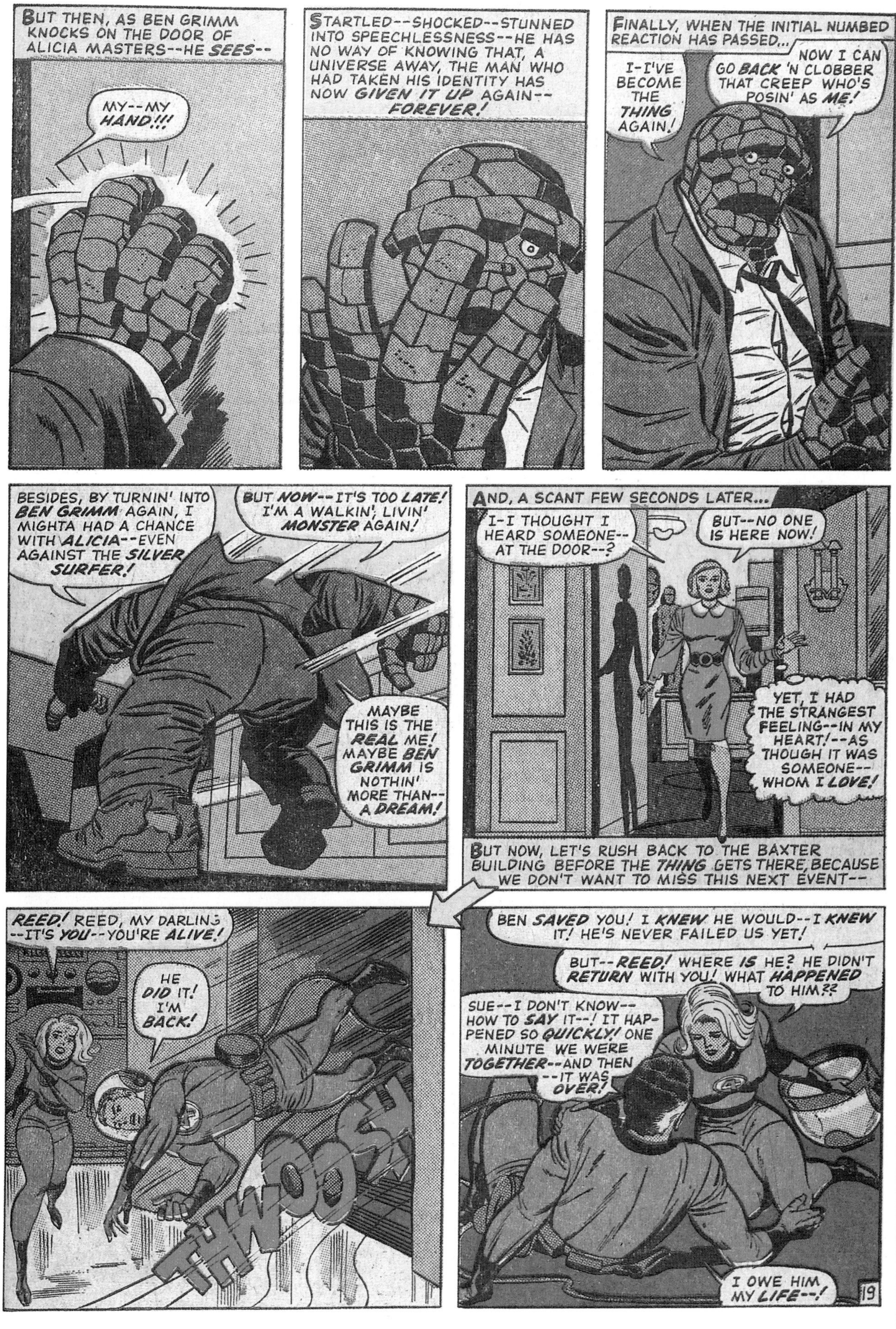
BUT THEN, AS BEN GRIMM KNOCKS ON THE DOOR OF ALICIA MASTERS--HE SEES--
MY--MY HAND!!!
STARTLED--SHOCKED--STUNNED INTO SPEECHLESSNESS--HE HAS NO WAY OF KNOWING THAT, A UNIVERSE AWAY, THE MAN WHO HAD TAKEN HIS IDENTITY HAS NOW GIVEN IT UP AGAIN--FOREVER!
FINALLY, WHEN THE INITIAL NUMBED REACTION HAS PASSED...
I-I'VE BECOME THE THING AGAIN!
NOW I CAN GO BACK 'N CLOBBER THAT CREEP WHO'S POSIN' AS ME!
BESIDES, BY TURNIN' INTO BEN GRIMM AGAIN, I MIGHTA HAD A CHANCE WITH ALICIA--EVEN AGAINST THE SILVER SURFER!
BUT NOW--IT'S TOO LATE! I'M A WALKIN', LIVIN' MONSTER AGAIN!
MAYBE THIS IS THE REAL ME! MAYBE BEN GRIMM IS NOTHIN' MORE THAN--A DREAM!
AND, A SCANT FEW SECONDS LATER...
I-I THOUGHT I HEARD SOMEONE--AT THE DOOR--?
BUT--NO ONE IS HERE NOW!
YET, I HAD THE STRANGEST FEELING--IN MY HEART!--AS THOUGH IT WAS SOMEONE--WHOM I LOVE!
BUT NOW, LET'S RUSH BACK TO THE BAXTER BUILDING BEFORE THE THING GETS THERE, BECAUSE WE DON'T WANT TO MISS THIS NEXT EVENT--
REED! REED, MY DARLING--IT'S YOU--YOU'RE ALIVE!
HE DID IT! I'M BACK!
THWOOSH
BEN SAVED YOU! I KNEW HE WOULD--I KNEW IT! HE'S NEVER FAILED US YET!
BUT--REED! WHERE IS HE? HE DIDN'T RETURN WITH YOU! WHAT HAPPENED TO HIM??
SUE--I DON'T KNOW--HOW TO SAY IT--! IT HAPPENED SO QUICKLY! ONE MINUTE WE WERE TOGETHER--AND THEN--IT WAS OVER!
I OWE HIM MY LIFE--!
19

"This is one of my favorite stories," says Stan Lee. "I liked it because, while it had a lot of fantasy, it was basically a character-driven story, rather than one that depended on gimmicks. I love stories that deal with characterization, and I thought this was a good example of the Marvel style."

"The Hunter," a Wolverine adventure written by Chris Claremont and drawn by Marshall Rogers, has an unusual history. It was created in 1987 for a book of Marvel stories sold exclusively through Sears stores around the United States, and as such it remains unfamiliar to many comic book fans. It was intended as a quick course to instruct the general public in the care and feeding of Marvel's most popular mutant, so Claremont refers to it as "Wolverine 101."

Penciler Marshall Rogers, who studied architecture, made the contrast in buildings an integral part of this story about a clash of cultures. Rogers has worked for Marvel on characters from Dr. Strange to G. I. Joe, but is perhaps best known for his superior work on Batman for DC Comics. Accidentally omitted from the art credits upon first publication were inker Randy Emberlin and colorist Bob Sharen.

MAN'S A HISTORY BUFF, SO HE BUILT HIMSELF A CASTLE. REPRODUCTION OF AN ANCIENT FORTRESS SUPPOSED TO HAVE STOOD ON THIS SITE.

IMPRESSIVE.

The unique first-person narration that Chris Claremont devised for Wolverine is spaced around the page to provide a dramatic sense of rhythm and timing.

PROTECTED, TOO.

I'M UPWIND, BREEZE BLOWIN' ACROSS THE BATTLEMENTS TOWARDS ME.

COUPLE O' BREATHS, I KNOW THE ODDS.

MOAT'S NO PROBLEM.

NEITHER IS THE WALL.

PERFECT LOCATION. NO GUARDS IN SIGHT, THIS STRETCH OF WALL SHROUDED BY SHADOW. TOO GOOD TO BE TRUE.

BUT ANYBODY BREECHIN' THE WALL WILL BREAK THE LASER SECURITY LINK--

--BEAM OF LIGHT SO FINE I CAN BARELY SEE IT.

PROBABLY RAISE A HECKUVA RUMPUS.

CLANGALANG

Wolverine may be unkillable, but the agony he so frequently experiences serves to make him an extraordinary super hero. There are no free rides for characters like this, and their complex appeal is not based solely on wish fulfillment.

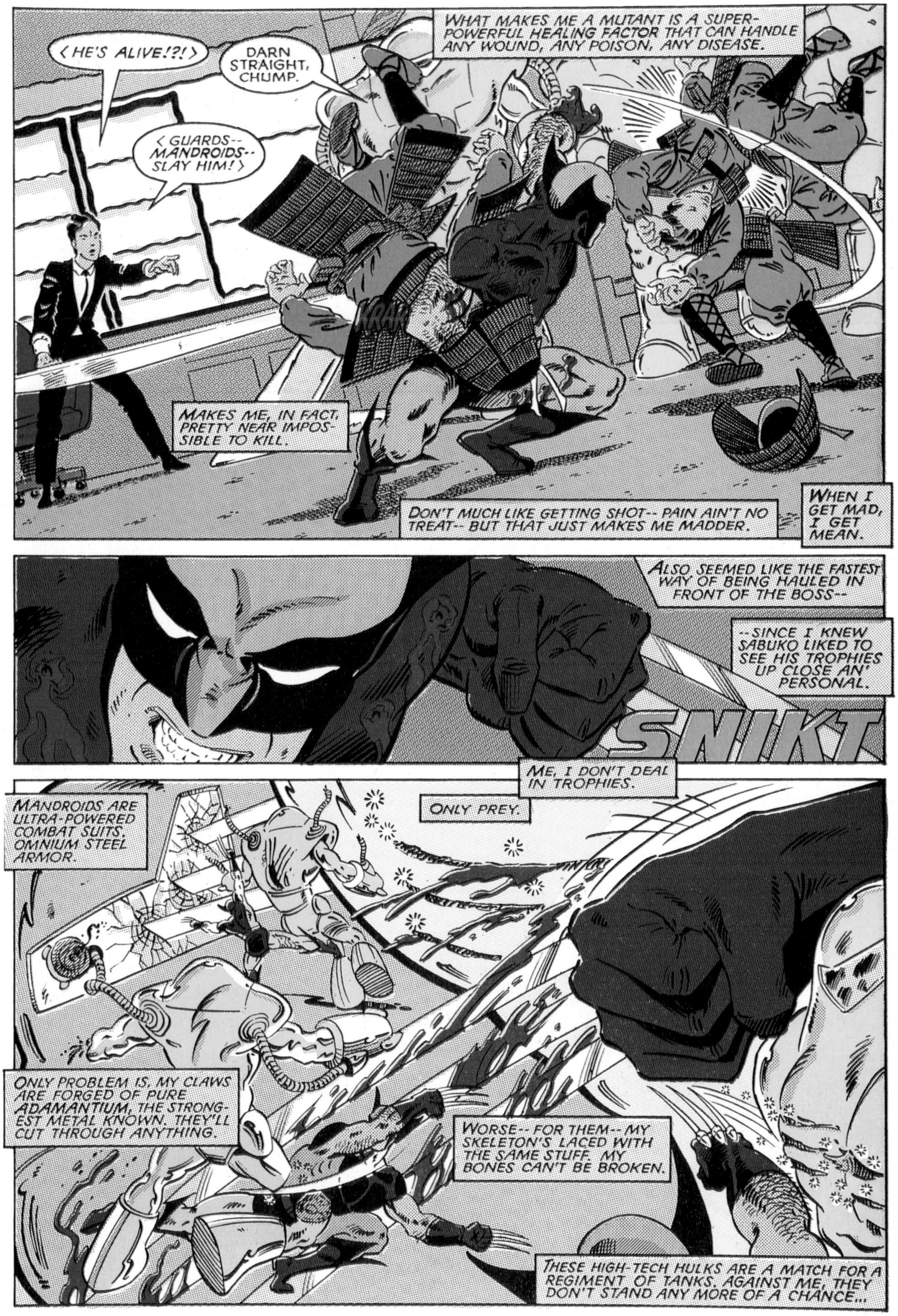
WHAT MAKES ME A MUTANT IS A SUPER-POWERFUL HEALING FACTOR THAT CAN HANDLE ANY WOUND, ANY POISON, ANY DISEASE.
‹HE'S ALIVE!?!›
DARN STRAIGHT, CHUMP.
‹GUARDS-- MANDROIDS-- SLAY HIM!›
MAKES ME, IN FACT, PRETTY NEAR IMPOSSIBLE TO KILL.
DON'T MUCH LIKE GETTING SHOT-- PAIN AIN'T NO TREAT-- BUT THAT JUST MAKES ME MADDER.
WHEN I GET MAD, I GET MEAN.
ALSO SEEMED LIKE THE FASTEST WAY OF BEING HAULED IN FRONT OF THE BOSS--
--SINCE I KNEW SABUKO LIKED TO SEE HIS TROPHIES UP CLOSE AN' PERSONAL.
SNIKT
ME, I DON'T DEAL IN TROPHIES.
ONLY PREY.
MANDROIDS ARE ULTRA-POWERED COMBAT SUITS. OMNIUM STEEL ARMOR.
ONLY PROBLEM IS, MY CLAWS ARE FORGED OF PURE ADAMANTIUM, THE STRONGEST METAL KNOWN. THEY'LL CUT THROUGH ANYTHING.
WORSE-- FOR THEM-- MY SKELETON'S LACED WITH THE SAME STUFF. MY BONES CAN'T BE BROKEN.
THESE HIGH-TECH HULKS ARE A MATCH FOR A REGIMENT OF TANKS. AGAINST ME, THEY DON'T STAND ANY MORE OF A CHANCE...

Wolverine's claws make him a very adept killer, yet he restrains himself by holding one of them in reserve. Like most of Marvel's best super heroes, he battles not only his enemies, but also himself.

INDEX

Page references in lightface are to the text; references in boldface are to captions. If a topic is referred to both in the text and in a caption on the same page, only a lightface reference is given, with the following exceptions in boldface: photographs and drawings of persons; comic book covers; and credits of artists and writers. Only the captions of illustrations are indexed, not the details of the illustrations themselves; in particular, visual depictions of characters have not been referenced. Titles in italics without qualification are names of comic books, e.g., "*Spider-Man.*" All other titles are qualified, e.g., "*Spider-Man* (TV movie)." Fictional characters are listed first name first, e.g., "Peter Parker" (not "Parker, Peter"). Alternative identities for super heroes are cross-referenced to the super hero's name, e.g., "Peter Parker. *See* Spider-Man."